WILLIAM J. BAUSCH

the STORY

REVEALED

Homilies that sustain,
inspire, and engage

TWENTY THIRD *23rd*
PUBLICATIONS
NEW LONDON, CT 06320
WWW.23RDPUBLICATIONS.COM

To Charles and Ella,
And their 60-year-old journey.
She gone. He waiting

Twenty-Third Publications
A Division of Bayard
One Montauk Avenue, Suite 200
New London, CT 06320
(860) 437-3012 or (800) 321-0411
www.23rdpublications.com

ISBN 978-1-58595-883-2
Library of Congress Catalog Card Number: 2012953232
Printed in the U.S.A.

Contents

ORDINARY TIME

FEASTS & OCCASIONS

FUNERAL HOMILIES

The SERIES

An Experiment: A Lenten Series on Technology and the Christian and the Series on Confession and the Series on the Local Church

Preface

The homilies in this book are both familiar and different. Familiar because they follow the style of my previous collections of homilies, namely, Scripture commentary wrapped in memorable stories; different because there is a whole swath of more dense homilies, longer with few stories and more directly challenging. These would be what I call the social justice and discipleship homilies. Read together as they appear in this book, they tend to be less attractive and more didactic, more like lectures than homilies. They probably make up a quarter of the book. The homilist can skip these or rework the material into a more palatable form.

There are, however, two things to remember that justify them. First, they were given over a period of two or three years; spaced thusly, they did not have the heaviness they have here when placed together. Second, they reflect a kind of contract between the homilist and the congregation, the reaching of a level of trust that has given me permission, so to speak, to preach the occasional, longer, more didactic homily supported by a compatible series of "questions for reflection" in the Sunday bulletin.

These homilies, as always, have been "audience tested." I recommend that the reader consult the Notes and Credits section, as sometimes there are critical suggestions or explanations that enhance or support a particular homily. Near the end, I have dabbled in another experiment. I have offered a set of series, three of them. One is on the digital age, the second on confession, and the third on the parish. They are good for series times, such as Advent or Lent, and they too tend (at least the digital age Lenten series) to be more lecture than homily and thus invite modification.

As always, it is my hope that these homilies might also serve as spiritual reading for those who do not ascend the pulpit.

The
ADVENT
CYCLE

1. The Sunday After Thanksgiving: Five Kernels

Some families I know have a peculiar Thanksgiving custom. They set on each plate five kernels of dried corn. Then, around the table, on Thanksgiving Day, each family member relates five things they have been thankful for that year.

That custom derives from an old legend about the Pilgrims. They were undertaking a perilous journey from England to Virginia; in fact, so perilous was sea travel in those days that it was always suggested that one make out one's will before boarding ship! The Pilgrims were blown off course, landing, instead, in New England. They suffered a harsh winter. By spring, nearly half their number had perished. During the winter months, it was not unusual to have two or three deaths a day. It was said that, during the worst of it, each person had only five kernels of corn to eat each day—and they were grateful for that.

So this morning, at the beginning of a new Church year, let's take our kernels, one at a time, and, in five offbeat random but related stories, contemplate what we might be thankful for.

First kernel: Advent. Think of Disney's *The Lion King*. Think of the scene where the spirit of Mufasa appears in the sky and speaks to his prodigal son, Simba, who has been hiding out in the deepest, darkest jungle, reclining in a life of self-centeredness and greed where only he, number one, counts. He's quite forgotten that he was born to be king. The ghost of his father challenges his spiritual blindness. Mufasa says to his son, "You have become less than you are."

Advent is our first kernel. We look at it and say: Thank you, God, for reminding us that you have come among us, have called us by name, have shared our humanity so that we may share your divinity. Yes, our dignity is that we are related. By taking our human condition on yourself you have made us a royal priesthood, a holy nation, a people set apart. So, thank you for Advent, our new year, our second chance, that calls us back to who we are meant to be.

Second kernel: that marvelous genius and storyteller, Garrison Keillor. In one of his celebrated Lake Wobegon tales, he tells of his childhood Thanksgiving dinners as the family gathered around the table and remembered the blessings of the past year. Uncle John usually gave the prayer, which caused everyone to squirm. As Keillor said, "Everybody in the family knew that Uncle John couldn't pray without talking about the cross and crying….Sure enough, Uncle John prayed, talked about the cross, and cried…." Then Keillor adds these memorable words, "All of us knew that Jesus died on the cross for us, but Uncle John has never gotten over it."

And that story reminds us that we have been bought with a great price. "Greater love than this no one has than to lay down one's life for his friend," said Jesus. He came to do that for us. Above all others, he loves us that much, and we should never get over this. Thank you, Jesus, for that.

Third kernel: a horse. One of the most famous racehorses ever was Seabiscuit—as you know from the movies and books about him. Seabiscuit was the son of a champion, but originally he was not destined to be like his father. The reason is that he was chosen to be the goat, the shill, the second banana, the fool. Which is to say he was forced to run with better horses so that they would gain confidence by beating him. So when he raced, he did what he was trained to do: fail, lose. Because of this demeaning treatment, Seabiscuit eventually became an angry, almost uncontrollable horse that nobody really wanted.

But one day a trainer considered to be past his prime, and a jockey considered to be too big to ride, came along, and they were willing to take a chance with him. In taking on Seabiscuit, the trainer had simply said, "You don't throw a life away just because it's been banged up a little." By and by, Seabiscuit began to thrive with these people who believed in him.

We've sometimes been treated poorly, made to feel we could never measure up, were a loser—they even called us that—but we know there is someone who has never, ever thrown away a banged-up life, and so, in the incarnation, has embraced ours. For that, thank you, Jesus.

Fourth kernel: bell ringers. A man tells about an experience he had. "Just up the road from my home," he writes, "is a field with two horses in it. Now from a distance each horse looks like any other horse. But if you stop your car, or are walking by, you will notice something quite amazing, quite amazing! Looking into the eyes of one horse you will find that he is blind. Obviously his owner has chosen not to have him put down, but to make a good home for him.

"Now if you stand there long enough and listen a while, you will hear the sound of a bell. Looking around, you will see that it comes from the smaller horse in the field. Attached to the horse's halter is a small bell. The bell lets the blind friend know where the other horse is, so he can follow. If you continue to stand there long enough and watch these two friends, you'll see that the horse with the bell is always checking on the blind horse and that the blind horse will listen for the bell, and then the blind horse will slowly walk to where the other horse is and nuzzle him, trusting that he will not be led astray. Later on, when the horse with the bell returns to the barn each evening, you will notice that it stops occasionally and looks back, making sure that the blind friend isn't too far behind to hear the bell, and then moves on till they're both safely back in the barn."

And that story leads us to give thanks for all the bell ringers in our lives: parents who nurtured and supported us, good friends who stuck with us, teachers who believed in us—anyone who pulled us through, inspired us, led us to a better, holier life. Thank you, friends of the past and present.

Fifth kernel: crosses. Toward the end of the movie *Little Big Man*, which starred Dustin Hoffman, there is a scene in which an Indian named Old Lodge Skins, sick and blind, knows he is dying and begins to pray to God a prayer of thanksgiving: "O Lord God, I thank you for having made me a human being. I thank you for having given me life and eyes to see and enjoy your world. But, most of all, I thank you for my sickness and my blindness because I have learned more from these than from my health and from my sight."

Life has often been hurtful, painful, and mostly unfair, and many people have turned their backs on a God who seems to be indifferent, absent, and silent. We can sympathize with that. But it is also true that, for many persons, hardship, betrayal, sickness, and loss have brought them to a new dimension, dragged them to a different, fuller life than they never imagined possible.

One thinks of John Bernardone, whose depression and imprisonment led him to become Francis of Assisi, or town drunk Matt Talbot, who became a model of piety and compassion, or parents whose children died of AIDS who set up hospices and centers to minister to those who are sick, or simply those who have known trauma and loss but whose prayer life deepened and whose charity expanded. They're all people who, like Old Lodge Skins, learned more from their crosses than from their crowns.

So, yes, thank you, Lord, for the crosses that shaped us, made us humble, brought us to our knees—a good place to be.

So, there we are. On the brink of a new Church year, with Thanksgiving still fresh in our memories, we are giving a different kind of thanks today, in fact, five kernels worth.

So we pray:
"For reminding us who we are,
for your loving us to the extremes of your life,
for embracing our brokenness,
for sending us bell ringers,
for the crosses of concealed graces—
for all these things, O Lord, we also give thanks.
Amen."

2. The Legacy

A friend of mine—at least I think he is a friend—sent me this email:

Dear Bill,
You may have heard that, beginning in January, the Federal Government, in a step to save the economy, has decided to stop deporting illegals and instead to deport old people. The reasoning is that old people are easier to catch and will not remember how to get back home.
   A tear came to my eye when I thought of you.
   See you on the bus.

Well…more changes coming for the new year and that segues us to our new year, our Church new year, which begins today: Advent. You already notice the obvious signs of change: different colored vestments, an Advent wreath with its four candles for the four weeks of preparation, a change of hymns—and, of course, this year, a change in some of the Mass prayers.

So, once more, it's Advent, and we search for a motif, a mantra, for our new Church year. Let me suggest one inspired by Alexander McCall Smith. He's the famous author of the wonderful, best-selling No. 1 Ladies' Detective Agency series starring Mma Ramotswe, the proud owner of the only ladies' detective agency in her beloved Botswana in Africa, a job that never fails to teach her something fascinating about human nature. Here's an excerpt of how she got started. Listen:

Mma Ramotswe set up the No. 1 Ladies' Detective Agency with the proceeds of the sale of her father's cattle. He had owned a big herd, and had no other children; so every single beast, all one hundred and eighty of them, including the white Brahmin bulls, whose grandparents he had bred himself, went to her. "I want you to have your own business," he said to her on his death bed. "You'll get a good price for the cattle now. Sell them and buy a business. A butchery maybe. A bottle store. Whatever you like."

She held her father's hand and looked onto the eyes of the man she loved beyond all others, her Daddy, her wise Daddy, whose lungs had been filled with dust in those mines and who had scrimped and saved to make life good for her. It was difficult to talk through her tears, but she managed to say, "I'm going to set up a detective agency. Down in Gaborone. It will be the best one in Botswana. The No. 1 Agency."

For a moment her father's eyes opened wide and it seemed as if he was struggling to speak. "But…but…" But he died before he could say anything more, and Mma Ramotswe fell on his chest and wept for all the dignity, love, and suffering that died with him.

And maybe there we have it, our Advent motif: legacy. The great and inspiring legacy of her Daddy: hard work, dignity, love, sharing, compassion, so that people will remember, not our bank accounts or the number of our financial or sexual conquests, our houses and cars, but our suffering for justice's sake, our dignity as children of God, our love that touched others, our sense of justice.

So let's, in broad strokes, take a look at some of our current legacies. They involve big issues of social justice—something, to be honest, we hate to hear about, especially from the pulpit. "Stick to the pieties, Father!" I would, except that the pope and the bishops—not to mention the gospel— keep pushing me otherwise. Anyway, put up with it as your Advent penance.

So let's dive right in. Whatever you think of the Occupy Wall Street movement—maybe Gingrich is right, they should take a bath and get a job; but, whether he's right or wrong—the statistic that does take our breath away is this: the top 1 percent of Americans possess a greater net worth than the entire bottom 90 percent, and the richest 20 percent of Americans own more than 80 percent of the country's wealth. Contemplate that for a while. The huge chasm between seven- and eight-figure salaries and the widespread foreclosures, unemployment, and poverty, and their attendant suffering in these United States is not a good legacy to leave.

Let's go to Celebrityville. The multimillion-dollar wedding—the wedding cake alone reportedly cost $20,000—of the reality show star Kim Kardashian and NBA star Kris Humphries, broadcast in a two-part special on E!, was watched by more than four million people—some of you included. It was a wedding followed—as we all know—only 72 days later by their divorce. He is now suing her for hundred of thousands of dollars to get back the wedding ring.

Surely we people of the Christian faith have to admit that such shallowness and excess doesn't fit well with the thousands of babies in Somalia who starve to death each year. What they would give for a few crumbs of that $20,000 wedding cake! Such extravagance and waste cry to heaven but, you know, so loud is the hoopla, so captive are we to the media, that we don't hear starving babies breathing their last. Such moral deafness is not a good legacy, is it?

Next, the sports page. On the front page of *The New York Times* is this story, and I quote: "Ohio State University hired Urban Meyer as its football coach Monday, giving him one of the richest contracts ever in college sports—the latest indication that the big business of college football is undeterred by the nation's broader economic woes or by concern about the prominence of sports on campus. The contract includes $4 million in base salary, bonuses for everything from players' graduation rates to playing in a national championship—up to $700,0000 annually—and lump payments in 2014, 2016, and 2018. The deal is worth more than three times the $1.32 million that the university president made in 2010...."

Contrast this to the front page story in the New York section just the week before in *The Wall Street Journal*: "Most City University of New York community college students drop out before graduating, squandering the system's resources as enrollment soars...The story by the Center for an Urban Future, a Manhattan think tank, highlights a problem with national implications: Too many students arrive at community colleges without having learned basic reading and math concepts...A CUNY spokesman... noted that 'almost four out of every five freshmen who arrive at its community colleges with a high-school degree require remediation in reading, writing, and mathematics."

Four million dollars for a coach. Not enough money to teach students. Not a good set of priorities or a balanced legacy to leave to the future, is it?

So there we are: the majority of the nation's wealth in the hands of a few, producing a severely unequal society, a media that compulsively spotlights celebrities and casts into the shadows the least of our brethren, the triumph of sports over education—all should make us pause and ask questions about our legacy to the future.

In summary: Advent, priorities, the "what you did for the least of my brethren you did to me" background mantra, should, at the beginning of our new Church year, make us think of our legacy—at least before we board the bus.

3. Three Cups of (Weak) Tea

Today, the first Sunday of Advent, marks, as you know, the start of the Christian year. It's the Church's version of a Happy New Year, beginning with the expectation of the coming of Jesus and ending with his resurrection. Advent sounds the theme of destroying the old ways—as you just heard in the vivid gospel reading—and putting on new attitudes.

So, in this context, I want to share a life and a lesson.

Unless you've read his book (and some of you have), you probably don't know the name Greg Mortenson. Let me tell you about him. First, be it noted, that although his parents were Lutheran missionaries in Tanzania, where he grew up, he doesn't seem to be explicitly religious. Born in 1967, Mortenson joined the U.S. Army as a young man and was trained as a medical corpsman. That, coupled with a love of adventure, led him to being included on mountain-climbing teams who loved having a medic aboard. In 1993 he was part of a team ascending the world's second highest mountain, only slightly lower that Everest.

The peak is part of the Karakoram segment of the Himalayas, located on the boarder between Pakistan and China. It is known as "Savage Peak" because of the difficulty of climbing it and the fact that, for every four who reach the summit, one dies trying to get there. All the climbers, of course, want to climb to the top, but Mortenson had an added incentive. The previous year, his 23-year-old sister, Christa, had died from a massive seizure after a lifelong struggle with epilepsy. Mortenson intended to dedicate his conquest of the mountain to her memory.

As it turned out, however, he honored his sister with a far more lasting result. It happened like this. After 78 days of struggle against the mountain, Mortenson got within 1000 feet of the summit. But then failing strength and altitude sickness forced him to turn back. A local guide helped him off the mountain, but by chance they got separated when Mortenson made a wrong turn. He ended up in a primitive mountain village in Pakistan. Too sick to go on, he stayed there under the hospitable care of the villagers while he got better. The people of the village he stumbled on are Muslim and belong to an ethnic group called the Balti, and many of them work as guides and porters for the many mountain climbers.

While in the village recuperating, Mortenson couldn't help but observe the harsh realities of life. The Balti lived in an isolated, remote mountain valley with a severe climate. Medical care is almost non-existent, and people die from things that would be routinely treated and cured elsewhere. One third of the children under 12 die, and there are no schools for those who live there, no way out of their pitiable poverty. Mortenson was touched, and although he had no money and no idea how to raise any, he resolved to build a school for the village. When he returned to California, he took a job as a emergency room nurse and started sending letters to celebrities and the Hollywood crowd and anyone he could think of who might help with the school.

The attempt failed, but eventually a rich man, a mountain climber buff, read about Mortenson's quest and donated the necessary money. Mortenson went back to Pakistan with building materials, but he was faced with the problem of getting the bulky materials to the village while fending off rival chieftains who wanted to steal them. However, the people there, accustomed to hauling large rocks from the frequent rock slides, carried all of the heavy materials over the hills on their backs to the village, a truly Herculean task.

After Mortenson's school was built, he returned to the United States, but he continued to be haunted by the needs of the people. To make a long story short, Mortenson resumed raising money so he could help other villages, and again and again he returned to Pakistan and Afghanistan and, as of a few years ago, has established more than 78 schools. He also paid out of his own pocket for the teachers in the rural and often volatile regions of those two countries. He hasn't profited one cent from all this. He draws a very small salary from his organization.

I might add that he has faced considerable dangers during those years, including an eight-day kidnapping by a Taliban group, who finally let him go when they became convinced of his good intentions. Some of them even donated money for his schools. In 2003 he escaped a fight between feuding Afghan warlords. He has been the target of Islamic mullahs who didn't like his helping girls receive an education. He has been investigated by the CIA. But, for the most part, he has gained the trust of Islamic leaders, government officials, military commanders, and tribal chiefs both in Pakistan and Afghanistan.

That's the life. Now the lesson.

Would you believe that after September 11, 2001, Mortenson has received hate mail and even death threats from Americans? Why? Because he is helping Muslim children to live, to receive an education. I hope his haters weren't Christians, because that's an affront to the gospel, to all that Jesus came and stood for. Let's remember this Jesus we soon will celebrate. Remember when the hated, ethnic Samaritans wouldn't let Jesus' group pass through their land on the way to Jerusalem? And one of Jesus' disciples asked if they should cast down fire from heaven to destroy those people? Jesus sighed and told them simply to take another route.

And then, a few Sundays ago, the gospel was about one of Jesus' disciples seeing someone not of their group helping people and casting out devils, and the disciples asked if they should stop him because he wasn't part of their group. Again, Jesus, patience wearing thin, said no; if one is not against us, they are for us. Let them alone to do their good deeds. And how about the times Jesus touched the worst of the outsiders, such as the untouchable leper, or drew a Samaritan woman into grace at a well, or cured the daughter of a foreigner or the servant of a hated Roman soldier, or embraced a despicable traitor—the tax collector Zacchaeus—or prayed for those who were crucifying him, thus giving bold witness to his words, namely, that his disciples should love their enemies and pray for those who persecute them?

Yet, for all of that, someone who is trying to educate children and help them live longer and rise out of poverty is threatened with death because he is helping that faceless "enemy," the Muslims, who, in some people's minds apparently, are all terrorists, just like all Jews are greedy, all Italians are Mafia, all Irish are drunks, and all Americans are crass. Did they forget so soon the image of Mother Teresa, who cradled the dying street-poor in India? She did not see a Buddhist or a Muslim. She said she saw Christ.

Friends, our lesson is this. Christianity, whose beginnings we are celebrating, is a pain in the...in the heart and mind. It is an aggravation. It keeps confronting us with a call to a wide spirituality that teaches us that we are all children of a God who makes his rain fall on the just and unjust alike, that giving a cup of cold water to the least, not the best, of our brethren is the way of salvation.

Look: we all pray for many things, as indeed we should—for family matters, fractured relationships, health, financial hurt—but on this inaugural Sunday, we should also remember to begin imitating the One who is coming, to pray for a large heart, the open heart, the generous heart, the Jesus heart.

We need to set out on the road laid out in Mortenson's book, which is entitled, as some of you know, *Three Cups of Tea*. The title refers to an old Balti proverb: "The first time you share tea with a Balti you are a stranger. The second time you take tea, you are an honored guest. The third time you share a cup of tea, you become family."

It also works that way with God.

4. Testimony of Two Women

One will be taken, one will be left … The Son of Man is coming at the time
you least expect. Nation will rise against nation, and kingdom against kingdom. There will be powerful earthquakes, famines and plagues from place to
place, and awesome sights and mighty signs will come from the sky.

These are unnerving words from today's gospel.

In the past, to be truthful, we considered such words fringe talk from another age for people who lived on the constant edge of war, famine, disease,
and poverty in hovels, tents, and caves in other parts of the uncivilized
world. Or we think of the cartoon characters who run around with signs
saying the end is near. We dismiss them.

Until now. Now the words are uncomfortably close, uncomfortably true,
uncomfortably ours. Nation is rising against nation, as terrorists level the
mighty buildings of our nation's greatest city and strike at the military
headquarters in our capital. Famine stalks Rwanda, and cholera Haiti, and
plagues like anthrax have already taken six lives and infected more than 30
others as it creeps toward us all from Trenton to Washington to New York.
Terrorists stalk our land.

There are awesome sights in the sky as our drones rain down bombs in
Afghanistan, and the Taliban return the fire. At home, waters flood the
earth, and tornadoes contort the land. Suddenly, it's the apocalyptic scenario of the gospel brought home. Suddenly, it's all too true, all too real, all
too here.

And here, once again, stands Jesus. And what does he say in the midst
of all of this? Go back to the gospel. He says that we will be seized by loss,

persecuted by terror, laid low by infection, and cowered by
says carefully and soberly, "It will lead to your giving testime
words in today's gospel. "It will lead to your giving testimony."

Indeed. Jesus is right. If we are to survive in anxious and fearful times,
it is time to use our Christian lives to give testimony—testimony that may
cost us to be sure—testimony against hate and violence and for our Christian values of forgiveness, compassion, and witness.

To make this gospel truth real to you, let me share the stories of two
women who gave such testimony in the midst of terrible times. A well-
known professor and psychologist named Alexander Shaia tells the first
story, about his grandmother. He writes,

> I was raised in Birmingham, Alabama, in the early 1950s during the time
> when Birmingham was not kind to immigrants and certainly not kind to
> Catholic immigrants like my family which had come to Birmingham in the
> 1900s from Lebanon…
>
> I was raised with a Semitic worldview. What I mean by that is the view that
> is shared by all the village people from Lebanon, Jordan, Israel, Palestine….
> As I grew up, I grew up in the old ways with my grandparents. My maternal
> grandmother—Sito in Arabic—and my paternal grandfather. I had the great
> honor and delight of sitting on my Sito's lap as a young child, not hearing
> folktales or fairy tales as children of other traditions may have heard, but for
> me it was to hear the gospels chanted in Arabic. And as I sat on her lap and I
> heard those melodies, I learned that there was something in the gospel text,
> there was something underneath the words. There was a rhythm or what
> we might call a grace that touched my heart and held me in awe in my early
> years.
>
> Now those years of hearing the gospels chanted and receiving them from
> my Sito, my grandmother, came together in a new way, a profound way, a
> true way when I was seven years old. I stood outside my Sito's house on what
> would have been a beautiful May evening, except on this May evening we
> stood with my family outside that house after it had been set on fire. Some-
> one or someones had broken into the house shortly after sunset and they had

done a particular way of burning the house which in Birmingham was the way that racists did it. They left a signature behind.

They went through the house and they gathered up everything in the house that looked like it had come from Lebanon and poured it into a pile on the living room floor. And then next they went into the house and gathered up everything that looked Catholic: statues, rosaries, and put those on top of the objects from Lebanon, and lastly they put on top of the pile crucifixes, doused it with kerosene, threw kerosene around the simple wooden structure, lit the match, and fled.

We horribly stood outside that burning house, made all the more horrible by the fact that we did not know where our Sito was. And that was quite unusual for her, even in those days long before cell phones, she was always on the phone to someone in the family. So we had the unmistakable impression that perhaps we were not simply watching her house burn, that we were also watching a funeral pyre. Fortunately, about an hour later she drove up. She had gone to church that night—there was a novena going on—and we joyfully received her presence but that was not the moment that most touched my heart.

It was five days later when all of my family was together yet again as we always were for Sunday dinner, and even in those days there were some 70 of us, who were gathered together, but this time we weren't in my Sito's home. We weren't sitting at a great table with fine china. We were sitting, I believe, in my aunt and uncle's basement, on metal folding chairs, around plywood tables set on wooden horses, but, as always has been true, my Sito led us in saying grace.

When she did, she sort of looked around the room—she had a way of her glasses sort of sliding down her nose—and she looked up over her glasses and looked around the room, in my memory, and looked at each one of us and held our gaze for a few seconds. Then after what was a profound silence she said simply, "No hate. No hate. No hate."

And in that moment she lifted the heart of my family into a far different discussion than the bitterness and anger that I had been hearing for five days, and she set our family on a new course. She kept our eyes on moving forward together and in love.

The story and testimony of a grandmother who was a true Christian. A grandmother who challenges us to live and to preach: no hate, no hate.

The second story comes from an obituary in the August 9, 2010, edition of *The New York Times*. It chronicles the life and death of actress Patricia Neal, who died at age eighty-four. The writer of the obituary discussed Neal's life and career in detail and noted that Neal won an Academy Award for Best Actress for her role in the film Hud (1963). Neal also later made a remarkable recovery from a series of strokes that she had in 1965.

In 1949 the twenty-three-year-old Neal appeared in *The Fountainhead*, an adaptation of Ayn Rand's novel, with Gary Cooper. During the filming, Neal fell in love with the older (and married) Cooper, and the two began a three-year affair. Neal eventually became pregnant. Under pressure from Cooper, who wanted to return to his wife and daughter, and from the fear that having a child out of wedlock would destroy her career, Patricia Neal had an abortion.

The obituary goes on, noting in passing that in her book *As I Am: An Autobiography* (1983), Neal recalled the guilt she experienced over the abortion. "If I had only one thing to do over in my life," she wrote, "I would have that baby." But this being the very pro-abortion *New York Times*, it could not bring itself to say more than that and omitted a significant and defining part of Neal's biography.

First of all, here is the full quotation that gives the measure of her anguish: "But for over thirty years, alone, in the night, I cried. For years and years I cried over that baby. And whenever I had too much to drink, I would remember that I had not allowed him to exist. I admired Ingrid Bergman for having her [illegitimate] son. She had guts. I did not. And I regret it with all my heart. If I had only one thing to do over in my life, I would have that baby."

Second, the *Times* could not bring itself to mention that Neal eventually converted to Catholicism (or that, independently, so did Gary Cooper), that she became a pro-life activist, that in 2007 Neal served as the honorary co-chair for the twenty-second Annual Charity Ball for Life. According to Msgr. James Lisante, who celebrated Neal's funeral Mass, Neal often told women who were thinking about having an abortion: "Don't make my mistake. Let your baby live."

So there we are. In a culture of hate and death, two Catholic women, two witnesses, one a born Catholic who preached love, another who converted to Catholicism and reclaimed it. In terrible times they gave testimony.

"Before all this happens, they will persecute you...[but] it will lead to your giving testimony...."

In troubled times, testimony to God's love and healing is the only way to go.

5. Mary Moments

In the Philadelphia Museum of Art there is a painting of the Annunciation by an artist named Henry Ossawa Tanner. It shows Mary as a young girl sitting on her disheveled bed, and there is this light in front of her. It must be right after the angel has spoken to her. And Mary is just sitting there, looking at the light with her mouth open, dumbfounded. She has this look on her face that says, "What, are you kidding? How can this be?" She is stunned, confused, scared to the point that the angel is compelled to say, "Do not be afraid."

There is a similar fresco at St. Michael's Chapel at Rutgers University. It depicts the topsy-turvy aspect of the event, as the angel appears to Mary upside down, uttering the word "blessed" backwards, indicating that Mary's life would be thoroughly upended.

And it would be. What God is asking is incomprehensible. In addition, in her tiny village, where everyone knows everyone else, and many people are related to one another, everyone knows that she and the man who is already her legal husband have not yet begun to live together. And all of them can count to nine. What will they say about her? What kind of nasty looks will they cast her way when her precious child is born too soon?

It is all too much: too much at stake, too much to ask. Yes, like so many others before her, Mary has just experienced the truth: that it's a fearful and messy thing to be encountered by God, to discover a mission, a conscience, to stand at the crossroads. As a Jew, Mary knew well enough the ancient stories. She thinks of Moses, who tried to duck his call by saying he was no natural leader like his brother Aaron. Pick him. Or Isaiah, who protested his call to be a prophet by saying he'd make a lousy one. Or Jonah, who ran

19

the other way when told to go to Nineveh. They wanted to be close to God, but not that close. Mary, too, knew that to flirt with God had its unspeakable joys but also its cost.

What I'm trying to do with these insights is to wean you away from those gorgeous Annunciation paintings of a serene Mary, robed in Renaissance attire, glowing with a halo and accompanied by cherubs in a resplendent room whose windows show a Tuscan landscape. The reality is quite the opposite.

Mary's sitting on a disheveled bed with hair undone trying to recover from what was like a slap in the face, realizing fully what it meant to say yes to God and fearful of the consequences. She knew what it wound up costing Moses and Isaiah and Jonah—that is closer to the truth, and, therefore, it made her yes, when she got around to it, all the more open and generous and heroic.

What I'm trying to do is to present to you this gospel as a "Mary Moment" to contemplate. The Mary Moment is one we all know: that sudden stop-in-your-tracks episode. Perhaps it's the loss of a family member or friend, a flash of self-disgust while watching online porn or engaged in loveless sex or binging. Maybe it's a movie or book or tender insight that made us pause, an incident that slowed us down, made us realize for a fleeting moment that a certain shallowness has entered our lives, that life is really about more than celebrity dances and Facebook and divorces and fashion, and *Hot in Cleveland* and endless stimulation—that we have other choices we should make.

A man relates a simple story. "One spring afternoon," he says, "my five-year-old son, David, and I were planting raspberry bushes along the side of the garage. A neighbor joined us for a few moments. Just then David pointed to the ground. 'Look, Daddy! What's that?' he asked.

"I stopped talking with my neighbor and looked down. 'A beetle,' I said. David was impressed and pleased with the discovery of this fancy, colorful creature. Then my neighbor lifted his foot and stepped on the insect giving his shoe an extra twist in the dirt. 'That ought to do it,' he laughed. David looked up at me, waiting for an explanation, a reason. That night, just before I turned off the light in his bedroom. David whispered, 'I liked that beetle, Daddy.' 'I did too,' I whispered back." The man concluded his story by saying. "We have the power to choose."

We have the power to choose how we will respond to every living thing that crosses our path. We have the power to love one another or not.

There are these Mary Moments when we are confronted with such an opportunity to choose, to realize that we can be better persons. We don't always have to use people. There are people who live on the edge, are poor or suffering, who need our concern and ministrations. There's a bad habit we need to deal with, an indifference we need fired up, an addiction that calls for attention, a relationship that needs healing, a priority that needs to be put in place. We need to embrace the holiness we secretly desire, no matter how much others make fun of us. The "Me" life, the shallow life, the surface life, is killing our souls, and yet, all the while, in the background, we vaguely sense that an angel is confronting us. These are Mary Moments.

Can we say yes? It's not easy. There will be a cost—Mary knew that, hence her fear—and there will be indescribable peace and joy. Mary also knew that when later she sang to cousin Elizabeth, "My spirit rejoices in God my Savior, for he has looked with favor on the lowliness of his servant...for the Mighty One has done great things for me and holy is his name."

But perhaps today, in the light of this familiar gospel now seen with fresh eyes, we can reconsider, perhaps even ask Mary to intercede for us—that, perplexed and fearful as we sit on the edge of our beds, we too may find courage to say "yes," to surrender to:

live simply,

give generously,

care deeply,

speak kindly,

to walk by faith and not by sight,

to utter fearfully but firmly, "Be it done unto me according to your word."

6. Christmas or Xmas?

As certain as the merchants hawking Christmas sales in September, you know it's the Christmas season when the atheists post signs in public places telling us to be happy this season without God, and the ACLU vigilantes ride the circuit ferreting out any signs of religion in public places. We in turn react by loudly complaining that they are taking Christ out of Christmas. And they are bent on doing so, no doubt about it; and we should resist them when they overstep their bounds. But today, fellow Christians, let me play the John the Baptist Grinch role—this will probably get me coal in my stocking and no presents under my tree—but it has to be said: if Christ is taken from Christmas, it won't be the secular folks' fault as much as ours, because we are using the wrong arguments and embracing the wrong myths. Let's tackle three of them.

Myth #1: Secular atheists are convincing the courts to remove all public displays of the nativity scene.

As it stands, this is not true. The Constitution guarantees the right to practice faith without government interference. Which means that if you or I or if any Christian wants to display the nativity scene on a private lawn, on church property, or in the window of their private business; or if any private company wants to broadcast or put on a religious show featuring the nativity, the courts will always uphold that right. In fact, the courts have. They have consistently ruled in the past on the side of private displays of faith in public forums and will always do so.

But, of course, it's a different matter when displays of the nativity are sanctioned by government agencies. That is in dispute, as it must be. Which

22

is to say that the same Constitution that guarantees freedom of private individuals or private corporations to display faith symbols such as the nativity scene, that same Constitution prevents the government from practicing and displaying faith symbols—Christian, Muslim, Jewish, Shinto, and so on in our polyglot world—because that would put the government in the business of "the establishment" of a religion. And so that's why, say, the nativity scene put up by a local town government is prohibited by the Constitution.

And in a way, we should be grateful for that. Think: do we really want our government to sponsor a faith, especially one not ours? Do we want government officials or employees to create and enact and thus set the standards of our religious practices? Governments did that in the past—and some still do—and it's hard, often to the point of persecution, on outsiders.

Do we want a town council or maintenance crew deciding to put Frosty, Rudolph, and Santa in the manger with Mary and Joseph? And if we protest Frosty in the manger, do we want the dispute to go to court and have the courts decide what a proper manger should or shouldn't look like? Do we want the symbols of a dozen or hundreds of religions on public property? No, it is better to keep the government officially out of religion and let people be free to practice their own.

Myth #2: When you see "Christmas" written as "Xmas," that is a sign of some hostile person crossing out Christ from Christmas.

This is not true. We get upset because, understandably, we don't know Greek. What we should know is this: that abbreviating Christmas as X-m-a-s is an ancient Christian shorthand way of using the first two letters in Greek for the full name of Christ, much like we might use NY or NJ to stand for New York or New Jersey.

You see, in the Greek alphabet, CH, the first two letters of the word Christ, looks in English like our letter X and sounds like chi or "kee." This "chi" or X in Greek became, as I said, shorthand for the full name of Christ. So "X-m-a-s" is really a combination of the Greek X or "Christ," and the English word "Mass" with the final s deleted. So X-m-a-s, when decoded, is really Christmas and therefore it should never be pronounced "Eksmas" but Christmas, for, when spoken, that is what it says in two combined languages. So "X-m-a-s," pronounced "Christmas," has an honorable pedigree.

Not to confuse you, but I might add that the third letter of "Christ," the "r," called "rho" in Greek, looks in English like a "P" with a long stem; and some of you older Catholics may recall how the "P" was dropped down the middle of the X, so you had an X with a P through its intersection. It was known as the "chi-rho," the first three letters of "Christ," and was used to decorate tabernacles and vestments.

Myth #3: Secular atheists are doing away with Christmas.

Yes, secular atheists, as we said, are bent on doing away with Christmas and Christianity. No question about that. But I tell you, if they succeed it will be because Christians have let it happen. The truth is, it is Christians who are allowing the religious and spiritual dimension of this holy day to evaporate. We're not happy to hear that, but let's try a little examination of conscience to check the facts.

What are the decorations inside or outside our houses like? Ask yourself this, and be honest: could a stranger go around your neighborhood and identify which homes are Christian homes? Is yours identifiable as one? With all the other decorations from inflated Santas and Snoopys, from lighted trees to blinking Rudolphs, is there somewhere out there a Christmas crèche? Is there one outside our homes, in our windows, or even inside our homes? Any sign of Jesus at all? How about any mention of Jesus in your home? In your home, what is the ratio between mentioning Jesus and mentioning Santa Claus? We read our children or grandchildren stories about Rudolph and the Grinch and Frosty. Do we ever read them the nativity story from St. Luke?

Do we make our children more excited about Santa's arrival than about Jesus' arrival? Perhaps, I suggest, we should write to Santa and ask him to take a more background role by bringing the more practical gifts like clothes while the parents, the true source of the gifts, give the cooler gifts. And perhaps the tags on our gifts can mention that the gift is given in honor of the Wise Men's gifts to the baby Jesus. Then, too, how about this: which is more important to us—exchanging gifts among those who can give back, or, as a family, giving to the poor? Good question.

Then there's our Christmas cards and stamps. What are they like? Santa, snow scenes, Dickens-like villages, adorable dogs and cats? Greetings like "Happy Holidays!" or "Celebrate Winter"? Is there any faith statement in the cards we send for this very holy day? If not, aren't we just like everyone else?

In short, is there any clue at all that makes us stand out from the secular, Disneyfied crowd? If not, the next time we say Happy Holidays rather than Merry Christmas, the next time Jesus is hardly mentioned in our homes or the gospel message hardly mentioned on our cards, or our care for the poor is not obvious, let's not blame the atheists for taking Christ out of Christmas, but ourselves, our own secular lives, our neutral homes, and our own private square. The reality is, if Christ is absent from our private "here" we should make no fuss if he's absent from the public "there."

How about this final thought: the nation is roughly 80 percent Christian. Think of the impact we'd have if 80 percent of the nation's population displayed crèches instead of the snowmen that cover their lawns, 80 percent sent religious cards, 80 percent read the nativity story to their children or grandchildren, 80 percent gave to the poor. What a powerful, visual impression, what a spiritual panorama, what a national wonderland of faith, hope, and love that would make. Those trying to take Christ out of Christmas wouldn't stand a chance if we Christians were more Christian.

Merry Christmas!

7. Two Images for Christmas

Christmas is full of fond images. Conjure up Christmas and you think of:
greetings, gifts, and gatherings,
family, friends, and feasts,
Santa, Scrooge, and snow,
tree, tinsel, and toasts.
The more spiritually attuned think of crib, Christ, and cross.

To emphasize, as we should, this spiritual tradition, let me share two images that cut closer to the mystery of what it's all about, two images of Christmas wrapped in two stories that will help us remember Christmas's meaning.

Abba Abraham was a monk from the fifth century, a holy man and a great ascetic. He had eaten nothing but herbs and roots for fifty years. Dressed in wild camel's hair like John the Baptist, he lived simply and very austerely in total self-discipline. It so happened one day that his only brother died and left a niece, Mary, and there was no one to care for her. So Abba Abraham, in his kindness, took her in and nourished and cherished her. She grew up to be beautiful both in body and in spirit. She followed Abba Abraham, prayed with him, and was filled with grace.

One day, a wandering monk came, as was their custom, to hear the word of God from Abba Abraham and was smitten by the beauty of Abraham's niece. He took advantage of Abba Abraham's hospitality, and while Abraham was out visiting a sick monk, the wandering monk was overcome by lust and violated the poor girl. She was so mortified and so ashamed that in desperation she fled before Abba Abraham could return home. She fled to the city, where, feeling so violated and disgraced, she became a "lady of the night." In vain did the distraught Abba Abraham look for his niece year after year, until he heard one day what had happened to her and that she was plying her trade at a certain tavern.

Abba Abraham took off his simple camel's hair shirt, disguised himself as a military man with all the regalia, and went to that town. He stormed boisterously into the tavern, ordered bottles of wine and rich, red meat, and loudly downed it all to his heart's content, to the amazement of the on-lookers. After he finished his dinner, he asked the innkeeper for that wench named Mary, for he shouted, "I have come a long way for the love of Mary!"

She was brought to him, rouged and coarse, worn by her trade, and she did not recognize this hard-eating and hard-drinking soldier. He grabbed her around the waist and twirled her around the dance floor, as she asked coquettishly, "What do you want?" He shouted sounding half drunk, "I've come a long way for the love of Mary!" And then after a few more twirls around the floor, he suddenly stopped. He looked deeply into her eyes and said very, very softly, "I have come a long way for the love of Mary." She rec-ognized her uncle, and she wept bitterly and returned home with him. She became known as "St. Mary the Harlot." But Abba Abraham, the simple hermit monk, became a hard-drinking soldier "for the love of Mary."

And, the story tells us, so has God. He has transitioned from eternity to time "for love of us." There we are, fallen, rouged, coquettish, and coarse; and there is God, boisterous, leering, drunk, and loud. God has come into our human condition and taken on our limitations so that he might dance with us. This is a wonderful Christmas image to embrace.

My second image of Christmas comes from a story told by an old man who, back in the early 1900s, was stricken with polio at the age of three. His parents didn't know what was the matter with him. All they knew was that times were hard and suddenly they had a crippled child on their hands. So they took him to a New York City hospital, left him, and never came back. The people who took him into their foster home had relatives on a Georgia estate, where he was sent in the hope that the warmer climate might help.

There he met a remarkable woman, the daughter of slaves. Her name was Maum Jean, a Georgian-slurred version of mama. All the kids, as well as her own, called her Maum Jean. Maum Jean was the first person called when there was sickness; she made medicines from roots and herbs that seemed to cure just about anything. Maum Jean's heart reached out to small, helpless things, so from the start she took particular interest in the timid, scared, six-year-old boy.

She quietly surveyed the polio damage and decided that, regardless of what the doctors might have said, something more ought to be done. She had never heard the word "atrophy," but she knew that muscles could waste away unless used. And so every night when her tasks were done she would come to the boy's room and kneel beside his bed to massage the boy's legs. He picks up on the story:

Sometimes, when I would cry out with pain, she would sing old songs or tell me stories. When her treatments were over, she would always talk earnestly to the Lord, explaining that she was doing what she could but that she would need help, and she asked him to give her a sign when He was ready.

A creek wound through the farm and Maum Jean said there was strength in running water. She made her grandson carry me down to a sandy bank where I could splash around pretty well. Slowly I grew taller, but there was little change in my legs. I still used crutches. I still buckled on the clumsy braces. Night after night, Maum Jean continued the massaging and praying.

Then one morning when I was about twelve, she told me she had a surprise for me. She led me out into the yard and placed me with my back against an oak tree. She took away my crutches and braces. She moved back a dozen paces and told me that the Lord had spoken to her in a dream. He had said that the time had come for me to walk. Then she looked at me long and softly. "So now," said Maum Jean at last, "I want you to walk over here to me." My instant reaction was fear. I knew I couldn't walk unaided. I had tried. I shrank back against the solid support of the tree. Maum Jean continued to urge me.

I burst into tears. I begged. I pleaded. Then her voice rose suddenly, no longer gentle and coaxing, but full of power and command. "You can walk, boy! The Lord has spoken! Now walk over here!" She knelt down and held out her arms.

And somehow, impelled by something stronger than fear, I took a faltering step, and another, and another until I reached Maum Jean and fell into her arms, both of us weeping. It was two more years before I could walk normally, but I never used the crutches again.

There is a sequel to his story. He continues,

For a while longer I lived in my twilight world. Then a circus came through town and when it left, I left with it. For the next few years, I worked with one circus or another. Then the night came when one of Maum Jean's tall grandsons knocked on my door. Maum Jean was dying. She wanted to see me. The old cabin was unchanged. Maum Jean lay in bed surrounded by silent watchers.

Her frail body covered by a patchwork quilt. Her face in shadow, but I heard her whisper my name. I sat down and touched her hand. For a long time I sat there. Now and then Maum Jean spoke softly, her mind was clear. She hoped I remembered the things she had taught me.

Then the old voice spoke, stronger suddenly, "Oh," said Maum Jean with surprise and gladness, "It's so beautiful!" She gave a little contented sigh and died. And then something quite unbelievable happened. In the semidarkness her face seemed to glow. No one had touched the lamp. There was no other source of light. But her features, which had been almost invisible, could be seen plainly and she was smiling. It lasted for perhaps ten seconds. It was most strange, but not at all frightening. I couldn't account for it then, and I can't account for it now. But I saw it. We all saw it. Then it faded and was gone. That happened a long time ago. But I still think of Maum Jean often. And I will always remember the main thing she taught me: that nothing is a barrier when love is strong enough.

Friends, for the spiritually sensitive, the tales of Abba Abraham and Maum Jean are the Christmas story retold. The monk who left the peace of the desert for the tawdry tavern, the woman who left her house to enter into the life of a cripple are, I suggest, powerful images of Christmas's meaning. Both stories evoke the ancient majestic Scripture, "The Word was made flesh and dwelt among us." Now we know why: because there is no barrier to love.

The LENTEN CYCLE

8. Lent Is Calling

Not everyone who claims me and devotedly calls me "Lord"; not everyone who does pious and churchy things, and those who wear the label of disciple but are short on action, those who talk out of both sides of their mouths without ever taking a stand—none of these will be saved.

Whenever I hear these gospel words of Jesus I always immediately think of the famous response of a Tennessee legislator answering a constituent's letter about the "whiskey situation." He wrote:

Dear Friend:

I had not intended to discuss the controversial subject at this particular time. However, I want you to know that I do not shun controversy. On the contrary, I will take a stand on any issue at any time, regardless of how fraught with controversy it may be. You have asked me how I feel about whiskey. Here's how I stand on the question:

IF, when you say "whiskey," you mean: the Devil's brew, the poison scourge, the bloody monster that defiles innocence, dethrones reason, destroys the home, creates misery and poverty—yes, literally takes the bread from the mouths of little children.

If you mean the drink that topples the Christian man and woman from the pinnacle of righteous, gracious living into the bottomless pit of degradation, despair, shame, and helplessness, then, certainly, I am against it with all my power.

32

BUT, if, when you say "whiskey," you mean: the oil of conversation, the philosophic wine, the ale that is consumed when good fellows get together; that puts a song in their hearts, and laughter on their lips and the warm glow of contentment in their eyes; if you mean Christian cheer; if you mean the stimulating drink that puts the spring in an old gentleman's step on a frosty morning; if you mean the drink, the sale of which pours into our treasury untold millions of dollars which are used to provide tender care for our crippled children, our blind, our deaf, pitiful, aged, and infirm; to build highways, hospitals, and schools, then certainly I am in favor of it.

This is my stand, and I will not compromise.

That's a clever reflection of the gospel, on those who prefer the shallow life to the authentic life. It's this kind of lip service that Jesus is warning against. But, I tell you, the need for authenticity has never been more urgent than today because today people are more spiritually hungry than ever. True, we have so much even in recession times—at least in our western world— houses, cars, endless electronic toys, pornography on demand, nonstop entertainment, travel, books, television, web sites—the litany is endless.

Yet, with all this busy, noisy abundance, which gives us a feeling of being important, there is a great spiritual hunger. One spiritual writer puts it like this:

Our society portrays us as "consumers" but misidentifies our hunger. We can devour all the hamburgers in the world and still not be satisfied. Obesity is the symptom of a society whose hunger cannot be quenched because we have forgotten what we long for, which is each other. We are starved of the happiness of those who are dying of malnutrition, unable to see that their flourishing is our own. Above all, we are hungry for God.

The lotions, makeovers, cosmetic surgeries, and billion-dollar public relations industries can't hide the hunger in our lives, where the lowest common denominator of conduct, greed, evil, and lying have numbed our sensitivities, a hunger not satisfied by a culture where anything goes because, as we know, when anything goes, nothing counts, and we need something to count, to live for, to die for.

We have a subtle, unarticulated sense that we are longing for a more substantial life, something that gives meaning and offers spiritual depth and joy. Like sheep without a shepherd, we are hungry, restless, and discontent. The body may be full to obesity but the heart is empty, and we don't know where to turn. We have grown weary of programs, promises, and pronouncements. We are drowning in words. Our cry is deep and painful: "Don't tell me. Show me! Show me the authentic life."

One writer says, "[People] want to witness someone, anyone—just one will do—living an authentic life, someone whose words are supported by the authority of his or her actions. Someone striving humbly but heroically to live by what is good, true, and noble in the midst of—and in spite of—the modern climate."

These words form the theme of today's gospel, and Jesus taps into it when he says that not everyone who talks a good game is a disciple, but only those who do God's will: those whose actions speak louder than words, those who are real, authentic. And he's calling us to be that authentic person.

As in this story: the reporter was interviewing an old man, a grandfather who was obviously still in intense grief over the shooting death of his teenage grandson. The grandson had been shot in a robbery of the family's little neighborhood store.

"Do you want revenge on those who did this," asked the very modern reporter. "Would you like to shoot the person who shot your grandson?" he asked again with relish, dreaming of getting higher ratings on TV.

But the old man only looked astonished at the question. "No, that's not possible," he said.

"Oh, I guess that's because you don't even know for sure who did this," said the eager reporter.

"No, no," said the grandfather. "It's not like that. It's that we are Christians. We are not permitted revenge."

And the reporter's mouth fell open. He simply could not comprehend that kind of a response. He encountered authenticity and could not handle it, even though, deep down, he secretly desired it.

Why am I going on talking this way? Because we're in the shadow of Lent. This Wednesday's dark ashes speak of limits, the time when the clock runs out on our stewardship. What will be our legacy? Who are we? What have we become? These are the questions of Lent. With the world's desperate need, desperate search for heroes, for witnesses to a more noble life, for authenticity—when the world looks at us, what does it see?

Maybe Lent's challenge this year is to strive to become an authentic person, to live as Jesus taught, to become a saint. The world needs kindness, compassion, generosity, forgiveness, acceptance, and love, but we have divided hearts of a thousand compromises. Let's undo some of them. Let's work toward authenticity. Be ourselves, embrace who we fundamentally are: children of God, disciples of Jesus, those who cry, "Lord, Lord," and mean it.

O.K. let me give you a break and lighten things up a bit. There's the story of the woman who was working in her front yard when a moving van pulled up next door. Her new neighbors drove up behind the moving van. While the movers were unloading, the new neighbors walked over and greeted the woman. She was a bit self-conscious because she was rather a mess. She had dirt on her hands and face and was wearing dirty old clothes. Well, a few days later the new neighbors invited the woman and her husband to an open house. This was the woman's opportunity to make a better impression than last time. So she colored her hair, put on a girdle, glossed her lips, applied eye shadow and false eyelashes, polished her fingernails, and popped in her colored contact lenses. She stepped to the mirror and admiringly told her husband, "Now the new neighbors will get to see the real me!"

Funny? Of course. But in the light of what we have said, also sad. This Lent, let the real me, the Jesus follower, the God collaborator, stand up and shine through. For Lent, the goal is to strive to become the best version of ourselves.

9. A Tale of Two Cities

The great Hindu religious leader of the nineteenth century, Swami Vivekananda, once said, "The intensest love that humanity has ever known has come from religion, and the most diabolical hatred that humanity has known has come from religion."

We shall see the truth of his words unfold in this homily, which I have titled, "A Tale of Two Cities," a take-off on Charles Dickens' famous book of the same name about the French Revolution. Only this isn't a story based in London and Paris, but in two cities worlds apart: Philadelphia in the United States and Tibhirine in Algeria. One is a tale of shame of the worst kind, the other of love of the deepest kind. As you'll see, maybe I should have titled this, "A Tale of Two Churches."

The tale of shame—and it pains all of us to recall this because is it so appallingly familiar—is summed up in the removal last month of 28 priests in the archdiocese of Philadelphia—the largest single suspension of clergy in U.S. history—against whom there are allegations of sexual abuse of minors. In spite of credible allegations that these priests were abusive, the archdiocese failed to follow the guidelines set out in 2002 and simply and outrageously moved these priests around to continue their evil. The monsignor in charge of clergy personnel, Msgr. William Lynn, has been criminally charged with child endangerment and, if found guilty, will likely serve jail time. The others are awaiting trial.

This ongoing scandal in Philadelphia and elsewhere continues to be an open wound in the Church, a wound that will fester for decades more to come. The Catholic Church is branded with a large scarlet letter that besmirches the gospel, tarnishes good priests, and shames Catholics everywhere.

Why would anyone stay in a Church like this? The answer may be found in another city, another country, Tibhirine, Algeria.

As you may know, a powerful movie filmed in Morocco has been made about that country. The name of the film is *Of Gods and Men*, a phrase taken from Psalm 81 where it says, "I have said you are gods; and all of you are children of the most high. But you shall die like men and fall like one of the princes." It won the Grand Prix in 2010 at Cannes, and has also been nominated as the best film of the year.

It's the true story of seven Roman Catholic Trappist monks at Our Lady of Atlas Monastery in Algeria during the 1990s Algerian Civil War. Their mission as monks—who are lay people, remember—is to live a life of prayer and contemplation and, in addition, to serve the wretchedly poor people in the area by giving them medical assistance, comfort, counseling, and education.

It's a dangerous place to live. Islamic terrorism is at every corner and grows more intense each day. The monks are increasingly witnessing with horror the ruthless murders of the townspeople. They have heard about the murder of European construction workers by terrorists and recoil on hearing about the stabbing by Islamic fundamentalists of a woman on a bus who was not wearing a veil. They begin to realize that they cannot long escape the same fate if they remain there.

In fact, the Algerian government has asked the monks to leave for their own safety. Ominously, it's not long before a group of fundamentalists show up at the monastery on Christmas Eve demanding medicine for their wounded colleagues. Though their request is refused—the monks need the medicine for the desperate local people—the abbot quotes the Koran to their leader, and they end up shaking hands, but the abbot knows in his heart that they will be back. And each monk also knows that, sooner or later, when they do come back, the monks will have to decide what to do: to flee or to stay.

Ultimately, in a most poignant scene, the movie takes us, the audience, into the monks' chapter room, where they candidly struggle to come to a decision that has to be unanimous. Shall they flee to safely or shall they stay with the understanding that they will most certainly be killed?

Their discussions are long, measured, respectful, quiet, with stretches of profound silence. We the audience are allowed to gaze into their searching eyes as each one lays bare his fears, his struggle, his ambiguity, his faith, his soul. The power of the film is such that we ourselves are invited to imagine ourselves around that table, to feel the agony, the weight of coming to a decision. Think: What would you decide? What would I decide?

Finally compassion and humility win out, and the monks decide to stay where they are and not abandon the people. They feel deeply that Jesus, who has sent them there to work and pray among the oppressed people of Algeria, would not want them to abandon them, no matter what the danger, the suffering. The monks, in effect, have decided to offer the world the possibility of another way to live and to die, to show what the world might look like transformed by grace.

The high point of the film comes when the monks re-create the Last Supper by sitting around a small table drinking wine and listening to a recording of Tchaikovsky's *Swan Lake*. As the camera pans from face to face, we observe a beatific smile on some faces, tears on others, apprehension on all. This is it.

We hear the abbot muse aloud. He says, "If it should happen one day, and it could be today, that I become a victim of terrorism, which somehow seems to encompass all the foreigners living in Algeria, I would like them to be able to associate this death, my death, with so many equally violent ones allowed to fall into anonymity. My life is of no more value than any other nor any less value. I have lived long enough to know that I share the evil which seems to prevail in the world and even in that which would strike me blindly."

Not long after their "Last Supper," in 1996, they are all beheaded. As he approaches his death, the abbot, obviously mindful of Jesus on Calvary, addresses the Islamic militant whose sword will kill him: "You, my friend, who do not know what you are doing, yes, for you too, I give you farewell and commend you to the God whose face I see in yours. And someday may we find each other happy 'good thieves' in Paradise, if it please God." And his head rolled into the dust.

Thus my sober tale of two cities, two churches. A tale meant for Lent because, when you come right down to it, Lent basically asks, over and over again, which city we inhabit, which church we inhabit. We may, of course, not be at the sick level of predators but we all have our compromises, we all are faced with countless little decisions, and some big ones, that define our moral addresses.

We can't get around it: if we don't leave the Church but decide to stay, then we are Catholic Christians either in name or in deed, in sin or repentance, in indifference or in decision. As Lenten pilgrims, for forty days we are presented with two ways, two cities, two churches. Lent, in short, is the time to sit around the table and decide who we are—sinner or saint—and which church we belong to.

10. Listen With Your Eyes

We priests, like many others, pass around in-house jokes and bloopers. In my early days it was said of one pastor that he was inaccessible on weekdays and incomprehensible on Sundays.

Or there's that snide thing they say about us preachers: "A preacher is someone who talks in other people's sleep."

And we all remembered the earnest priest who concluded a wedding ceremony with, "Go, the Mass and the marriage are ended."

Our all-time favorite is the one where, at a funeral homily, this priest, gesturing toward the casket, intoned solemnly, "What we see before us is the mere shell. The nut is gone."

Despite that delightful nonsense, I want to turn serious on this first Sunday of Lent and share some evocative themes. To keep you awake, I am going to do this is by telling you some stories, three of them to be exact, two that are about us and one that is about Jesus. I ask you to listen, not with TV ears and hearts, but with faith ears and hearts. These stories are not to entertain. They are stories that offer images to put us in the mood for Lent.

My first story concerns a Dr. Scott Peck, who was, way back, a celebrated, best-selling author and psychiatrist—some older folk here may remember his name. He once told a story about counseling a man who was a career sergeant in the army stationed in Okinawa in the 1940s and 50s. This sergeant was in serious trouble because of his excessive drinking and was being counseled by Dr. Peck. In their sessions the sergeant denied that he was an alcoholic, or even that his use of alcohol was a problem. "There's nothing else to do in the evenings in Okinawa," he said in justifying his behavior, "except drink."

Peck then asked him if he liked reading, and the sergeant said he loved to read. So the doctor asked him if he couldn't read a book instead of going out drinking

"Nah," said the sergeant, "the barrack's too chaotic with all the guys."

"You could go to the library," Peck suggested.

"No, the library's too far away," was the response. Confronted with the fact that the library was no farther away than the bar, the sergeant claimed he wasn't really that much of a reader after all. The doctor suggested fishing, which the sergeant liked, but he said he wasn't available in the day and Okinawa didn't have night fishing. Peck came back with an offer to put the sergeant in touch with a number of people who were enthusiastic night fishers, and suddenly the sergeant said that, well, he wasn't much of a fisherman either.

"So," Dr. Peck said, summing things up, "There are things you could do here besides drink, but given the choice, you're going to choose drinking over any of them."

"Guess that's right," said the sergeant.

"But since it's getting you in all kinds of trouble, seems like you've got a pretty severe dilemma on your hands."

With anger the sergeant answered, "This island would drive anyone to drink!"

It's a story, but we surely get the point and recognize that the sergeant is us, routinely rationalizing our less-than-Christlike behaviors. It's a story, a parable, made for Lent; for Lent, like Dr. Peck, is here to tell us to stop kidding ourselves, to confess our sins, not our excuses. It's time to strike our breasts and call it like it is, crying out, "O God, be merciful to me, a sinner!"

My second image-story is a familiar one to all of us these days. It's about a mother named Sue who was standing at the kitchen sink, working diligently on dinner preparations, her mind totally committed to the task at hand, peeling potatoes. Her middle son, three-year-old Steven, was playing nearby. Within a few moments she felt a tug on her skirt proceeded by the words, "Mommy..." She nodded something like "un-huh" or "yes?" and went on peeling the potatoes. There were more tugs on her skirt and more little sounds: "Mommy..." Again, she gave a brief verbal comment and yet stayed right at her task.

Five minutes passed. Steven continued to chatter and then she felt those tugs on her skirt again. This time the tugs seemed harder and more persistent. She finally put her potatoes down in the sink and bent down to her son. Steven took her face in his two little chubby hands, turning her directly to his line of vision and said, "Mommy, will you listen to me with your eyes?"

That rings a bell, for there we are: multitasking, treating the people who have needs, the people we love, like they're a distraction from "what really matters." You know: cell phone to the ear, attention to the computer screen, fingers to the text board, head turned toward the TV. And all the while, all that our loved ones want is that we listen with our eyes so that they know they are important to us; and the poor, the sick, and the needy want to hold our faces to their line of vision so that, like Mother Teresa, we see them and respond to them.

So never mind the grand schemes of "doing something for Lent." There's these telling little spiritual challenges right in front of us, laden with the invitations to a deeper spirituality.

Now, for the Jesus story.

Father Bob Roberts received a call from a hospital. The operator informed him that Mary, a member of the church, wanted to see him because her child had just died.

Fr. Roberts sped off in his car to a hospital several miles away. He had a vague idea who Mary was. She had been involved in the young adult group, so he knew her enough to say "hello." Yet he couldn't ever remember seeing her with a child, so he was shocked to hear that her child had died.

When he got to the hospital, he was directed to a dark, quiet corridor where he found Mary, just outside of her son's room. "Thank you so much for coming," she said. As he and Mary paused in the hall, she told him the heartbreaking story of her son, Jimmy. Jimmy had been born with multiple physical and mental handicaps. As they spoke they went into the room where Jimmy's body lay. All the tubes and wires were still connected to him. Fr. Roberts was totally shocked by what he saw. Jimmy was tiny, much smaller than a normal seven-year-old boy. His little body was badly twisted and deformed. The priest found it difficult even to look at him without wincing.

But not Mary. She looked upon her son with eyes of uncompromised love. She touched his face and spoke quietly to him, even though he couldn't hear anymore. She tenderly kissed his cheek many times. Mary told Roberts how much Jimmy had meant to her, and how much she would miss him. Then the priest had a kind of epiphany. He realized that where he saw Jimmy as someone marred in his appearance, almost beyond human resemblance, Mary saw him as a beautiful, lovely human being, and she lavished undeserved, unabashed, unquenchable love on her child.

We get the picture, don't we? Jesus sees us the same way. However we are, however others see us—unlovely, broken, sinful—Jesus loves with a redeeming, unquenchable love. And while for Lent we confess our sins and do our penances as we should, we must remember that Jesus' compassion, forgiveness, and love are also a part of the Lenten equation.

End of stories and end of homily, but I have a parting suggestion. If you want to carry around a kind of spiritual mantra or image for Lent, how about picturing Jesus as little Steven and hear him saying to you what Steven said to his mother: "Listen to me. Listen to me with your eyes!" That is, "Put aside the distractions and give me your full attention these 40 days of Lent. Yes, listen to me with your eyes—and with your heart."

11. The Temptation Chronicles

FIRST SUNDAY OF LENT, A, MATTHEW 4:1–11

We have an ancient storybook that has nourished our lives for millennia. It's called the Bible. It's an anthology of stories because, the ancients—unlike ourselves, who are negatively addicted to what we call "objective" data and erroneously equate facts with truth—the ancients more wisely wrapped truth in story. That's why we remember them.

Think, for example, of that first-century rabbi called Jesus. Someone once asked him, "Who is my neighbor?" And, being the good Semite that he was, he smiled and replied, "Have I got a story for you!"

He then proceeded to make up entirely out of his head an interesting tale about a priest, a Levite, and a Samaritan (notice the standard storytelling device of "three") encountering a man who had been viciously mugged. It was all made up, of course: there was no priest, Levite, or Samaritan on the road from Jericho. Factually, it never happened. Ah, but the truth of that story has challenged and nourished us ever since, hasn't it?

I bring this up because we have a wonderful instance of a provocative story in today's readings. In Jesus' life, as his disciples knew and witnessed, Jesus encountered many challenges, many temptations to bank on his status and misuse his power. He faced them all down. When, decades later, the first-century gospel writers wanted to display this particular truth, they automatically turned to story as a means to do it.

Fortunately, they had a ready-made plot at hand that every Jew knew deep in his bones. Ancient Israel, so went the traditional tale, was led into the desert and there was tempted threefold. Only the Israelites didn't do so well. So the gospel writers—especially Matthew, the most Jewish of them all—took the plot outlines of that tale and rewove a new story that, while factually not true, was morally true, That is, they told a deep truth about Jesus when they had him meet the same three temptations the ancient Israelites encountered. Only Jesus conquered, while they caved in. That reworked story is our gospel for today; for this first Sunday of Lent it couldn't be better.

First temptation: "Are you hungry?" asked Satan knowing, as the story tells us, that Jesus had just fasted for forty days (a storytelling number, like three and twelve). He went on: "God's Son, if you are that, shouldn't be hungry. That's beneath your dignity. Change the stones into bread and don't sweat it out." It's the same temptation that ancient Israel underwent. They were God's chosen people, and chosen people by definition shouldn't be hungry, and when they were, they felt that God didn't love them anymore, and they proceeded to protest and complain and rant at God.

But Jesus gives us a powerful truth that too many Christians have never accepted. In the story he says in effect to Satan, "You say, if I am God's son, I should not be hungry. I should trade in my connections and do a cheap miracle. I am God's beloved, his son, but let me tell you, being beloved, being God's son, does not mean that I will never be hungry, that I will never be vulnerable, never hurt, never cry, never die. My Father's love is no guarantee of non-stop bliss. On the contrary, my Father's love is the guarantee that he will always stand by me in my pain." Jesus would show the truth of his words when one day, in deep agony, he would have to struggle to move from "Father, take this chalice from me" to "Into your hands I commend my spirit."

This is the answer Jesus gave in contrast to ancient Israel, and how we have missed it! I've heard this lost lesson enough: "How could God take my child? How could I get cancer? How could I lose my job? How could my marriage fail? Why is life so unfair? I'm a good Catholic. I go to church every Sunday, am honest, live a good life. How could God do this to me? I've been so faithful, and look at this! Why is God punishing me? What did I do to deserve this? God doesn't love me anymore!"

These are the cries of crisis, and they are understandable, but notice the false assumptions that Jesus tried to overturn: "God and I have a contract—I live a good and faithful life, and God in turn guarantees me no pain, no disappointment, no loss. I am, after all, God's son, God's daughter."

Jesus would say that love doesn't deal with legal contracts. It deals with fidelity. "Behold I am with you all days, even to the end of the world." We should never say God doesn't love us. We should never "punish" God by dropping out of church or ceasing to pray. What kind of concept do you have of him? He's not your lawyer. He's not the magician turning life's stones into bread. He's the parent at the child's bedside, the friend comforting a loss, the hospice worker preparing for death. He's the tears Jesus wept over Lazarus.

He is faithful. He does not subtract pain. He adds faithful love. When a distraught parent once yelled at me, "Where was God when my son died?" I could only answer, "The same place when his son died." God is not indifferent. God does not withdraw his love. Our anguish is not unnoticed, unfelt. Position does not negate pain.

So, in the gospel, Jesus said outright that, just because I am the Son of God, I am not immune from what life will do to me. Being God's Son does not mean turning stones into bread. It means turning the hard things of life into compassion, charity, and trust that my Father will keep his word and make all things new again. We need to ponder his words.

Quickly, the other two temptations are the same. The second: play Lois Lane and jump off the Empire State Building, and angels, like Superman, will bear you up. Israel's pride led them to such foolishness. Jesus replied that we're not to pull God's chain and walk into temptation with our eyes open and expect no consequences.

Finally, Satan's sweet invitation to fall down and adore him and Jesus will be marketable, a high roller, an instant celebrity doing two shows a day in Las Vegas, and you'll have more houses, cars, and sex than you can handle. This is the life! Celebrate yourself! Jesus simply points out that that kind of life is death, the death of empathy, community, justice, and charity. We were made to exist beyond bread.

If the three temptations of Jesus are the evangelists' story version of Israel's three temptations in the desert, then we are meant to ponder them. The ancient people embraced privilege, pride, and power. Jesus rejected that triple temptation and embraced trust, humility, and service.

12. Give Them What They Want

Since we are celebrating the first Sunday of Lent with its story about temptation, let me update its theme with another story. Once there was a well-known, very wealthy industrialist who decided to purchase, of all things, a zoo. It was not meant for the public. It was meant just for him, his personal pleasure, something to show off to his equally wealthy friends. So he collected animals from all over the world, and his zoo soon became one of the most complete collections ever.

One day the man heard about a rare and beautiful type of gazelle from Africa. No other zoo had this animal, so he was determined to be the first. He mounted an expedition to Africa, where the natives told him that he could never capture rare gazelles. They were too fast, too strong, too smart. He was told he would never take one alive.

That made him more determined. He told a reporter, "I'll get one; in fact, I'll get as many of them as I want. Won't be a problem." And he did; and this is how he did it.

When his men located a herd of these gazelles, he poured sweet feed—a blend of oats and barely rolled in molasses—on the ground in an open area in the middle of the night, and then left. The next night, he would scatter the feed again. For two weeks he spread the feed, night after night. The animals, of course, came in and ate this delicious concoction. Then, on the first night of the third week, he scattered the feed and sank an eight-foot post in the ground twenty feet away. The next night, he scattered the feed and sank another post into the ground twenty feet in the opposite direction. Every night he added a post. Then he started putting boards between the posts while scattering the feed.

Six weeks rolled by. He continued adding posts and boards until he had a corral built around the feed. Every night the gazelles, lured by the easy treats and focused on the easy sweets, would find gaps between the posts and would come into the corral and feed. They were quite oblivious to the fact that they were gradually losing their freedom. Temptation does that. It blocks out peripheral moral vision.

Finally, the man watched one night as the entire herd squeezed through the final gap. He moved in behind them and nailed the last board into place. The animals were trapped inside the corral. He then proceeded to choose the animals he wanted to take back to his zoo, and he let the others go. When he was asked how he knew how to catch them, he said, "I treat animals the same way I treat people. I give them what they want. In exchange they give me their freedom."

A nice and obvious parable about how the gradual seductions of temptation work, a parable of how our lives are being slowly lured away from the freedom of children of God. Some are lured into becoming less than who they are by bold and grand schemes and crass greed—think Bernie Madoff—and we've have lots of examples of that in the past few years, examples that have ultimately cost us economic freedom. Most of us, however, are lured by something smaller, something more pervasive and subtle, and that is the pursuit of the trivial. I hasten to add at the outset that trivia is not all that bad. We all need some mindless distraction, some diversion, a bit of relief in our lives. We know it, enjoy it, and then let it go.

The trouble comes when we don't let it go, can't let it go because even good people like ourselves become addicted to the trivial and accept it as substance. Like the gazelles fixed on sweets, we become fixated on a world of the shallow and the hollow, the banal and the inane. We no longer realize how captive we are, how much our lives are shaped and determined by how we look, how much we consume, how much we hang on every word that comes from the mouth of Charlie Sheen.

As someone famously said, we are being entertained to death. Tutored by a mass media, we are endlessly distracted by things that are nice but which don't really matter, causing us to live unreflectively on this unnourishing diet of bread alone. We find ourselves following every directive from self-appointed fashion critics like botoxed Joan Rivers.

Fortunately, just before the last board is nailed into place, as it were, Lent comes along and, like a quivering arrow just shot into the tree we're about to pass, claims our attention and demands that we stop and think that maybe we need to escape, to do some sorting, some pruning, some prioritizing. Lent comes along to remind us that there are flies and death and stuff out there that need our attention, our ministry, our compassion, our love.

Lent calls our attention to life's more profound realities, like the wake-up call portrayed in this story. Many years ago Fr. John Powell told of a student he had in his religion class, a boy named Tommy who, as resident cynic, was a pain in the back pew, always scoffing, always asking if he would ever find God, and Fr. Powell always shooting back sarcastically, "No, but he'll find you." Fr. Powell was happy to see him move on. Tommy eventually graduated and then, out of the blue, years later, he came to visit Fr. Powell. There he was. No more long hair, no more macho body. Tommy had terminal cancer. Fr. Powell found himself asking Tommy what it was like to be 24 and dying.

"Well, it could be worse," Tommy replied, "like being 50 and thinking that booze, seducing women, and making money were the real biggies in life."

Then Tommy went on to say that, when he got cancer, he banged against the doors of heaven, but God did not come out, and so he just quit banging and decided that, whether there was a God or not, he would spend his remaining days doing something more profitable. He said he recalled some words Fr. Powell had spoken in class: "The essential sadness is to go through life without loving. But it would be almost equally sad to go through life and leave this world without ever telling those you loved that you loved them."

"So," said Tommy, "I began with the hardest one, my dad."

Tommy went on to describe it. "He was reading the newspaper when I approached him.

"Dad?"

"Yes, what?" he asked without lowering the newspaper.

"Dad, I would like to talk with you."

"Well, talk."

"I mean… it's really important."

The newspaper came down three slow inches.

"What is it?"

"Dad, I love you, I just wanted you to know that."

The newspaper fluttered to the floor. Then, Tommy said, his father did two things he could not remember him doing before. He cried, and he hugged him. And they talked all night. "It felt so good to be close to my father," Tommy told Fr. Powell, "to see his tears, to feel his hug, to hear him say that he loved me."

It was easier with his mother and little brother. But Tommy added this, "Then, one day, I turned around and God was there. He found me even after I stopped looking for him." Tommy had discovered that the surest way to find God was to get out of his small, self-absorbed world.

By the way, Fr. Powell asked Tommy to come and share his story with his class. Tommy promised, but he never made it. He died before the scheduled date.

The point of the Tommy story is the point of the gazelle story is the point of this homily on Lent's first Sunday: our isolated lives are circumscribed with seductive, attractive, appealing trivia, fluff that really doesn't matter. We need to shake free of some of it. We need to drop some of it before the last board is in place and we become simply unthinking clones of some celebrity. We need to resist like Jesus and be like Jesus.

So turn off some TV. Toss aside the tabloids. Read a portion of St. Matthew's gospel each day. Put down the cell phone and the iPad for a stretch. Look around: There's people out there who need to know that we love them. There's people out there—too many of them—who don't have laps much less laptops. They need our charity. In short, there's a world out there that needs our love, our compassion, our purpose in life. There's a God out there who needs to be discovered.

That's what Jesus dramatically showed us in today's gospel: We do not live by bread alone, even reduced fat bread that will make us slim.

13. The Transfiguration

SECOND SUNDAY OF LENT, A, MATTHEW 17:1–9

Jim was sitting at the blackjack table and wondering what he was doing there.

Just then he remembered seeing a sign in the casino that read, "If you have a gambling problem, call 1-800-Gambler."

Jim pulled out his cell phone and made the call.

"Hello?" a man on the other end answered.

Jim replied, "I have a gambling problem."

"It's good you called," the man on the other end said. "I want to acknowledge you for taking a step in the right direction. Now, let's get a bit more specific about your problem."

"Okay," Jim answered, "I have an ace and a six. The dealer has a seven. What do I do?"

That's not quite what the man on the other end expected—and this gospel is not quite what we expect or think it is either. We expected, as I read it, a reporter's account of what happened on a mountaintop a long time ago. But Matthew, the creative author, is not a reporter. He wasn't even there. He was, rather, a Jew, a first-century Semite, who did not make up reports. When he wanted to get across a truth, he, like his Mid-East contemporaries, wrote symbol stories.

For this story of what we of a later age title "The Transfiguration," Matthew pulled in all the old themes and metaphors familiar to every devout Jew, and he reworked them into a truth about Jesus. What were those themes and metaphors he employed? They were the old standards: a mountaintop, because that's where the ancients thought the gods dwelled; a cloud, the usual signal of God's presence; a bright face that recalled Moses'

51

shining face after his encounter with God; two old, reliable champions of the law and the prophets, Moses and Elijah, and so on. Matthew put all these memory-laden symbols together, shook them up, and came up with a tale, a parable, of what we call the Transfiguration that, like Jesus' made-up story about the Good Samaritan, would encapsulate a truth to ponder.

Then the next thing Matthew did was to carefully position his tale right smack between the two major moments of Jesus' life: Jesus' call at his baptism when all was promise—"This is my Beloved Son. Listen to him"—and his passion and death when all was failure—"My God, my God, why have you abandoned me?" The transfiguration story was to be an important interpretative bridge between them. Remember that.

And this is what it meant, There was so much joy and promise at the beginning of Jesus' life, and so much sadness and disappointment at the end of it, that his disciples were beginning to wonder where God was in all of this. Matthew's transfiguration story strives to deal with that problem. His story was also meant to challenge generations of Christians ever after because, sooner or later, everyone would have promise and disappointment, and everyone would ask at one time or another, "My God, my God, why have you abandoned me?"

The marriage, the children, the job, the health, the security, the project—all start out well and promising and then, for whatever reason, one day they turn to horrid ashes and bitter disappointments.

And when the failure is stunningly massive and global and utterly beyond human comprehension—think of the earthquake in Japan that took tens of thousands of lives, displaced millions, destroyed drinking water, food, and shelter, and left nuclear fallout to poison generations—and the burden is staggering, the question of abandonment by God cries to heaven.

So, let's go back and see how Matthew sets up the dilemma. There is Jesus, and Peter and James and John contentedly traveling with their beloved friend. Suddenly Jesus changes, and his face and clothes shine like fire. He is brilliant with promise, hope, joy. Then the two old symbolic prophets, Moses and Elijah, are conversing with Jesus, and a voice from that cloud says, "This is my beloved Son in whom I am well pleased." It's a memorable, stunning moment, never to be forgotten. Then the scene fades. The apostles are bowled over, and they head for home, awed and charged up—until Jesus says, "By the way, don't tell anyone what you've experienced until I am raised from the dead."

From the dead? Where did that come from? All this springtime of light and cloud and a voice-giving affirmation, and Jesus talks winter? St. Luke's version of the story makes the dissonance even more noticeable. He says that in their conversation with Jesus, Moses and Elijah were actually discussing Jesus' suffering and death. So, razzle-dazzle on the one hand, pain and death on the other. The apostles looked at each other. "What gives?"

What gives is hope. When Jesus is no longer greeted by the praises of a crowd waving palms but is vilified by a nasty mob hurling hate speech, when Jesus no longer shines but is covered by the shadow of death, the disciples are to remember the story of the transfiguration when God was with Jesus and with them and to take hope from that. They are to retrieve and retell that story, for it told them that, no matter how desperate, how evil, how deep the suffering, the pain, the loss, the death, they are to trust in God's presence, God's voice, and God's words of blessedness and peace.

When in horror his disciples eventually see Jesus dying in agony on the cross and placed dead in a cave—all is over, all hopes are dashed—they are to force themselves to remember a story that took place on a bright day on a mountaintop and know in their hearts that this tragedy cannot be the last word—not when they heard other words of hope and saw other visions of victory.

In other words, the transfiguration story is, as it were, an ace up the Christian sleeve, a story to be told when all is ashes. A beloved Son knew glory; and a beloved Son—God's own Son—was not immune to betrayal, humiliation, suffering, and death; and a beloved Son, while he was dying, remembered the mountaintop experience, and forced himself to pray, "Father, into your hands I commend my spirit"; and a beloved Son's trust was vindicated in the resurrection.

The transfiguration incident was meant to be a memory card for the disciples to play when they needed it. And they would need it later when they were faced with the death that Jesus mysteriously spoke about at the time. They would remember that there was a splendiferous Jesus, and there was a God calling him beloved; and that gave them hope. God would not forget his beloved.

Ford Francis Coppola gave us not only arguably the best motion picture ever made in *The Godfather*, but also the beautiful movie *The Black Stallion*. You may recall it is the story of a boy and his father and some horses on a ship that sank. Only the boy and a black stallion survive by getting to an island. The story tells of the gradual bonding between the horse and the boy.

What kept the boy going in his lonely time on the island was a small statue of a horse, Alexander the Great's horse, Bucephalus, that his father had given him. He cherished that horse because it brought back memories of his father, who loved him deeply. Even after the boy and the stallion were rescued and eventually entered and won a big race, that little toy horse was his keepsake, the felt presence of his dad, his icon of hope when times were difficult.

The transfiguration story functions like the toy horse. In the difficult times when our promises turn to disappointments, we are not to despair. We are not immune to hurt, any more than Jesus was, but we are always and everywhere, like Jesus, beloved sons, beloved daughters, in whom God is well pleased, even when we're laid low. We are to remember that hard and painful times are not signs that God has withdrawn his love from us any more than he withdrew it from Jesus. Just as the transfiguration story gave the apostles hope, so it is meant to do the same for us.

The voice of God, muted in times of deep distress, is still the voice of God, and we are still beloved.

14. Encounters

*[In the lectionary, this gospel is clumsy even in its shortened form.
I have reworked it here to conform to the homily.
On the homily itself, see the Notes.]*

A Reading of the Holy Gospel According to John

At that time Jesus had to pass through Samaria, and his journey brought him to the Samaritan town named Shechem near the site of Jacob's well. Jesus, tired and thirsty from his journey, sat down at the well. The hour was about noon.

While his disciples had gone off to buy provisions, a Samaritan woman came to draw water, and Jesus said to her, "Give me a drink." Astonished, the Samaritan woman said to him, "You are a Jew. How can you ask me, a Samaritan, and a woman at that, for a drink?" Jesus replied: "Ah, if only you recognized God's gift, and who it is that is asking you for a drink, you would have asked him instead, and he would have given you living water."

"Sir," she challenged him, "you don't have a bucket and this well is deep. Where do you expect to get this flowing water? Surely you don't pretend to be greater than our ancestor Jacob, who gave us this well and drank from it with his sons and his flocks?" Jesus replied evenly, "Everyone who drinks this water will be thirsty again. But whoever drinks the water I give him will never be thirsty. No, the water I give shall become a fountain within him, leaping up to provide eternal life." The woman, intrigued, said to him, "Give me this water, sir, so that I won't grow thirsty and have to keep coming here to draw water."

Ignoring her request, Jesus suddenly shifted ground as he told her, "Go, call your husband, and then come back here." "I have no husband," shot back the woman. "You are right in saying you have no husband!" Jesus exclaimed laughing. "The fact is, you have had five, and the man you are living with now is not your husband. What you said is true enough."

The woman, taken aback, answered weakly, "Sir, I can see you are a prophet." Then quickly changing the subject, she said, "You know, our ancestors worshiped on this mountain, but you people claim that Jerusalem is the place where men ought to worship God." Jesus closed his eyes and said in a soft voice, "Believe me, woman, an hour is coming when you will worship the Father neither on this mountain nor in Jerusalem. I tell you, the hour is coming, and is already here, when authentic worshipers will worship the Father in Spirit and truth."

The woman said to him: "Well, I know there is a Messiah coming and when he comes, he will tell us everything." Jesus opened his eyes and replied simply, "I who speak to you am he."

There was a pause as they looked at each other for a long time in silence. Strangely, the woman realized that she was thirsty no longer. She felt refreshed, refreshed in a deep and profound way. After a while, wordlessly, the woman left her water jar at the well and hurried off into the town where she said to the people: "Come and see someone who told me everything I ever did! Could this not be the Messiah?" With that news they all set out from the town to meet him, for many had come to believe in Jesus on the strength of the woman's word of testimony. The result was that, when these Samaritans came to him, they begged him to stay with them awhile. Later on they told the woman: "No longer does our faith depend on your story. We have heard for ourselves, and we ourselves know that this really is the Savior of the world."

The gospel of the Lord.

Even in the shortened gospel version we heard, we catch the dynamics of the carefully crafted story the evangelist has left. A man and a woman from opposite sides of the tracks have an accidental meeting at a well. What they have in common is thirst, he for her wholeness, she for water. They are a man—Jesus the Jew—and the nameless woman—a Samaritan; Jesus, the holy Messiah, and the woman, a moral cripple. At this well the fallen woman moves slowly from bravado and hostility to surrender and freedom.

It's a classic Christian theme, and, to give it a fresh look, I would transpose this well-known story of the first century in Judea to the beginning of the 20th century in the 1900s in the southern United States where, in a sense, the same encounter occurred. You must listen carefully, which is to say, actively, by entering into the story, by taking on the character of the crippled man who told the story. Listen.

I was a timid six-year old with braces on my legs, a frail, lost, lonely little boy when I first arrived at the farm in Georgia. Had it not been for an extraordinary woman, I might have remained that way, crippled all my life. She lived on the farm in a two-room cabin where her parents had been slaves. To an outsider she looked like any of the black people on the farm, in her shapeless gray dress. But to those who knew her she was a spiritual force whose influence was felt everywhere.

She was the first person called when there was sickness; she made medicines from roots and herbs that seemed to cure just about anything. She had a family of her own, but all the children in the area felt that they belonged to her. Her name reflected this. In the soft speech of the Georgia lowlands, the word "maum" is a slurred version of "Mama." We called her "Maum Jean." Maum Jean talked to the Lord often and we all suspected that when she did He stopped whatever he was doing and listened and took appropriate action. Her heart reached out to small, helpless things, so she took particular interest in me from the start.

When I was stricken with polio at the age of three, I'm sure my parents didn't know what was the matter with me. All they knew was that times were hard and suddenly they had a crippled child on their hands. They took me to a New York City hospital, left me, and never came back. The people who took me into their foster home had relatives on the Georgia estate where I was sent in the hope that the warmer climate might help. From a distance I could feel the presence of Maum Jean. In her quiet way, she looked at me, hurt and crippled, often. Her sensitive emotional antennae instantly picked up the loneliness and withdrawal inside me. Moreover, her marvelous diagnostic sense surveyed the polio damage and decided that, regardless of what the doctors might have said, something more ought to be done.

She responded. Maum Jean had never heard the word "atrophy," but she knew that muscles could waste away unless used. And so every night when her tasks were done she would come to my room and kneel beside my bed to massage my legs. Sometimes, when I would cry out with pain, she would sing old songs or tell me stories. When her treatments were over, she would always talk earnestly to the Lord, explaining that she was doing what she could but that she would need help, and she asked him to give her a sign when He was ready.

A creek wound through the farm and Maum Jean, who had never heard of hydrotherapy, said there was strength in running water. She made her grandson carry me down to a sandy bank where I could splash around pretty well. Slowly I grew taller, but there was little change in my legs. I still used crutches. I still buckled on the clumsy braces. Night after night, Maum Jean continued the massaging and praying.

Then one morning when I was about twelve, she told me she had a surprise for me. She led me out into the yard and placed me with my back against an oak tree. She took away my crutches and braces. She moved back a dozen paces and told me that the Lord had spoken to her in a dream. He had said that the time had come for me to walk. Then she looked at me long and softly. "So now," said Maum Jean at last, "I want you to walk over here to me." My instant reaction was fear. I knew I couldn't walk unaided. I had tried. I shrank back against the solid support of the tree. Maum Jean continued to urge me.

I burst into tears. I begged. I pleaded. Her voice rose suddenly, no longer gentle and coaxing, but full of power and command. "You can walk, boy! The Lord has spoken! Now walk over here!" She knelt down and held out her arms. And somehow, impelled by something stronger than fear, I took a faltering step, and another, and another until I reached Maum Jean and fell into her arms, both of us weeping. It was two more years before I could walk normally, but I never used the crutches again.

There is a sequel to his story. He continues,

For a while longer I lived in my twilight world. Then a circus came through town and when it left, I left with it. For the next few years, I worked with one circus or another. Then the night came when one of Maum Jean's tall grandsons knocked on my door. Maum Jean was dying. She wanted to see me. The old cabin was unchanged. Maum Jean lay in bed surrounded by silent watchers. Her frail body covered by a patchwork quilt. Her face in shadow, but I heard her whisper my name. I sat down and touched her hand. For a long time I sat there. Now and then Maum Jean spoke softly, her mind was clear. She hoped I remembered the things she had taught me.

Then the old voice spoke, stronger suddenly, "Oh," said Maum Jean with surprise and gladness, "It's so beautiful!" She gave a little contented sigh and died. And then something quite unbelievable happened. In the semidarkness her face seemed to glow. No one had touched the lamp. There was no other source of light. But her features, which had been almost invisible, could be seen plainly and she was smiling. It lasted for perhaps ten seconds. It was most strange, but not at all frightening. I couldn't account for it then, and I can't account for it now. But I saw it. We all saw it. Then it faded and was gone. That happened a long time ago.

But I still think of Maum Jean often. I remember the first day she looked upon my brokenness and tears. And I will always remember the main thing she taught me: that nothing is a barrier when love is strong enough. Not age.

Not race. Not sin. Not pain. Not life's unfairness. Not hurt. Not death. Not anything!

I have just related to you a true story of a crippled man at a stream in Georgia, a story that is a modern version of the old story of a thirsty woman at a well in Samaria. One was physically crippled and met a Christ figure in Maum Jean, the other was spiritually thirsty and met Jesus face to face.

It happened then. It happened now. Lent is the time for it to happen again, a time to bring our crippled-ness of sin and our thirst of soul to Jesus Christ.

15. The Untying

The gospel writer John has constructed a complex story for us. It's like a one-act play full of drama that displays a full range of emotions, as befits the doleful subject he's dealing with: death.

Take the disciples. They are full of confusion. And why not? Jesus receives word from two sisters that their brother—and Jesus' very dear, very close friend—Lazarus, is seriously ill. "So," the disciples say, "let's get moving," and they grab their walking sticks. Jesus says, "Hold it. No hurry," and hangs around for two more days while his disciples look at one another totally confused and wondering if Jesus really cares about his friend.

When Jesus finally gets moving and takes another two days to arrive at Bethany, he finds that Lazarus had died in the meanwhile. Lazarus' sister Martha is beside herself and makes no bones about it. She rather testily says to Jesus, "Look, if you had come when you got our message, you could have saved him from dying. Some friend you are!"

She can barely hide her annoyance, her anger, but she immediately feels ashamed as soon as she says those words, so she hastily tries to make amends as she says, though not totally convincingly, "Still, even now, I know that God will hear you if you wish to do something."

Ultimately it all becomes too much for Jesus—the death of a friend, the distraught sisters, the crowd, the wailing—and it clearly upsets him. On the way to the grave he breaks down and cries. And this is not the suppressed, swallowed cry of us Westerners. No, this is the typical Near East wailing with tears freely flowing with head tilted up to the sky. When Jesus finally gets hold of himself, he speaks to the sisters words of comfort and hope; and then, composed, he turns to the tomb. There he commands Lazarus to come forth from it, and then, to the amazed and slack-jawed people, he speaks those final profound, world-shaking words that would ring out forever, "Untie him and let him go."

Untie him and let him go.

These words—untie him and let him go—are the key words of the gospel. These are the words we should cling to and remember, for they describe what has happened to our loved ones. If in the gospel story there are, as we said, lots of emotion—shock, disappointment, confusion, anger, grief, hurt, tears, awe—these are also the feelings so many of us here remember so painfully when we have lost a loved one.

But pause. Go back for a minute to Lazarus. When Jesus said "Untie him and let him go," he was referring to the ancient custom of wrapping the body with strips of cloth from head to toe until, mummy-like, it was ready for burial. And so it was with us.

Do you remember? So often every day, every week, every month, we noticed another strip of confinement and diminishment, physical and mental, slowly wrap around our sick loved ones until one day, little by the little, immobile, the last strip was in place, and they died, and we wept.

And yet faith tells us that this gospel story, this Lazarus story, was repeated with our loved ones. It tells us that, into that moment of death, beyond our shock, anger, confusion, numbness, and unstoppable tears, the weeping Jesus came along and said with compassion to his angels what he said to the crowd at Lazarus' grave, "Untie him and let him go."

"Yes," Jesus continued, "Untie him. Unwrap these strips from head to toe, one by one. Take away the IVs, the tubes, the oxygen, the medicines, the pills, the therapy, the injections, the blood pressure, the chemo, the doctor, the nurse, the hospital, the wounds of the body. Take away the incoherence, the wicked darkness and ravings of the mind. Untie him. Let him go free, let her go free, so that he or she can stand new and shining and renewed and enter into my kingdom." Yes, the Lazarus story says, the physical and mental constrictions of death that we so brokenheartedly witnessed were not the last word. The untying was.

In a very real way the whole Lazarus incident is a preview of Jesus' own terrible death, his mother's unbearable grief, and his crying out to his Father exactly what Martha and Mary cried out to him, "My Father, if you had been here, I would not be dying like this. My God, My God, why have you abandoned me?"

His Father heard and wept and called him out of the tomb on Easter Sunday and said to his angels, "Untie him and let him go. Take away the nails. Take away the thorns. Take away the flogging marks. Take away the blood. Take away the spit. Let him go. Let him go to announce to the world the good news that death is now no longer the last word. It is the next to the last word. After the untying, the last word is life everlasting. It is love. It is freedom."

The Lazarus story, as we said, is a preview of the coming Jesus story we will hear two weeks from now. Both the Lazarus and Jesus stories do carry the themes of death, grief, anger, and abandonment, but they also carry the untying—always the untying. And know this. The same thing that has happened to Lazarus, Jesus, and our loved ones will happen to us. In our Creed we proclaim this conviction when we say, "I look forward to the resurrection of the dead and the life of the world to come."

So the bottom line is that, just as Jesus told a grieving Martha and Mary to believe in God in spite of their hurt and loss, and Jesus himself had to believe in his Father in spite of his sense of abandonment, so we too are asked to believe. Believe in what? Believe that, in the end, for Lazarus, for Jesus, for our loved ones, for ourselves, in spite of all of the wrappings of death, there is the untying.

And after the untying, freedom forever.

The
EASTER
CYCLE

16. The Easter Church

In the Passion narrative this past week, we heard this episode: Jesus was with his disciples in the Garden of Olives. While he was speaking to them, Judas arrived with a large, armed crowd. He went up to Jesus and kissed him (the prearranged signal to the soldiers), saying, "Greetings, Rabbi." And Jesus asked, "Friend, why are you here?"

Today I have the same question. Friends, why are you here? This, after all, is the Catholic Church of the media headlines, the devious and corrupt Church, the Church branded with a large scarlet letter that besmirches the gospel, tarnishes good priests, and shames Catholics everywhere. So, friends, why are you here?

Beyond your own private responses, let me suggest an answer. We're here because of what I call the Easter Church, the bedrock church. By that I mean the everyday church, the two-thousand-year-old church that continues to display quiet, persistent, daily heroism outside the radar of the media. For over 2,000 years ordinary people have done the deeds of love, forgiveness, charity, and compassion in the name of the risen Savior. Among them are the people who taught us how to read and write and preserved civilization during the dark ages, the people who founded and, to this day operate, the hundreds of thousands of schools, leprosarias, hospitals, orphanages, and the largest AIDS support in the world. The people in our history who include a deacon, Francis of Assisi; a wife and widow, Catherine of Siena; a soldier named Ignatius of Loyola; an archbishop from San Salvador, Oscar Romero, who, while celebrating Mass in the cathedral, was assassinated and fell onto the altar, his blood mingling with that of Jesus in the chalice—an assassination ordered by the controlling power because he spoke out against their oppression of the peasants.

Closer to home, there is our contemporary convert Dorothy Day of Staten Island, who founded the Catholic Worker Movement and whose cause is up for canonization, not because she once was a communist, a common-law wife, or had an abortion, but because she discovered in our Easter Church the risen Jesus and showed a heroic and profound concern for the poor.

Then there are the 19 million people who entered the Easter Church last year. That's 2,169 for every hour, or 36 for every minute of the year. There are the millions upon millions who come to Mass every weekend, the massive crowds who come on Ash Wednesday and Palm Sunday, Christmas, and Easter.

There is the Easter Church of Catholic Relief Services, the largest single private charitable organization in the world, and which is given the highest marks by secular committees for almost all of its collected money going to its target.

I could go on, but listen to columnist Nicholas Kristof whose *New York Times* Op-Ed piece sums it up. He wrote:

In my travels around the world, I encounter two Catholic Churches. One is the rigid all-male Vatican hierarchy that seems out of touch …Yet, there's another Catholic Church as well, one I admire intensely. This is the grass-roots Catholic Church that does far more good in the world than it ever gets credit for. This is the Church that supports extraordinary aid organizations like Catholic Relief Services and Caritas, saving lives every day, and that operates superb schools that provide needy children an escalator out of poverty.

This is the Church of the nuns and priests [and lay people] in the Congo, toiling in obscurity to feed and educate children. This is the Church of the Brazilian priest fighting disease... This is the Church of the Maryknoll Sisters in Central America and the Cabrini Sisters in Africa [who risk their lives] in Swaziland to visit AIDS orphans…

So when you read about the scandals, remember that the Vatican is not the same as the Catholic Church. Ordinary lepers, prostitutes, and slum-dwellers may never see a cardinal, but they daily encounter a truly noble Catholic Church in the form of priests, nuns and lay workers toiling to make a difference....

To these words let me piggy-back an excerpt making the blog rounds. It's from a man named Sam Miller, a prominent Cleveland Jewish business-man. He writes:

Why would newspapers carry on a vendetta on one of the most important institutions that we have today in the United States, namely the Catholic Church?

Do you know the Catholic Church educates 2.6 million students every day at the cost to that Church of 10 billion dollars, and a savings on the other hand to the American taxpayer of 18 billion dollars? The graduates go on to gradu-ate studies at the rate of 92%. The Church has 230 colleges and universities in the U.S. with an enrollment of 700,000 students. The Catholic Church has a non-profit hospital system of 637 hospitals, which account for hospital treat-ment of 1 out of every 5 people—not just Catholics—in the United States today.

Now if all that doesn't suggest why you are here, let me end by taking you to the movies.

As some of you may know, a powerful movie, filmed in Morocco, has been made about that country. The name of the film is *Of Gods and Men*. It has won the Best Foreign Language Film of the Year, and the Grand Prix in 2010 at Cannes, and has been also nominated as the best film of the year.

It's the true story of seven Roman Catholic Trappist monks at Our Lady of Atlas Monastery in Algeria during the 1990s Algerian Civil War. Their mission as monks—who are lay people, remember—is to live a life of prayer and contemplation and, in addition, to serve the wretchedly poor people in the area by giving them medical assistance, comfort, counseling, and education.

It's a dangerous place where they live. Islamic terrorism is at every corner and grows more intense each day. The monks are increasingly witnessing with horror the ruthless murders of the townspeople. They have heard about the murder of European construction workers by terrorists and recoil on hearing about Islamic fundamentalists stabbing a woman because she was not wearing a veil. They begin to realize that they cannot long escape the same fate if they remain there. In fact, the Algerian government has asked the monks to leave for their own safety. Ominously, it's not long before a group of a fundamentalists show up at the monastery on Christmas Eve demanding medicine for their wounded colleagues. Though their request is refused—the monks need the medicine for the desperate people—the abbot quotes the Koran to their leader, and they end up shaking hands, but the abbot knows in his heart that they will be back. And each monk also knows that, sooner or later, when they do come back, the monks will have to decide what to do: to flee or to stay.

Ultimately, in a most poignant scene, the movie takes us into the monks' chapter room where they candidly struggle to come to a decision that has to be unanimous. Shall they flee to safely or shall they stay with the understanding that they will most certainly be killed? Their discussions are long, measured, respectful, quiet, with stretches of profound silence. We, the audience, are allowed to gaze into their searching eyes as each one lays bare his fears, his struggle, his ambiguity, his faith, his soul.

Finally compassion and humility win out, and the monks decide to be the Easter Church—to stay where they are and not abandon the people. They feel deeply that Jesus, who had sent them there to work and pray among the oppressed people of Algeria, would not want them to abandon them, no matter what the danger, the suffering. The monks, in effect, have decided to offer the world the possibility of another way to live and to die, to show what the world might look like transformed by grace.

Then the high point of the film comes when the monks recreate the Last Supper by sitting around a small table drinking wine and listening to a recording of Tchaikovsky's *Swan Lake*. As the camera pans from face to face, we observe a beatific smile on some faces, tears on others, apprehension on all. This is it.

Not long after their "Last Supper," in 1996, they are all beheaded. As he approaches his death, the abbot, obviously mindful of Jesus on Calvary, addresses the unknown Islamic militant whose sword would kill him: "You, my friend, who do not know what you are doing, yes, for you too, I give you farewell and commend you to the God whose face I see in yours." And his head rolls into the dust.

These monks were imitating Jesus who gave his life for others.

Friends, why are you here? I think you are here because of those monks, because, whatever your journey, whatever your misgivings, whatever your doubts, whatever your faithful or unfaithful observances, whatever the faults of the media Church, you somehow intuitively recognize the persistent presence of the risen Jesus in this Easter Church where there is still the same bread, the same wine, the same teaching, the same Scripture, the same gospel, the same baptism, the same forgiveness, the same outreach, the same healing, the same quiet heroes, the same faith, hope, and love—all in the name of the One who was raised 2,000 years ago and is with us today.

Yes, the felt presence of this Jesus is here in this Easter Church of ours. Mock him, beat him, disfigure him—and, Lord knows, we've done it all— he remains. His words and his works remain. His Church remains. He is here. And that's why I am here, and perhaps, deep down, you also.

So thank you for being here, and have a blessed Easter.

17. Why Is This Meal Different?

FOURTH SUNDAY OF EASTER, A, 1 PETER 2:20–25

At the Jewish Seder Meal the youngest child asks the oldest person, "Why is this night different from any other?" The response is the long recounting of Israel's national epic: who they are, how they came to be, how they are different, and how they gained freedom from slavery under the guiding hand of Yahweh and his prophet, Moses. The meal, replicating the Exodus plot and the story that interprets it, has been the glue of Jewish identity for some 3,000 years. Even secular Jews celebrate Passover—if not as a religious event, then as a national event—this is their history. This is who they are as a people, and Passover never lets them forget it. That's why they have lasted so long.

But that's what national epics do: they embody the values, the ideals that give a people an identity and something to measure themselves by. So the Greeks have their Homeric sagas, the Romans their emperor worship, the Germanic peoples their Nordic sagas, the Indians their tribal tales, the Muslims their Mecca and Medina, the Jews their Passover, and Christians their gospel stories and Eucharist. Through ritual and symbol all these peoples regularly celebrate their stories, thus re-cementing their identity as a people and reconnecting with the values they believe in.

When conquerors want to subjugate and assimilate a people, it is not surprising that the first thing they usually do is to dismantle the national sagas in order to take away the people's identity. It makes sense. So they destroy their shrines and statues. They co-opt their sacred symbols, tear

71

down their monuments, rename their cities and streets—think of the Communists changing St. Petersburg to Leningrad—burn their books, curtail their speech and, most of all, distract the people with new and glitzy promises until their assimilation is complete, their stories forgotten, and their memories gone.

Two things we must understand about all this. First, this is what was going on in Jesus' time—suppressing the memory—and when Jesus tried to call the people back to remembering who they were as the chosen children of God and how they should act like it, the memory erasers, those with vested interests, killed him. Yes, the truth is, Jesus died from being a subversive, a prophet who spoke against the false stories and the fabricated values imposed by the "thieves and robbers" crowd of his time. In fact, Jesus' whole life was a challenge to those who were obliterating the biblical memory of his people. Jesus' deliberately provocative stories and actions said it shouldn't be this way.

As an instance of Jesus' subversion, take Palm Sunday. Note that Jesus entered Jerusalem by the East Gate on a donkey with the poor people, because the week before Pilate had entered the West Gate on a mighty steed and with powerful people and a large military force. It was a calculated move on Jesus' part, a slap in the face to the powers that be, a deliberate counter-value system he was offering by his move: justice for injustice, love for force, sharing in place of greed. Much later, Mahatma Gandhi would imitate Jesus. When he came to England he didn't arrive in diplomatic dress with high-powered staff and pay his homage to the powerful political leaders in London. Rather, wrapped in a sheet and wearing a diaper, he first went to the exiled textile workers in Liverpool hurt by the English boycott.

Jesus continued his mission. He went right on telling pointed stories about the rich man and Lazarus, while others got their fat bonuses. He went right on telling stories about good Samaritans, the hated enemy, while others preached revenge. He went right on eating with outcasts and public sinners, while others kept them in their segregated ghettos. He went right on showing mercy to the woman caught in adultery, while others would stone her. He went right on challenging inequity, while the powerful would secretly promote it to their own gain. No wonder his enemies had to silence him. But he didn't care. He had to risk death in order to help people remember.

Now fast forward: there are still those today who would suppress the Jesus story, those who want to silence and kill us, who don't want us to be different, who want us to forget who we are. These people will not put us on a wooden cross. Unlike in other countries, these people do not imprison or behead us. They just slowly neuter our identity and erase our memories. They systematically force our stories out of public institutions, replacing them with around-the-clock, plugged-in entertainment. They ban religious talk from the public square, remove sacred images, seduce us with materialism, substitute Lady Gaga for Mother Mary, replace Sunday worship with soccer and shopping, undermine Merry Christmas with Happy Holidays, and undercut the stupendous mystery of Easter with Spring Break. They give us a society that glorifies consumerism and celebrity and whose motto is the very opposite of the gospel story—preaching, as it does, that we do live by bread alone and the more bread the better, even if that means that others go hungry.

A good example of clever suppression: I am always amused to see statues of St. Francis of Assisi on sale at the garden departments of the malls— those cathedrals of consumption. Merchants can tolerate making him a hippie who talks to birds. That's "in." But they would never, could never, permit the full truth, never permit his real story to be known: that he was the son of a very rich merchant, that, although his baptismal name is John, his friends nicknamed him "Frenchy" or Francis because of his love of French consumer brands, or that, at one point, tired of his empty life, he decided to take seriously the Jesus stories he heard all of his life and, one day, to the chagrin of his father, walked away literally naked from the mall parking lot, leaving the equivalent of his BMW and Armani suit to wear rags and go and preach to the marginal and embrace what he called Lady Poverty. That story would never be allowed. Bad for business.

Anyway, the secular folk are constantly seeking to replace or voice over the voice of the Good Shepherd. They want us all to forget who we are and to become one of them—and they're pretty good at it.

But the fact is, all is not lost, for here we are—and I am not sure that you fully appreciate that being here and the choices you have made are subversive acts. Think: you gave your money to build this gathering space for yourselves and your family. There is no merchandise, no commercials in this building continually stroking your desires, convincing you that you need the latest gadget to make you happy. No images of celebrities are plastered on the wall. Instead we have an outrageous oddity: we have a prominent central image of a half-naked dead man on a cross. No perfect abs, no white teeth, no plastic surgery, no pleasant smell, no credit cards. He's up there because he dared to speak gibberish about washing one another's feet—no self-respecting CEO would do that to his plant's cleaning crew. He said that the one who would rule must do so by being the servant of all. That makes no sense and certainly won't wash in a power-hungry, I'm-number-one society. His "forgive your enemies" talk is off the wall, and movie producers who specialize in searing, cruel, and graphic revenge don't like his hitting at their bottom line.

That's our celebrity up there *[pointing to the crucifix above the altar]*. He's our national epic. Certainly a sign of contradiction. We must be crazy. A secular culture—that tries to make human beings out to be a bundle of insatiable desires that need the constant stimulus of brand names to make them whole—can't understand us. We need to be muted.

Then, look around at our *other* celebrities, the saints. Look at the statues and images not permitted elsewhere. There's Mary and Joseph, and we recall the stories of their trials, their struggles, their faith. There's a statue of St. Thérèse over there, who died of consumption at age 24 and who, without ever leaving her convent, became a powerful force in the spirituality of the modern world. And in the window there's the image of the Dove to remind us that we are a Spirit-filled people.

There's a painting of St. Catherine of Siena in the back, our patron saint. She's there, not because she made it on *American Idol*, but because, sensing a call from Jesus, she left the so-called good life to help the poor and sick and personally walked with prisoners about to be executed on the gallows. She counseled others, scolded the pope for not doing his job, and dictated wonderful letters—she could not read or write—that nourished many and still do.

Finally, there's our Eucharist. We shall soon share in our Passover, the ancient countercultural ritual of the bread and wine—the body and blood of Jesus, "given for you"—in the hopes that we will remember that this is what we too are about. We're here to remember all this, to remember that we are a people of a different story, the Jesus story, a people who are also supposed to give our body and blood for others, a people to take up the cross as an inevitable yoke to carry on behalf of justice and mercy for the sad, the hurting and needy, the poor and the disenfranchised.

So, with all this being said, we come full circle and return to our opening question: Why is this two-thousand-year-old meal here today different from any other? Answer: because it reminds us of who we are. It reminds us of our basic identity as children of God. It jars our memories. Yes, we belong to Jesus. We are to follow him in witnessing to a set of values, a set of stories, a set of heroes different from the secular culture.

It is to your great credit that you took this hour to pull back a bit from a culture that gives us endless entertainment, endless commercials, endless preening, endless distraction from what really matters. I'm sure some think you're a bit crazy for being here, "wasting your time." But I know you're here because you wanted to reaffirm a different perspective, a different take on life, a different path to walk and, mostly, I suspect, to find like-minded people who support you on the path you have chosen.

It's hard being a Christian in a world that mocks or subverts it. We need this space, this time apart. That's why we are here. We need each other to help us remember who we are: disciples of Jesus, children of God, related to the saints, and a people who should be broken bread in his memory.

I, for one, am glad you're here. It helps me. Thank you.

18. Mary, Raymond, and Me

One of the more poignant moments in the cycle of the post-Easter stories we have been hearing lately in our liturgy is the one about Mary Magdalene. You know it well. Resigned to Jesus' terrible fate, feeling that it was all over, Mary went to the gravesite to anoint his body. As you recollect, there had been no chance to do that earlier because the entombment was a hasty one before the start of the Sabbath.

So she was understandably confused and dumbfounded when she arrived at the gravesite and found that the stone had been rolled away. Instead, according to the story, she encountered two angels, who told her that Jesus was not there and asked her why she was weeping. She sobbed in reply that it was because someone had stolen the body and she had no idea where it was.

She had no sooner said these words than she sensed someone behind her, someone who also asked her why she was weeping. By this time she had covered her face with her hands in distress and said to the stranger whom she thought was the caretaker, "If you're the one who has taken him away, tell me where you have put him, and I will take him and anoint his body and give him a decent burial."

There was a long deep silence that hung in the air finally to be broken by just one word, "Mary!" And immediately she knew. She knew who it was who called her name, and she dissolved in joy as she turned and saw her friend, Jesus.

Framing the scene as he did, I think the gospel writer wanted to dramatize and emphasize the importance of that one word, "Mary." He wanted to underscore its impact, what it meant for this woman to hear her name in the depths of her confusion and despair. Think of a lost, frightened, little child suddenly hearing his father call his name in the dark, and you catch the feeling. So Mary exploded in relief, in holy shock. There he was. He is alive. And he called me by name! My name.

I ask you to savor this scene and identify with it, for this episode reflects everyone's experience in two ways. First, everyone, from the beginning of time, at one time or another, has felt lost and abandoned like Mary. You know: where was God when this or that tragedy hit? Where was God when I was lost and frightened and afraid and terribly hurt by life's unfairness?

Second, how painful the memory when others, for so long, have called us by titles other than our name, mocking our nationality, our color, our status, our body—the hurtful word, the degrading and nasty putdown names they hung on us, names designed to put us in our place, that marked us out as lacking, inferior, stupid, labels that made fun of us, that wounded us deeply.

This episode of a weeping woman in the chill of the morning suddenly and compellingly being called by her name is meant to convey a great spiritual truth to live by. And it is this: no matter what anyone else in our lives has ever called us, whatever labels they stuck us with, whatever ridicule they heaped upon us, there has always been one who has been present in our confusion and sadness, stood by us in our shame, pronounced us a son or daughter of God, and called us by name. And that truth is something to cherish, and it makes all the difference.

Sometime back, there was a speech given by Tom Kalinske. He's the chairman of an outfit called LeapFrog, the maker of creative educational games for children. Kalinske began his speech with a story, a true story that originates from a friend of his who was hired to shoot a documentary film about computers and education. The film was about an experiment in a Southern California junior high school, a test of a new computer system that was programmed with learning games that reinforced the fundamentals of math and reading and writing. This particular school was chosen in order to make the computer's job as tough as possible because, year after year, its students scored in the lowest statewide percentiles in every subject.

This experiment took place a dozen years ago, when computers were still pretty exotic contraptions to find in a public school. Naturally, the principal wanted to minimize the risk that the computers would be damaged in any way. And so he made a decision to exclude the special education class from the experiment. Well, the fact is, the special education kids were always a bit out of control.

That would have been the end of the story if it weren't for a very dedicated special education teacher. When she heard that her kids were going to sit on the sidelines while everyone else got time on the computers, she made such a fuss that the principal gave in.

And so, the special education kids got their four hours a week at the computers. And when, in just one semester, some of these kids learned more than in the preceding ten years, the administration realized that something very special and unexpected had happened.

There was, for example, a Hispanic girl who was placed in special ed. because she just never learned to read. And she was terribly intimidated in class, so she never was able to communicate that she simply didn't get the basic phonic concepts. But the computer didn't intimidate her, and in one semester she'd begun to read at her proper grade level.

The most touching story, however, was about a kid named Raymond, who had every problem in the book: a dysfunctional home, acute shyness, bad eyesight, and zero academic performance. But in the one semester he had with the computer, Raymond caught up seven years of math.

Well, he became the poster boy for the school. They got him in front of the camera for an interview, and he was asked how it was that he blossomed so magnificently.

"Well," he replied, "you see, all the kids here call me retard. The computer calls me Raymond."

Mary. Raymond. You. I.

Remember: Whatever desperation we're in, whatever else people call us, there is one who calls us by name. In your mind and heart, imagine Jesus standing behind you seeing you through his love and calling your name. Listen. Taste it. Turn it around. Embrace it. Rejoice in it. How sweet the sound.

19. As I Have Loved You

The man is destined to die tomorrow. He's in a room with some friends and is wondering how to break the news to them for they, he knows, will be shattered. More, he is wondering what he can leave them as a legacy, something to hold on to in their grief, their loss, their bewilderment.

He knows, of course, that there's only one word that will do it. That word is "love." So he gets up, walks nervously around the room as they watch him, sensing something profound is about to happen, and he breaks the silence by saying to them, "As I have loved you so you also should love one another."

That brief sentence said it all. Now we of another age try to digest those words, break them down. Ultimately, after centuries of reflection, we discover that Jesus has compacted in those simple words a threefold expression of love, and this morning we explore them together. One: love is the "as" of Jesus. Two: love is not repaid but passed on. Three: love without justice is an empty—and dangerous—sentimentality.

First, love is the "as" of Jesus. If you want to know the meaning of that "as"—as I have loved you so you also should love one another—simply look at Calvary. Calvary shows us what "as" means. It means we are to love to the extent and fullness of Calvary.

A man who experienced the Auschwitz Nazi concentration camp relays an incident of love given on the Calvary of that wicked place. He writes,

> You know everything was terrible in Auschwitz. There was no food, there was no water; there was cold, you didn't know whether your father or mother lived.

79

I worked in a factory. One day it was almost Christmas and the snow that fell was like a table set for guests; it was so white and beautiful. And of course we had to work inside starting at 5 o'clock in the morning and finishing at 5 o'clock at night and not having food or anything we needed. The foreman watching us every minute making sure we were making every ammunition supposed to be made. And then the foreman looked at me and called me over. I was sure I was going to be punished because all the way walking there the SS man is whipping his whip. You don't work fast or you don't do the work like it's supposed to be done, they beat you. I was 15 years old and my legs were shaking. I am trying to tell him please don't hurt me. Please, I will work faster. And the foreman says bend down over and over and I feel that he is about to beat me when he whispers, "Here, take this bread, put it under your coat, and go out fast." That was my Christmas. What an incredible man. The SS man was behind him and saw the whole thing but did nothing. He also put his life on the line to give a child a chance. You know what a slice of bread meant? Could you imagine that I am starving? Instead of beating me he gave me bread.

Just like Jesus. That's the "as" of Jesus.

Second, real love is not repaid but passed on. Let me also wrap that truth in a story, the story of the "Secret Santa." A few years ago, someone tracked down a man known, up until then, as the "Secret Santa" and asked him, "Why do you do this? Why do you secretly help out people?" The man replied how life had blessed him with an extremely successful business venture. But this was not always the case. In 1971, he was an out-of-work salesman who was reduced to living out of his car. One morning he had not eaten for two days. He was incredibly hungry, so hungry that he walked into a diner in Houston, Mississippi, to order breakfast with no intent of paying for it. He couldn't. He had no money, but he was so hungry.

As he hungrily ate his breakfast, he wondered how he was going to pay for this meal or how he was going to get out of paying for this meal. When the check came, he fumbled around in his pockets pretending to have lost his wallet. The owner of the diner had already sized him up and knew he didn't have the money. The owner came around the counter, approached the man, and bent down as if to pick up something. The owner said to the man, "Well, lookie here! Looks like you dropped this $20 bill." Now the man had enough to pay for breakfast and a little more to keep for the road. He never forgot this totally undeserved act of generosity and goodness. He now gives to others as someone once gave to him.

Real love is passed on. To hug it to oneself is to suffocate it.

Finally—and this is most important—love without justice is empty sentimentality. Unfortunately we have a lot of this in our "feel-good" society, which puts "me first" first. Not so this father.

His son was eleven years old and went fishing every chance he got from the dock at his family's cabin on an island in the middle of a New Hampshire lake. On the day before the bass season opened, he and his father were fishing early in the evening, catching sunfish and perch with worms. Then he tied on a small silver lure. The lure struck the water. When his pole doubled over, he knew something huge was on the other end. His father watched as the boy skillfully worked the fish alongside the dock. Finally, he very gingerly lifted the exhausted fish from the water. It was the largest one he had ever seen, but it was a bass.

The boy and his father looked at the handsome fish. The father lit a match and looked at his watch. It was 10:00 P.M.—two hours before the season opened. He looked at the fish, then at the boy.

"You'll have to put it back son," he said.

"Dad!" cried the boy.

"There will be other fish," said his father.

"Not as big as this one," cried the boy.

He looked around the lake. No other fishermen or boats were anywhere around in the moonlight. He looked again at his father.

Even though no one had seen them, nor would anyone ever know what time he caught the fish, the boy could tell by the clarity of his father's voice that the decision was not negotiable. He slowly worked the hook out of the lip of the huge bass, and lowered it into the black water. The boy suspected that he would never again see such a great fish. That was thirty-four years ago. Today, the boy is a successful architect in New York City. His father's cabin is still there on the island in the middle of the lake. He takes his own son to fish from the same dock.

And he was right. He has never again caught such a magnificent fish as the one he landed that night long ago. But, he says, he does see that same fish—again and again—every time he comes up against a question of ethics, of matters of right and wrong, of choosing to do what is right when no one is looking.

Love cannot work without justice. Like: real friends don't let friends drink and drive. Real friends squeal on friends who are doing drugs. On the domestic level, real parents do not allow their child to break a commitment because something better comes up, and he wants to be there. To allow this is not loving him. To allow this makes them both feel good, but, without justice, it's the worst kind of sentimentality. On the contrary, real love with clarity says, "I know you want to go to Alice's party but you promised to be at practice and you must keep your word. You can't let the others down." It's the just thing to do.

So to summarize this gospel: Jesus' pattern of loving as he does means three things:

Real love is patterned after the "as" of Jesus, that is, the full gift of himself to us all on Calvary.

Real love is not repaid but must be passed on.

Real love does justice first.

As I have loved you, so you also should love one another.

20. *If You Love Me*

Sixth Sunday of Easter, A, John 14:15–21

Three Englishmen were in a bar and spotted an Irishman. One of the Englishmen walked over to the Irishman, tapped him on the shoulder, and said, "Hey, I hear your St. Patrick was a drunken loser."

"Oh, really. Hmmm. Didn't know that," replied the Irishman. Puzzled, the Englishmen went back to his buddies, "I told him St. Patrick was a loser and he didn't care."

The second Englishman remarked, "You just don't know how to set him off...watch and learn."

So the second Englishman walked over to the Irishman, tapped him on the shoulder, and said, "Hey, I hear your St. Patrick was a lying, cheating, idiotic, low-life scum!"

"Oh, really, hmmm, didn't know that neither," said the Irishman.

Shocked beyond belief, the Englishman went back to his buddies. "You're right, He's unshakable!"

The third Englishman remarked, "Boys, I'll really tick him off, just watch." So the third Englishman walked over to the Irishman, tapped him on the shoulder and said, "I hear St. Patrick was an Englishman!"

"Yeah, that's what your buddies have been trying to tell me," the Irishman replied.

When I start off like this, you know it's the only laugh you'll get as I set you up to tackle a serious subject: today's gospel.

"If you love me, you will keep my commandments." You could hear this saying of Jesus the wrong way. You could hear it like imagining Jesus shaking his finger at his disciples and telling them that if they really, really loved him they would do what he tells them to do. Sounds more like blackmail than friendship. Something like a wife might tell her husband or a friend another friend. "Look, if you say you love me, then you'll do this for me." That's how Barbara Stanwyck got Fred MacMurray to kill her husband in the classic film *Double Indemnity*. But Jesus is not saying "If you love me you will keep my commandments" that way. He is saying that, *if you are inspired by my love for you, the way I treated you, then this is the way you will just naturally treat others.*

Case in point. A teenage girl was out on a date one night. Unfortunately her boyfriend had no moral center other than what he got from watching too much TV, so he suggested that they go to a party where there was going to be alcohol and drugs and, of course, lots of sex. This young woman had a different moral background and said outright, "No, I don't want to go there. I don't want to do that and if you're going to do that you can take me home." The boyfriend countered with the standard pressure: ridicule. He said sneeringly, "What's the matter? Are you afraid your daddy will hurt you?" She replied, "No, I'm afraid I will hurt my daddy." She was beholden to her earthly father and her heavenly Father.

So, where did the boy get his values and where did she get hers? They were both born the same year, both started out on the planet the same way. Yet, they wound up with different attitudes toward life. Where did they get them?

David Brooks has a fascinating book called *The Social Animal,* in which he explores what the social science experts have discovered about us human beings. In the chapter on self control, he cites the example of students walking into a classroom, some of whom have no respect whatsoever for the teacher and, when angry, may curse at the teacher or even throw a punch at him or her. Other students would never dream of doing such things. He asks, why? Where does the difference come from?

He writes,

The answers are lost in the midnight river of the unconscious. But somehow, over the course of their lives, they have had certain experiences. Maybe they came to respect the authority of their parents and now extend that mental framework to authority figures in general. Maybe they have absorbed certain stories in which they observed people treating teachers in a certain way...

[Whatever the case] a certain pattern of perception has emerged, a way of seeing... [so] upright people tend to see other people's property in a way that reduces their temptation to steal. They learn to see a gun in a way that reduces their temptation to misuse it. They learn to see young girls in a way that reduces the temptation to abuse them. They learn to see the truth in a way that reduces the temptation to lie.

These commonsense words affirm what we already know. That's why we presume that the girl in our story who saw life in a certain way learned it from her parents and was reinforced by relatives and friends. As for the boyfriend, we can only guess. From the start, was his view of life a matter of cutting corners, a steady diet of disrespect for himself and his family? How did he learn to see the way he does? Was he just typically what is called a "nice kid" but nothing deeper?

Was he like the kid described in this letter a man sent Ann Landers? He wrote, "This is for the woman who was distressed about her son. I would like to ask her some questions about the boy. Is he disrespectful? Has he been arrested for drunken driving? Has he been kicked out of college for cheating? Has he made his girlfriend pregnant? Does he get failing grades? Does he steal money from your purse?... If you can answer 'No' to all these questions," says this writer, "stop complaining. You have a great kid."

Here is how Ann Landers answered him: "Your letter showed just how much times have changed. You said that if a kid today isn't on drugs, doesn't get failing grades, hasn't been arrested for drunken driving or kicked out of college for cheating, hasn't made his girlfriend pregnant, or stolen from your purse, that he's great. But you make no mention of achievement. There's not a word about integrity, a sense of responsibility, decency, morality, or service to others."

We wonder if that's a snapshot of the boyfriend. Did he ever hear about integrity, a sense of responsibility, decency, morality, or service to others? Did he even attempt to practice them until they became second nature?

Years ago there was a popular little book by William Glasser called *Positive Addiction*. We usually think of addiction only in negative terms, such as drugs, alcohol, or porn. But Glasser was interested in the opposite addictions, the positive ones, such as, for example, exercises like running, which can become addictive, where people come to need it, and look forward to it, and if something interferes with it, they are irritable and disoriented.

But these positive addictions are beneficial—running, gardening, swinging a bat, swimming, knitting. They can help us lose weight, lower blood pressure, regulate body sugar, and so on. Positive moral addictions are also beneficial—virtues we call them. Like your coming to church faithfully, like bringing your children to hear the subversive stories of Jesus, like your charities, like your choosing attitudes of decency, morality, service to others, and other values and actions that imitate those of Jesus.

These are the ways we try to live out this gospel. Lord knows we don't always succeed at these things, certainly not all the time, but remember this truth: the trying itself is the way we keep his commandments and the way we love Jesus—and he us.

21. Gospel Mirrors

SIXTH SUNDAY OF EASTER, B, JOHN 15:9–17

Once a young man proposed to his girl as they sat looking over a beautiful lake. "Darling, I want you to know that I love you more than anything else in the world. I want you to marry me. I'm not wealthy like Johnny Brown. I'm not rich like Johnny Brown. I don't have a yacht or Rolls Royce like Johnny Brown, but I do love you with all my heart." She thought for a minute and then replied, "I love you with all my heart, too—but tell me more about Johnny Brown."

This homily is like that, except I am going to tell you less about Jesus Christ. Which is to say I want to experiment with something different this morning. I want to focus on the wisdom of the gospel but without ever directly mentioning the gospels themselves. I want to tell you some stories and let you claim them, think about them, embrace them as wisdom for the spiritual life, and let your imaginations make faith associations.

So I begin.

Long ago a rich jewelry merchant in the East told this story: I was overtaken by a great storm. It buffeted me and my caravan this way and that until I was separated from the caravan and became completely lost. I kept moving for days, until I discovered that I had wandered around in circles. It was then that I realized to my horror that I had run out of food. I was half dead from starvation and in dire need of nourishment or else I would soon die.

In a fit of panic, I unloaded every bag on my camel's back, hoping desperately to find a morsel or two tucked away somewhere. I searched through every bag again and again, but there was no food to be found. But suddenly my heartbeat with new hope when I came upon a small pouch I had overlooked. My hands were shaking and, with trembling fingers I tore open the pouch. My heart then sank with despair.

All that the pouch contained were pearls.

This story is an aha! moment. Think about this tale and think gospel wisdom. How about Jesus' saying that we do not live by bread (pearls) alone or his warning about saving up treasure to make oneself rich with this world but not rich with God?

The great preacher Fred Craddock tells of meeting a man one day in a restaurant. "You a preacher?" the man asked.

Somewhat embarrassed, Fred said, "Yes."

The man pulled a chair up to Fred's table. "Preacher, I'll tell you a story. There was once a little boy who grew up sad. Life was tough because my mamma had me but she had never been married. Do you know how a small Tennessee town treats people like that? Do you know the words they use to name kids that don't have no father?

"Well, we never went to church 'cause nobody asked us. But for some reason or other, we went to church one night when they was having a revival. They had a big, tall preacher visiting to do the revival, and he was all dressed in black. He had a thunderous voice that shook the little church.

"We sat toward the back, Mamma and me. Well, that preacher got to preaching, about what I don't know, stalking up and down the aisle of that little church preaching. It was something.

"After the service, we were slipping out the back door when I felt that big preacher's hand on my shoulder. I was scared. He looked way down at me, looked me in the eye and says, 'Boy, who's your Daddy?'

"'I don't have no Daddy.' That's what I told him in a trembling voice, 'I ain't got no Daddy.'

"'Oh yes you do,' boomed that big preacher, 'you're a child of the Kingdom, you have been bought with a price. You are a child of the King!' I was never the same after that.

"Preacher," he told Craddock as he left, "for God's sake, preach that."

I just did. For God's sake.

Rose Russell was twenty-five. She was far more successful than most men fifty years of age. She was a partner in a real estate and investment firm in Newport Beach, California, which, next to Beverly Hills, is the place to live in southern California. She was also in partnership on quite a string of properties in the beach area. She drove her own silver Mercedes, and it was paid for. But at twenty-five, with all this apparent success, she went to a motel room, sat down and wrote a plaintive note, and took her own life. Her brief suicide note read simply: "I'm so tired of clapping with one hand."

My thought on this? The gospel wisdom would have told her that she was worth more than many sparrows.

Hardly anyone here, I suspect, knows the name of William Lawrence Bragg. But he has considerable claim to fame. At twenty-five, he was the youngest person ever to win the Nobel Prize in physics. Bragg was also an avid amateur gardener and herein lies the story.

When he moved to London to head the Royal Institution, he reluctantly left behind the beautiful Cambridge garden he had spent so many years perfecting. Before long, life in a city apartment made him restless and unhappy—until he found an ingenious solution to his problem.

Dressed in old gardening clothes with a spade over one shoulder, he patrolled the streets of a nearby wealthy district until he found a house whose garden tempted him. Then he rang the bell and, tipping his hat respectfully to the lady of the house, introduced himself as "Willie," an odd job gardener with one free afternoon a week. His employer found Willie an absolute treasure.

Until, alas, one day, a knowledgeable visitor looked out through her window and gasped, "Good heavens, what is William Lawrence Bragg doing watering your garden?"

This prompts my imagination to look through the window of the Upper Room and ask, "Good heavens, what is God doing washing feet?"

Finally, for the 10th anniversary of 9/11, the city of New York is ready to open the newly erected memorial at Ground Zero. One of the exhibits slated for the vast memorial museum is one you might remember, for its photo was shown all over television and the newspapers at the time. Two large beams in the exact shape of a 17-foot-tall cross were found in the foyer. It is awesome. There is a good chance, however, it will not be in the museum, for an American atheists group has been quick to sue, raising the usual separation of church and state alarms.

However it fares, we need to remember an event from the Great War, when people were less divided. On the night of November 4, 1940, the city of Coventry, England, already battered in several fierce raids by the Germans, was subjected to a continuous, 9-hour hail of incendiary and high-explosive bombs.

The town center was reduced to a charred wilderness of rubble and twisted metal. All that remained of Coventry's cathedral of St. Michael, a church dating back nearly 1000 years, were the lower walls and the 300-foot tower and spire. After the war's end, and after a great surge of rebuilding, the beautiful new St. Michael's Church was dedicated in 1962.

And it is striking. At the altar end of the building hangs a huge tapestry, the largest in the world—picturing the triumphant Christ. The altar itself was constructed from stones taken from the charred rubble. A cross made of charred beams from the bombed-out roof was placed above the altar.

On the altar itself was set a cross made up of 600-year-old iron nails that were recovered from the rubble. And above the altar and the crosses, the words Christ spoke from his execution cross are inscribed: "Father, forgive!"

If you ever visit Ground Zero, you can ponder this story and say to yourself, "It's a shame I won't see those gospel words here, but I can think them. I can pray them. And I will."

22. The Ascension

Most people have a wrong notion about the feast of the Ascension. They think it's about Jesus. It's not. It's about you and me, and I don't think you hear this fact enough. So let me recall a scene from the movies that will help us understand this better. The movie is *Good Will Hunting*.

Will Hunting, played by Matt Damon, is a mathematical genius. His best friend, Chuckie, thinks Will Hunting is the moon, sun, and stars, the best there is. He also believes, however, that Will is burying his talent in the ground—that Will has enormous potential that is being wasted.

One day the two of them are working on a construction site. During a break, the question arises about what Will's future holds. Will says he's going to live his life right there in the neighborhood, get married, and raise kids. This leads Chuckie to speak straight to Will. He says, "Look, you're my best friend, so don't take this the wrong way, but in twenty years if you're still living here, coming over to my house, watching the Patriots games, still working in construction—I'll kill you. That's not a threat, that's a fact, I'll kill ya."

"What are you talking about?" Will grunts.

"You've got something none of us have …," Chuckie continues.

But before he can go on, Will butts in: "Oh, come on! What? Why is it always this? I mean, I owe it to myself to do this or that. What if I don't want to?"

And now Chuckie butts in: "No, no, you don't owe it to yourself, you owe it to me. 'Cuz tomorrow I'm gonna wake up, and I'll be fifty, and I'll still be doing this [stuff]. And that's all right. That's fine. I mean, you're sitting on a winning lottery ticket and you're too much of a jerk to do something about it. I'd do anything to have what you've got. So would any of these guys. It'd be an insult to us if you're still here in twenty years. Hanging around here is a waste of your time…."

That's real friendship, isn't it? To support a friend, to encourage him to better things, even if it means there will be a vacant spot in your own life?

Fast forward backward. The disciples of Jesus were surely disappointed at his pending departure. They loved this man. There was nothing they would not do for him. He was their friend, their teacher, their Lord. Now he would be missing from their company. It was a moment of great sadness.

But, like Chuckie in his love for Will Hunting, they did realize that Christ was too big for Galilee, too big for Jerusalem, too big even for Earth. The physical world could not contain him. He needed to be set free from the confinements of his earthly body so that his Spirit might soar and be accessible to all. They were right, and so that Spirit was bequeathed to them. The Ascension is that turning point, that transitional point.

Ascension celebrates the passing on of that Spirit to that assembly of disciples who collectively would eventually be known as the mystical body of Christ, the Church. The Spirit was given to ordinary people to witness to Jesus, to do the works of Jesus in this world, to celebrate his memory and invoke his presence in the sacraments, especially the Eucharist.

The Ascension is, then, if you will, our swearing-in time. "Men of Galilee, why are you dawdling, looking up to the sky?" chides the angel. "You are now Church. Get busy. Your best friend has empowered you, like Chuckie tried to empower his friend, and the message is the same: People of Galilee, hanging around here is a waste of time…You have been empowered to witness to the wonderful works of God. Move!" Yes, we—all of us—are Church, all of us have been given the Spirit, not just a few.

Or try looking at it this way: Ascension is, as it were, an announcement of the institution of the priesthood of the faithful that would be given on Pentecost. That's why St. Peter could remind his parishioners, as I am reminding you, "You are a royal priesthood, a holy nation, a chosen race, a people set apart."

That's you: the priesthood of the faithful. You were promised so at the Ascension and made so at Pentecost. You are Christ in the world, and the job of the very small minority of the Body of Christ—about 2%—known as the ordained priesthood, like me, is serving the priesthood of the faithful like you and reminding you of your calling—which again, like St. Peter, is what I am doing.

Once more, today's feast of the Ascension is your feast, a preparation for the gift of the Holy Spirit to you. It is a kind of handing on of the baton. It is a feast to remind you of your dignity, your calling, your power, your mandate, and your duty. Together—you, the priesthood of the faithful, and I, representing the priesthood in service to your priesthood—are reminded today that together as Church we are to profess what we believe and live what we profess.

As Jesus said to his disciples in today's gospel—men and women of all walks of life—"Behold, I am sending the promise of my Father upon you."

Remember, you have received that promise at baptism. Remember, you are Church.

23. Pentecost:
The In-Between Time

A, B, C

Jesus has died. The disciples have scattered. Hope has been dashed, promises left unfulfilled. Rumors of an empty tomb only serve to underscore their empty hearts. It seems as if the disciples of Jesus are destined to live out their lives in that dry listless desert stillness known as the in-between time, the land of just existing.

The in-between time is a wearying and tantalizing kind of life, forever swinging as it does between hope and despair. When it goes on for a long time, a person eventually ceases to live but just marks time.

We all know the in-between time…waiting for word about your son caught in one of those senseless suicide attacks in Afghanistan: Is he wounded, alive, dead? The in-between time of waiting for the biopsy report. Out of work now, for what? a month, a year, now two years trying to live without despair in that seemingly endless time between unemployment and employment. An unhealed family rift that has gone on for so long; a depression that never takes a vacation; a sickness that has turned out to be a life companion; a hurt so deep that still festers after all these years; a deceased spouse or child, and you wonder if the tears will ever stop; an adult child who seems to be locked forever in addiction, perpetual adolescence, without a center or purpose; a dry spiritual life that God, it seems, hasn't watered in decades. The in-between life goes on and on.

In one way or another, we sometimes feel we're like the disciples. We're behind firmly locked doors. We can't get out. No help, no release, can get in. We are emotionally and spiritually stretched out on the rack of the in-between time. And it's gone on so long.

What do we do? Frankly, I don't know. Sorry to disappoint you. All that I can do is offer a handful of random stories and let you figure it out.

A little boy was on a train for a long, long trip between two western cities. It was a hot, dusty day, very uncomfortable for traveling, and that particular ride was perhaps the most uninteresting day's journey in the whole land. But the little guy sat patiently watching the fields go by until a motherly old lady leaned forward to ask in a sympathetic voice, "Aren't you tired of the long ride, dear, and the dust and the heat?"

The little boy looked up brightly and smiled. "Yes ma'am, a little. But I don't mind it much because my father is going to meet me when I get to the end of it."

A man slid his pickup truck off a road and ended up in a ditch. A farm-house was nearby, so the motorist asked the owner if he had a tractor he could borrow to get his truck back on the road.

"Nope, but I got my mule, Blue," said the farmer.

"I doubt a mule is strong enough to pull my truck out."

"You don't know Blue," said the mule's proud owner.

So Blue was hitched to the truck.

"Pull, Blue!"

The truck didn't move. And the farmer called out, "Pull, Elmer!"

The truck moved a little. Then the farmer called, "Pull, Biscuit!" and the truck was free.

"Thanks so much," said the truck owner. "But I have a question. You called your mule by three different names. How's that?"

"Simple," said the farmer. "Blue is blind. And if he thought he was the only one pulling, your truck would still be in the ditch!"

Finally, during the Great Depression, a government agency had the task of traveling through backwoods mountain areas in search of poor farmers to whom they gave some grant money for the purchase of seed or repairing their homes. One agent came upon an old woman living in a shack. It had no floor. Several windows were broken and covered over with tar paper. The old woman had but basic essentials and was just barely scratching out a living on a miserable plot of land. The agent said to her, "If the government gave you $200, what would you do with it?" Without skipping a beat, she replied, "I'd give it to the poor."

Back to the gospel. On the evening of the first day of the week, when the doors were locked where the disciples were stuck in their in-between time of fear and despair, Jesus came with peace on his lips and a Spirit to bestow.

This gospel, I hope you realize, is simply a variation of the stories I just told, stories that all had a dangling afterthought that made us think.

The first story of the little boy traveling a long, long time through the dusty, uninspiring land buoyed by the thought of his father at the end, tells us of Jesus' promise that he will not leave us orphans. The second story of the mule that pulled more than his weight when he thought he was not alone makes us think of Jesus, who said he would give us another abiding Spirit to be with us always. So why do we think we are pulling alone? The third story of the chronically poor woman who instinctively moved beyond "poor me" to think of people worse off than herself tells us that the way out of a funk is always an act of Spirit-inspired charity. And the fourth story, the gospel story itself, of Jesus passing through walls? It tells us that no barrier is able to keep Jesus and his peace from our in-between lives.

All the stories seem to have the same message about Pentecost. In the end is a Father who will make all things new again. We do not pull all alone. Out of failure there arises the prize of God's love. We inevitably make progress when we reach out to others. And lastly, through any sealed, closed door of mind and body, Jesus is able to come.

Pentecost is about gift, promise, presence, and surprise. It is a comfort for the in-between times.

ORDINARY TIME

24. Five A Day

A woman tells of the time she was feeling alienated from the church. Her local pastor was an elderly priest who terrified the parishioners. She was distressed when he fired an excellent school principal without consulting or telling anyone. It all happened around Holy Week, and, with all that, she just couldn't bring herself to go to her parish church.

So she and her family spent the Triduum—Holy Thursday, Good Friday, and Holy Saturday—at a Benedictine monastery. Without the ever-present tyrannies of the TV, cell phone, noise, and shopping, it turned out to be a transformative experience, and it paved the way for how she and her family would take the experience back home.

It developed this way: She knew, as most people do, about the familiar idea of a five-a-day fruit and vegetable diet for physical health. As a doctor, she was also familiar with the five-a-day mental health program: being physically active, connecting with others, taking time to notice our surroundings, learning something new, and giving to our neighbors and community.

Reflecting on these two patterns she came up with a five-a-day routine for spiritual health. They are: prayer, holy reading, silence, giving to others, and "enough."

This five-a-day spiritual routine is designed to bring us closer to God, just as a physical routine brings us closer to good health. It helps us achieve holiness—a holiness that reflects God's presence and light, but also a holiness that, realistically, does not necessarily reduce the challenges in a person's life. That is to say, holiness doesn't remove freckles or baldness or habits. The experience of grace clearly did not change some well-known saints' personalities, struggles, or mental health. One thinks of irritable St.

Jerome or depressed Mother Teresa. St. Francis de Sales had trouble controlling his temper—as when he pitched his manservant out of a second-story window. But their holiness blessed others.

This five-a-day spiritual discipline of prayer, holy reading, silence, sharing, and enough is best done—as are all routines, like AA, for example—within a supportive group. Which means that people who are serious about their spiritual lives connect for mutual support. They come together from time to time. For example, they might go on a day of recollection or retreat together. They claim holy space: going to Mass, sending an email reminder or a prayer to one another. Some say the Our Father at the same time every day knowing that others are doing the same. They enter silence by turning off the phone and TV for a spell and reading a spiritual book; and perhaps they even have a book club to discuss it.

The point is that, just as the five-a-day fruit and vegetable routine steps back from the ubiquitous fast-food diet that has produced an obese nation and instead promotes physical health, so the five-a-day spiritual routine promotes spiritual health, spiritual insight, a spiritual landscape to work from: prayer, holy reading, silence, giving to others, and enough.

OK, let's see: maybe this is too abstract. Let me put some drama to what I am saying: a story told by writer Philip Yancey about Dr. Paul Brand, an American physician who worked with lepers in India.

One day the patients had come together to pray and worship. Dr. Brand came in late and sat in the back. They saw him and insisted that he speak. He stood silent for a moment looking at the assembled patients. He began to look at their hands. Many of them had "claws" from their leprosy. Some of them had no fingers, just twisted, deformed stumps where their hands had once been. Many of them sat on their hands or hid them from view.

Dr. Brand began to speak. "I am a hand surgeon, so when I first meet people, I can't help but look at their hands. I can tell what trade you were in by the position of your calluses and the conditions of your nails. I can tell you something about your character. I love hands," he continued. "I've often wondered what it would have been like to meet Jesus and study his hands. There were the hands of Jesus the carpenter, rough and bruised from working with saw and hammer. There were the hands of Jesus the healer, radiating sensitivity and compassion. Then there were his crucified hands. It hurts me to think about the soldiers driving nails through his hands because I know what would happen to the nerves and tendons. His healing hands became crippled and gnarled, twisted and shut on the cross.

"Finally," the doctor continued, "there were his resurrected hands. You and I think of Paradise as a place of perfection, but when Jesus was raised up from the dead, he still had his earthly wounds, and he showed them to his disciples."

When he finished speaking the effect on the audience of lepers was electric. Christ had crippled, claw-like hands like mine? Christ showed his hands to his disciples when he was raised from the dead?

Suddenly this whole room full of less-than-perfect lepers began pulling their hands out of their pockets and holding them in the air. They knew Christ was one of them. They recognized him in their midst, and he lifted them out of their shame.

The point of the story is that people don't think, feel, talk, and act like this wonderful doctor unless they have tapped into the well of prayer, holy reading, and silence to give them a certain perspective about life. People don't value the misfits unless they have taken the time to escape the ten billion commercials hawking the perfect body and creating ever-new needs. They don't gather with moral or physical lepers unless they have learned to step back from their obsessive worship of celebrities. They don't even display their deformities and weaknesses to Jesus Christ unless they have first met him in prayer and silence and know that he loves and accepts them. All this takes a holy discipline, a special mindset, a way of seeing as Jesus sees, a spiritual routine.

So, look at our hands. Have they clasped in prayer or grasped in greed, held a holy book or plugged into more noise, reached out to others or hugged oneself, laid bare our deformities to Jesus or projected our carefully groomed image? What would the doctor say about us? Would he guess our profession, calculate our holiness?

I think we have to realize that just as so many of us in America need to go on a five-a-day fruit and vegetable regimen, so we do need a five-a-day spiritual regimen: prayer, holy reading, silence, giving to others, and an awareness of enough. Our spiritual health depends on it.

That last item, by the way—enough—will be the topic of next week's homily.

25. Enough

SEVENTH SUNDAY IN ORDINARY TIME, C, LUKE 6:27–38

If you're visiting New York City you can still pick up one of those funny maps at the souvenir shops that line Seventh Avenue. I mean those maps of the United States that show the borough of Manhattan filling 95 percent of the map, with the rest of the country scrunched into a little area down in the corner. While the map may boast of New York City pride or sense of humor, it's a bit skewed to say the least.

Yet, consider this map—only one that is accurate: Someone who's a whiz at math figured this one out. If you could condense the entire population of the world down to 100 people while maintaining its mathematical proportion and fit them into this church building today, our congregation today would consist of:

57 Asians
21 Europeans
14 Americans, North, Central, and South
and 8 Africans

In our congregation this morning there would be:
52 women and 48 men
30 Whites and 70 non-Whites
30 Christians and 70 non-Christians

Hmm, people like me are a minority. Well, take heart. We 14 Americans may be a minority but we can comfort ourselves with owning and enjoying the majority of the world's wealth and resources. Yes, if we have a full re-

101

frigerator, clothes on our backs, a roof over our heads, and a place to sleep, we are wealthier than 75% of the world's population. If we currently have money in the bank, in our wallet and purse, we—you and I—are among the 8 out of the 100 people in this church who have it. We have, in fact, more than enough of everything, more stuff than we can handle. Which is why we have yard sales.

Comedian George Carlin has a classic routine called "Stuff." He says: "You can see that when you're taking off in an airplane. You look down and you see everybody's got a little pile of stuff. And when you leave your house, you gotta lock it up. Wouldn't want somebody to come by and take some of your stuff. Especially shiny stuff. That's what your house is—a place to keep your stuff, while you go out and get…more stuff!"

How much more stuff? The book *How Much Is Enough?* answers that with a staggering statistic. It reports that Americans alone, between 1940 and 1992—that's just in 50 years—had used up as many of the earth's mineral resources as had all the previous people who had ever lived on the earth before them. Try to wrap that around your minds. In fifty years we used up more minerals than the whole human race before us back to Adam and Eve.

Let's move on. We enjoy feeling shocked and righteous when we hear that the executive pay for the CEO of Viacom last year [2010] was eighty-four million dollars plus, or that hedge fund manager John Paulson made nearly five billion—yes, billion—last year while millions of Americans are struggling. We get angry and disgusted at such news, but that's all.

There are those people. But what about you and me? Our over-stuffed lives are never challenged. Not in our society, whose economy is built on non-stop consumption, where our presidents tell us in this time of recession to get out and consume. "Shop until you drop" is preferable to "Share until you care."

The thing is, intellectually we know that we have more than enough, even the most financially modest among us know this, but we're just plain outgunned. This man speaks for us: "I'm tired of the lies. I hear them daily, read them nightly, watch them before I go to bed. They are so prevalent that I have a hard time knowing what is truth and what is fiction. Do cars really make you sexy? Are diamonds forever? Is a purchase the best way to show love? Is my worth tied to my waistline and my wallet? Am I worth loving based on my productivity or stature? I know that the answer to each of these is no. I know that these are lies, and yet I can't help but wonder. Somehow the father of lies is seeping into my subconscious and making himself at home."

That's us. Good people, but brainwashed by a totally saturating advertising culture that constantly strokes our desires—even if what we are made to desire we really don't need or want. As I was composing this homily I glanced at the title of a *Wall Street Journal* article: "How Stores Lead You to Spend: displays, music, layout make $98 pillows…look like must-haves."

Well, we have all so succumbed to the "must-haves" that we have spawned a multi-million-dollar phenomenon, the self-storage industry, to house our excesses. Yes, the non–stop, ever-present, 5,000 to 7,000 commercial messages we receive every day without realizing it stimulate our desires while carefully hiding from us the fact that undisciplined, infinite desire, sooner or later, will outrun our finite resources and sterilize our environment.

But, as I said, we are not allowed to stop and think of such truths. "Enough" is a subversive word absent from our national as well as our spiritual lexicon. Yes, we may have 30 pairs of shoes or 25 sweaters in our closet, but we simply have to have one more, especially if our favorite TV celebrity wears it and that ubiquitous "everybody" has one. As spiritual writer Ronald Rolheiser observes, "When excess enters, enjoyment departs, as does freedom. Compulsion sets in. Now we begin to seek a thing, not because it will bring joy, but because we are driven to have it."

He's right. We haven't yet personally cried "enough" and taken a serious look at our spiritual lives. As one writer puts it: "What is it that we celebrate as a culture? as believers? One can celebrate love and honesty, mercy and forgiveness, justice and truth. On the other hand, a person may also celebrate power, prestige, greed, corruption, and pride. But one thing is certain: 'We become what we celebrate.'"

We become what we celebrate. If we celebrate obsessive consumption and celebrity and must-have clutter that advertises that we are what we have, then what happens is that we become so full of stuff that the personal, spiritual, and gracious things of life have no room left to take root, much less flourish.

Jesus, who fed the hungry in today's gospel, was right to give us warnings: "Be on your guard against all kinds of greed, for one's life doesn't consist in the abundance of possessions" (Matthew 12:15). In the parable of the rich fool Jesus bemoans those who "store up treasures for themselves but are not rich toward God" (Matthew 12:21). And he repeats the old wisdom, "What does it profit a person to gain the world and lose his or her own soul?"

So, go back to our New York map. We think we're 95 percent of the world when in reality we're only 14 percent. We're wealthier than three quarters of the world and each day consume the world's resources at an alarming rate while other people are starving, and ten-year-old children are mining our gold in Africa and making our throwaway clothes in Malaysia.

All this is not to make us feel guilty—a cheap emotion—but to feel called. Called to ask, "Do I really need this? Can I live without it? Can I downsize? Can I live more simply? Can I live the simple life that will free me up to be spiritually alive, sensitive to others' needs, and compassionate? Is it time to cry "enough stuff" in my life and make space for beauty, goodness, and sharing? Maybe we ought to tinker around with the Great Depression axiom: "Use it up, wear it out, make do, or do without."

That's all this homily is about: an urging to take a look at our lives and declare "enough!" Or, to put it another way, if Jewish humor can protest "Enough, already!" Christian piety should claim that expression, turn it around, and use it as words to live by.

26. The Cost of Discipleship

*[It is critical for the homilist to take time with this
and to read the gospel—with which, as you shall see,
I have taken some liberties—deliberately and thoughtfully.]*

You have just stood up for the gospel and now I'm going to ask you to sit down again.

We're going to do something different this morning. We're going to make a verbal sandwich: two commentaries on either side of today's gospel.

This first commentary requires that we make an effort to put aside all the preconceived mental and emotional images we have of Jesus. Forget, too, for the moment, all the doctrines and titles about him. Try to think of a first-century Jew living in occupied territory, looking, not like Charlton Heston with wavy hair and blue eyes, but just like the rest of the dark Mid-Easterners you see these days on television news as the Middle East explodes. Jesus would be hard to distinguish from any other Arab or Palestinian Jew of today.

Wipe out the titles also. Eliminate them: Lord of Lords, true God from true God, King of Kings, Second Person of the Blessed Trinity, and all the rest. See him only as his contemporaries saw him. Put desert clothes on him and take away the golden crown, the royal robes, the bright halo of countless centuries of art, the other-worldly look. Think of him, if you can, before there was a Vatican, a papacy, cardinals, bishops' conferences, canon law, chanceries, and dioceses. Think of him even before we had monsignors!

Use your imagination and see Jesus from the nondescript village of Nazareth—he didn't have the title messiah or "Christ" yet, which would evolve into a kind of last name. See this itinerant rabbi standing there surrounded by a crowd of people, some friendly, some hostile. Watch their faces as he spouts out some of the most outrageous words ever uttered. Some think he's mad—that's on record—some are intrigued though skeptical that such a program he outlines is possible to live by. "He's kidding, isn't he?" was a comment overheard more than once.

Jesus begins to preach what is basically a radical way of life or, as we would say in hindsight, what following him would mean and cost. Luke, our recorder, got this material from some eyewitnesses, and whether Jesus said these things all at once or here and there in his preaching, Luke has brought them all together as a manifesto of discipleship. So now, put yourself into the scene. You're one of the crowd; listen with fresh ears as if this were the first time in your life you're hearing these words. Stand with the others who were there.

The Gospel

At that time, Jesus looked around, took a deep breath, and began to say to those who would wish to be his disciples:

"To you who are hearing me, who would follow me, I say: Love your enemies, do good to those who hate you; bless those who curse you, and pray for those who mistreat you." (Murmurs and puzzled looks here. "Love your enemy? Pray for people out to get you?" Jesus pauses and looks around to see if they're still with him.)

He goes on, "When someone slaps you on the one cheek, turn and offer the other so he can slap that one too. When someone steals your coat, let him have your shirt as well." (A few are starting to make circles near their foreheads with their fingers.) "Give to all who beg from you. When someone takes what is yours, do not demand it back. Do to others what you would have them do to you."

Jesus glances around once more. His audience has thinned somewhat.

He goes on, raising his voice, "If you love those who love you, what credit is that to you? Even sinners love those who love them back. If you do good only to those who do good to you how can you claim virtue? Sinners do as much. If you lend to those from whom you expect repayment, what merit is there in it for you? Even pagans lend to pagans expecting to be repaid in full.

"I tell you"—his voice is getting louder—"Love your enemies. Lend without expecting repayment. Be compassionate to others as your heavenly Father is to you. Do not be judgmental and you will not be judged. Do not condemn and you will not be condemned. Pardon and you will be pardoned. Give and it will be given to you. Remember— are you listening?—the measure you measure with will be measured back to you."

And here he stopped and awaited a response.

The Gospel of the Lord.

As we give the other commentary, you may be seated.

When Jesus finished, the audience response he got was silence, the silence of disbelief. Some people's mouths were hanging open. "Is it possible for anyone to live like that?" they seemed to say. It was an honest response, more honest than our own, for we in practice have found a way to neuter Jesus' charter for discipleship. We cleverly ran off in another direction and invented doctrines about Jesus, and so distracted ourselves from the words of Jesus. We opted for orthodoxy, right belief, over orthopraxis, right living.

We must immediately add that right belief is critical and necessary, and we owe a lot to those who labored to make it clear. It's just that orthodoxy alone soon became the criterion for true discipleship. We were deemed to be true disciples—Christians, Christ followers—if we believed the approved doctrines, even while all the time we hated our enemies, plotted evil against them, harbored revenge, and refused to pray for or forgive them. We did not give to beggars; we loved only our in-group. We were not always compassionate and have been terribly judgmental and resentful. Those who were "different" were shunned or declared to be beyond the pale. We often made laws against them and punished them for not being "one of us," thus bringing to mind Oscar Wilde's words: "When one looks through the pages of history one is positively appalled, not at the crimes of the wicked, but at the punishments of the just." We freely condemned others and refused to be reconciled. "After all, I have my pride," we declared. But we believed. Oh, yes, we believed. If we might not live the faith, we would willingly die for it. Deny the Trinity? Never! Pray for those who mistreated us?

Never!

If we would seriously live the spiritual life and live it as Jesus taught; if, in short, we would be his disciples, be true Christians, then we have to take a good look at ourselves and start measuring our lives, not by the articles of the Creed—"Not everyone who calls me 'Lord, Lord' will enter the kingdom of heaven"—but by the articles of the gospel: love enemies; do good to those who hate us; bless those who curse us; give to all who beg from us; lend without repayment; be compassionate; do not condemn; forgive; and move our love beyond our circle of family and friends.

It is an outrageous agenda, and who can really follow all this? We might easily dismiss it as pie-in-the-sky fantasy—except that the one who taught us these things actually lived by them. "Father, forgive them, they know not what they do."

This gospel, I think, should be made into some kind of an alternate creed to replace the one we're going to recite shortly. This one is a wonderful list of things we believe, and it costs nothing. The gospel creed, on the other hand, is another matter. It costs everything; and I for one find it uncomfortable and hard and wish it would go away, but, somewhere along the line, I know that if we love God, if we really want to be saints (our fundamental calling), if we call ourselves Christian, then we have to embrace it and struggle with it.

When Jesus originally spoke those words, some back then also found them a bit much, and some walked away. At least they were honest. Still others—a minority I suspect, ourselves among them—stayed.

Why? What difference has it made?

27. The Saga of the Paralyzed Man

SEVENTH SUNDAY IN ORDINARY TIME, B, MARK 2:1–12

As is common knowledge, over the years some folk have been known to have had brushes with the authorities on their way home from social occasions.

One man tells of his experience. "Last night," he says, "on New Year's Eve, I was out partying with some friends and had a few too many beers and some rather nice wine. Knowing full well that I may have been slightly over the limit, I did something I've never done before. I took a bus home. I arrived home safely and without incident—which was a real surprise, as I have never driven a bus before and am not sure where I got this one."

It's the old set-up and twist gag—which is my introduction to this familiar gospel story of the paralyzed man let down through the rooftop. My contention is that there are surprising hidden twists and turns that we might miss in this story—but they can reveal a lot about ourselves and our spiritual journey. So let's take a look.

To begin with, visualize the scene. The storyteller, Mark, opens it with a large crowd of people in the house and spilling out into the street. Think Christmas Eve: the church was packed. We had to send people to the hall. People couldn't get into the church.

So it was in Mark's story: there were so many people that they were blocking access to Jesus. And right away this gospel detail evokes a twist, a telling metaphor, as we think of how at times the Church with its rigid rules and regulations, its obstinate spirit, its bureaucratic mindset, has blocked access to Jesus; how the bad example of some Christians, the proud with-holding of forgiveness and compassion, the disdain and pride of so-called good people, the hypocrisy of the religious have all blocked access to a merciful and healing Lord. That crowd blocking Jesus from "outsiders," a hidden image in this gospel, uncomfortably mirrors our behavior.

Another twist: there is a taken-for-granted subtext to the gospel story, namely that people in Jesus' time firmly believed that illness and bad for-tune were related to sin. This or that person was physically, socially, or mentally afflicted because they or their parents committed some sin, and the affliction was God's punishment. In other words, they deserved what they got, and so the people in that house had little sympathy and much disdain for the man lowered on the mat.

The gospel subversively reminds us that this attitude is still with us in the people, for example, who say that the homeless person asking for a hand-out deserves to be ostracized from our company because he has chosen to be lazy and live off the system. Some do this, but in these days of high un-employment and foreclosures, decent people are, for the first time in their lives, going to food shelters, and it's not so easy to make that judgment.

Some people say that the out of control alcoholic or drug addict deserves to be denied financial help or housing because it's his or her chosen way of life—in spite of what we know about the fierceness and power of alcohol and drugs and how hard it is to deal with them—and how fortuitous it is that AA, for ex-ample, has taken a different view. The gay man deserves to be abused because he has chosen a sinful lifestyle, and the righteous God is right to afflict him with AIDS for his immoral behavior. But then one thinks of the great tennis pro Arthur Ashe: a virtuous man, father, Christian, athlete, who was infected by the AIDS virus in a blood transfusion and died at the age of forty-one.

His bright and charming little daughter was six at the time. In a poignant letter to that little girl, a letter full of hope and the most tender love, Arthur Ashe assured her that he would be with her all the days of her life after his death. He encouraged her to cultivate a deep, personal relationship with God, suggesting that a good way to do this would be to continue in the practice of her mother's Catholic religion. What do you do with Arthur Ashe and innocent babies born with AIDS if God is bent on revenge?

Recently one blogger wrote that clearly God sent the horrible death from cancer to the late Christopher Hitchens because he was an atheist and deserved to die.

The gospel story upends all this and tells us that God is bigger than our judgments: Jesus did not disdain the so-called sinful paralyzed man, but quickly offered him healing both of spirit and body. Maybe the message is that pain is not a penalty but an opportunity.

Next, let's note the detail of Jesus' command: *stand up*, he ordered the man, and carry your mat home. The Stand Up, the preeminent Easter symbol, reminds us that we are constantly in the process of dying and rising. Life is a pilgrimage of ups and downs, and Jesus is there to lift us up. As for taking home the mat—what carried the man in, he carries out—this is possibly meant to be a reminder of the man's former life, like a scar that shows where he was healed, a reminder of the amazing grace that touched him. Or perhaps the keeping of the mat was meant to be a kind of "show and tell," an occasion, many times, to proclaim the good news of Jesus, to evangelize.

Finally, let's not forget the four determined friends: there would be no forgiveness, no cure, without them. That's what friends are for. The message here is loud and clear: we need each other. We depend on each other. We must reach out and, by deed and witness, bring people to Jesus.

So, this fabulous and vivid gospel story has lots of drama—including, I might add, the practical, as when, in a bible study group, in reference to the four friends breaking through the rooftop and sending debris all over the place, a man wanted to know who was going to pay for it all. He was an insurance man.

But there it is: blocking access to Jesus, playing God in our judgments, true friendship, evangelizing—it's all there in twelve verses: a colorful gospel with provocative twists.

28. Do Not Worry

"Do not worry about tomorrow," says Jesus. We sit here and ask ourselves, what planet is he on?

The Mid-East is boiling over. There are demonstrations and deaths in the streets. There are angry mobs in Wisconsin and Ohio. Recession on Main Street remains intact. Unemployment still hovers around 9 percent. Taxes and the cost of food and gas are climbing. Earthquakes, floods, and repetitive blizzards pound our houses and hearts. Communities and families are frayed.

The drug trade, with its aggressive murders, flourishes. Kids, claiming stressed lives, mutilate themselves and put their pictures on Facebook. The Church is mired in scandal. People are worried about their life, having enough to eat, and the wherewithal to clothe themselves. And Jesus spouts off about not worrying about these things? What is he thinking of?

I come to his defense—as if he needed it. Jesus is not unaware of our needs and stresses. His point, rather, is in the solution he offers: "Seek first the kingdom of God and his righteousness and all these things will be given you besides." That is to say, we need to start all over again and build on a better foundation than greed and selfishness. "Seek first the kingdom of God and his righteousness."

For it is no secret—and every week a new book comes out to back it up—that so much of our troubles go back to the hubris and indifference of some Wall Street moguls and lax and complicit government agencies: the Enrons, the banks, and the Bernie Madoffs who eroded trust and promoted greed that affected millions and millions of lives.

Celebrities have replaced saints; spin has replaced truth; "lifestyles" have replaced friendships and fidelity.

We need to start over and put our focus on right relations, compassion, sharing, truth-telling, righteousness. All our multiplied laws, committees, and agencies will fail without this. We need people whose lives show us an alternate way of living besides consumption and arrogance, who, as we would say, put first things first. Seek first the kingdom of God.

Let me move from these generalities and translate Jesus' message into some stories. First, let me share an old Chinese folktale. It goes like this:

Once upon a time, the emperor summoned children from all over the empire and announced that one of them would become the next emperor. "As you leave today," he explained, "you will be given a seed. You must nurture and care for it. In one year's time, you will return here with your plants, and by looking at them I will know who is the new emperor." Each child received a special seed and hurried home with great excitement to plant it. One boy, Ling, faithfully planted his seed and tended and watered it. But it failed to sprout. He listened with dismay as his friends, abetted by their parents, all boasted about how large and beautiful their plants were becoming.

A year later, Ling still had nothing to show for his work, He was afraid to go back to the emperor, but his mother convinced him it was his duty to obey the emperor's command. By the time he arrived at the palace, the great hall was already filed with beautiful plants and even some small trees. Ling stepped quietly into the shadows, holding his pot of bare earth.

The emperor arrived but seemed oddly unimpressed by the thriving plants. Then his eyes fell upon Ling, and he commanded his guards to bring the boy into the royal presence. Laughing at the spectacle of this boy with his empty pot of earth, the guards brought him forward. Ling was shaking with terror, certain that he would be put to death. So he listened in astonishment as the emperor declared, "Today, I have chosen your new emperor. Behold! It is this boy!"

"I don't understand," said Ling, "I failed to grow anything from my seed!"

"That is exactly the point," said the emperor. "I gave each of you a boiled stone, not a seed. No one could have grown a plant from any of them. Only this boy had the courage and honesty to return today and tell me the truth. He has the makings of an emperor!"

Or, as we would say, he has the makings of a saint, the makings of a good citizen. I don't have to hit you over the head with the meaning of the story. Your heart caught it immediately. And that's what Jesus was talking about: integrity. Seek God's ways first, and you won't have so much to worry about.

Another story from a different culture. "One day," writes this man, "when I was about five, I told my grandfather a lie. It was not a very black lie. My grandfather asked our gardener to bring a long ladder and place it against the front of the roof. When the ladder was firmly in place he said to the gardener, 'Our boy had taken to leaping from housetops. The ladder is for him to use when he so desires.' I knew at once what this meant, for one of the proverbs in our village was 'A lie is a leap from a housetop.'

"I brooded in silence. It was awkward to have the ladder before the front door. I began to fear that it would be there forever if I did not do something. I found my grandfather reading a book, and I went quietly up to him and buried my face in his lap. 'Grandpa,' I said, 'we do not need the ladder anymore.' He seemed very happy. He called the gardener and said to him, 'Take the ladder away at once. Our boy does not leap from housetops anymore.' I will never forget that incident."

Repentance, forgiveness, and love are better than pride, revenge, and hate. They are the stuff of righteousness.

Finally, a story about someone who was the hero of every kid long ago—they even made a movie about him. Today he is unknown, replaced by celebrities, but in the nineteenth century, David Livingston left his comfortable home to spend 30 of his 60 years on earth as a missionary in Africa. He became internationally famous because of his travels and his work for the Royal Geographic Society. He discovered the source of the Nile and many other wonders westerners had not encountered before. He worked to abolish the slave trade.

Among those affected by Livingston was a reporter named Henry Stanley. He was sent by the *New York Herald* in 1869 to find Livingston, who was thought to be dead because no one had heard from him in such a long time. Stanley finally found him in Tanzania in 1871. Of his encounter he wrote these words, "I went to him as prejudiced as the biggest atheist in London...I saw this solitary old man there, and asked myself... 'Is he cracked or what? What is it that inspires him?' For months after we met I simply found myself listening to him, wondering at the old man carrying out all that was said in the Bible....Little by little his sympathy for others became contagious....I was converted by him, although he had not tried to do it."

"Do not worry...seek first the kingdom of God and his righteousness...." That translates as the integrity of Ling, the truth of a boy, and the witness of a saint.

Integrity, truth, witness. When they begin, worry ends.

29. Spiritually Teasing Stories

Like his contemporaries raised in an oral culture—the literacy rate was about 2% in his time—Jesus spoke and taught in stories. All the ancients did this because stories were so effective. They had so many levels of meaning that you couldn't canonize only one, and that made them challenging, diverse, and rich. Moreover, the stories had hidden hooks in them, messages that might only become apparent after you thought about them for a long time. Then it would hit you. Stories also, by nature, expand and evolve over time so that they are able to stimulate the moral imaginations of future generations.

There are the quick throwaway ones like the couple who came upon a well. The wife said, "Let's make a wish." So she made a wish, bent over the well, and tossed in a coin. The husband said, "Why not?" So he also made a wish, but as he bent over to toss in his coin, he bent too far and fell down the well and drowned. His wife said, "Hey, it works!" We laugh but even this surface joke has deep roots in the age-old battle of the sexes and the tensions of life's most intimate association.

But let's go deeper as I share other stories with you. On the surface they appear to be entertaining, but in hindsight, they confront us. They make us think morally.

The dour, sardonic Danish philosopher Søren Kierkegaard, gave us this to chew on: "I went to a church with a marble floor and sat on the velvet pew. I watched as the sun came shining through the stained-glass windows. The minister, dressed in an elegant robe, opened the golden gilded Bible, marked it with a silk bookmark, and proceeded to proclaim, 'If any man will be my disciple, said Jesus, let him deny himself, take up his cross, and follow me.' And I looked around, and nobody was laughing."

The silence tells me that, like a swig of limoncello, it will hit you later, when you might think of the distance of the often-elegant trappings of religion and the one who had nowhere to lay his head.

The priest received a phone call from a very irate father who told him in no uncertain terms, "I hold you personally responsible for this!" He was angry because his newly graduated daughter had decided, in his words, "to throw it all away and go do mission work in Haiti with the Jesuit volunteers. Isn't that absurd!" he went on, "She has an M.B.S. degree from Scranton and she's going off to dig ditches in Haiti! I hold you responsible for this!"

"Why me?" asked the priest.

The father said, "You filled her mind with all this religious stuff."

The priest was not intimidated and shot back, "Sir, weren't you the one who had her baptized?"

"Well, yes," said the father, "but what does that have to do with anything?"

"And didn't you send her to CCD classes when she was a little girl?"

"Well, yes."

"And didn't you allow your daughter to go on those trips to Appalachia when she was in high school?"

"Well, yes. I thought it would look good on her résumé. Again, what does that have to do with anything?"

"Sir," said the priest, "You're the reason she's throwing it all away. You introduced her to Jesus, not me."

"But," protested the father, "all we wanted was for her to be raised Catholic."

"Well, sorry, sir, but you messed up. You've gone and made a disciple."

"Yeah, but…."

And that, "Yeah, but…" exposes our shallowness, doesn't it? We want to be résumé Christians but not serious ones.

This man writes: "I've read a great deal over the years about the unhappy

Franz Kafka but never read anything by him. His life and his weird, surreal stories seem to be surrounded and impregnated by so much gloom that I had no desire to risk being pulled into that world. Nevertheless, there must have been something special about a man who could do what he did in the final months of his life when he was dying of tuberculosis.

"Kafka met a child on the street, crying because she had lost her doll. He explained to her that, while the doll had indeed gone away, he, by a happy coincidence, had just met it and that the doll had promised to write. In the weeks that followed, Kafka did, indeed, write letters to the little girl in which the doll told about its travels and presumably brought sweet magic into that child's life. Who would have suspected this of that miserable man?"

And the story perhaps probes our quickness to pass judgments.

A Jewish delight. You'll enjoy this: Wonderful smells wafted up and down Roosevelt Road and the New South Loop. People flocked to Brodsky's Better Bagel Bakery and carried away dozens of fresh bagels—everyone, that is, except Sam. Every day, Sam came just to smell the bagels. He stood on the sidewalk sniffing the air with a smile on his face. This made Brodsky crazy.

"Sam, why don't you buy something?! You're just taking space away from my customers!"

"I'm on a small pension and can't afford to buy. The onion, poppy seed, and garlic smells remind me of my childhood days in Brooklyn."

Some of the people waiting took sides. "Leave him alone, Brodsky, you bully!"

"Yeah. Brodsky, he's not taking up much room,"

Others disagreed. "You know, Brodsky, he's stealing the smells of your bagels! Take him to TV court, Judge Jackson's Jiffy Justice."

"Yah, I've seen that dude. He's a hoot!"

The next Thursday, Brodsky took Sam to TV court. The bailiff ordered everyone to stand. A tall, stern looking man in a dark robe entered and banged his gavel. "Be seated. I am Judge Jackson and I dispense Jiffy Justice. Let's get started. Mr. Brodsky, what is your complaint?"

"Well, your honor," he said, pointing to Sam, "this man stands in front of my bakery taking up space, and he steals the smell of my fresh bagels. He never buys anything!" I'd like full compensation for the smells he steals."

"I see. What do you have to say, Sam?"

"Well, Judge, I do come for the wonderful smells and the fond memories of my childhood. I can't afford to buy."

"Thank you both," said the judge. "I'll be back with my decision in a jiffy." And so he was: "This was a difficult case to decide quickly. However, I rule in favor of Brodsky."

Grumbles were heard throughout the courtroom. The judge banged his gavel.

"Sam, do you have money with you?"

"Yes, I have a few coins in my pocket."

"Will you shake them, please?" Sam did as he was told.

"Mr. Brodsky, did you hear those coins?"

"Yes, I did, now when do I get paid?"

The judge smiled, "Mr. Brodsky, you've been fully compensated. The sound of Sam's coins just paid for the smells of your bagels."

Now that's jiffy justice.

Don't be deceived. Let the story sink further into your hearts as you consider personal issues of small-mindedness, pettiness, narrowness of outlook. See if the story can inflate your hearts to larger issues of grace.

Finally, this one. A man was being tailgated by a stressed-out woman on a busy boulevard. Suddenly the light turned yellow just in front of him. He did the right thing, stopping at the crosswalk even though he could have beaten the red light by accelerating thorough the intersection. The tailgating woman was furious, and she honked her horn angrily, screaming in frustration and shouting obscenities as she fumbled her cell phone. She was still in mid-rant when she heard a tap on her window and looked up to see a stern police officer. He ordered her out of the car with her hands up and took her to the police station where she was searched, fingerprinted, photographed, and placed in a holding cell.

After a couple of hours she was escorted by a very embarrassed arresting officer back to the desk and given her personal effects. The officer said, "I'm really very sorry. You see, I pulled up behind your car while you were blowing your horn and cursing a blue streak at the guy in front of you. Then I noticed the 'What Would Jesus Do?' bumper sticker, the 'Choose Life' license plate holder, the 'Follow Me to Sunday School' bumper sticker, and the chrome-plated Christian fish emblem on the trunk. Well, naturally," he continued, "I assumed you had stolen the car."

30. Becoming Rachel

Two recent headlines:

First, Sandy Vietze—the 18-year-old, golden athlete headed for the Olympics from Vermont's Green Valley, $43,000-a-year tuition ski academy—has been detoured. On an air flight, the 18-year-old was so drunk that he exposed himself and urinated on the floor next to a sleeping 11-year-old girl.

Second, The "Dougherty Gang," as they are called—3 siblings in their 20s, two brothers and a sister—were finally caught in a wild car chase after a series of robberies, not to mention shooting at police and other crimes; not to mention they're all on drugs.

Thus two, well-publicized headlines. The cynic asks, can the book, the TV interviews, the mini series, and the movies be far behind? The cynic asks this because he knows that we can't get enough entertainment, no matter what the subject, because everything in America has a market value, everything and everyone is a commodity to turn a profit; and, let's face it, self-absorbed people seem to fascinate us.

That's not the entire shame of it. The real shame is that noble stories are lost in the ratings war. But I want to correct that at least for the few minutes we have here this morning. I want share a story this morning. Nicholas Kristof (8/11) tells it in a *New York Times* Op-Ed piece. It concerns a nine-year-old girl named Rachel Beckwith. Rachel died on July 25, 2011.

When Rachel was 6, she learned at school about an organization called Locks of Love that uses hair donations to make wigs for children who have lost their own hair because of cancer and other diseases. Rachel was deeply struck by this and went home and asked her mother if she could cut off her own hair and send it to help other kids. She explained that when it grew back after a few years, she could donate her hair again. Her mother said yes, and so she did. A remarkable gesture for one so young.

Two years later, when she was 8, her church began raising money for an organization called Charity: Water, whose purpose was to sink wells in Africa. Like so many of us, Rachel was stunned to learn that children didn't have what she and everyone else living here take for granted. She couldn't imagine children dying from thirst or not having clean water, so once more she asked her mother for a favor. This 8-year-old asked her mother if she could skip her forthcoming ninth birthday party and instead have the kids donate $9 each to the water project in Africa. So she did. She was hoping for $300 but got only $220. She was disappointed but happy to get what she got.

Then tragedy struck. A month later when riding with her family on a highway, two trucks collided, causing a 13-car pile up, including Rachel's car. Rachel was critically injured and went into a coma. Everyone was devastated. Seeking to comfort and support her and her family, friends began donating on her home page. Before long, Rachel's initial $220 for the African water charity went well past $300, until finally the total was near a staggering $50,000, all of which was sent to Africa. Her parents proudly told their daughter of this, although they were not sure Rachel could hear them.

Rachel, age 9, died. Her parents, moved by their daughter's love, donated her hair and her organs to other children. Soon, word of Rachel's life, compassion, and death began to spread. More and more contributions for Africa began pouring in, going well over $100,000 and eventually topping three quarters of a million dollars—and it is still growing. Amazing, what a little girl started.

Scott Harrison, the man who founded the African water project called Charity: Water, remarked in awe of how a little girl was able to inspire so many adults. Harrison himself, I might mention, is only 35, and he founded the water project when he was 30 while other thirtysomethings were looking in the mirror.

Rachel's mom, by the way, on the anniversary of her daughter's death, is planning to go to Africa to see some of the wells being drilled in her daughter's name and meet the children who would have died without her.

Remember the gospel incident when Jesus' disciples asked him who was greatest in the kingdom of heaven, and he called over a child and replied, "Unless you change and become like children you will never enter the kingdom of heaven. Whoever becomes humble like this child is greatest in the kingdom of heaven"? Think Rachel.

So there we are. A drunken 18-year-old and a trio of twentysomething druggies have captured the headlines. A nine-year-old has not captured headlines, but has captured hearts. I hope she has captured yours. I hope she is a reminder that there are really a lot of people out there who do march to a different drummer than the tunes of consumption and celebrity. There are the Rachels and the Scotts and countless others out there who have caring and compassionate hearts and who will turn things around.

Can we join them?

31. The Woman Who Taught Jesus

The story we just heard of a risky encounter, a sharp confrontation, is one of those provocative gospels that call for all of us to sit around a table and discuss it and what it means to us. It is so rich and challenging, I wish I could hear your thoughts on it.

However you heard it, let me throw out some tantalizing suggestions.

"Have pity on me, Lord, Son of David!" the woman cries out.

Now, remember, this is a Gentile woman from a tribe that is the traditional enemy of the Jews. She's from the other side of the tracks. She knows it, and so does Jesus, but he has something she needs. So she startles him by shouting, "You, Son of David"—in effect meaning, "Hey, Jew, how about some mercy?"

The disciples react. Remember they're always the foil in the Jesus stories, something like Watson to Holmes. So, true to form, they immediately think the problem is with this crude, vulgar woman shouting after them. But, as usual, the truth is otherwise. The problem's not with the woman. It's with Jesus. His job is to save Israel. He's a Jew with a mission to his fellow Jews, so he reminds her, "I was sent only to the lost sheep of the house of Israel."

And here lies the tension, the standoff, of the story. Here are two people on either side of an issue. So, notice what she does. She tries a second time. The second time around, she drops the "Son of David," the Jew title, and simply calls him "Lord, or "Sir." "Help me," she says. In other words, she drops his particularity and appeals to his universality. She's saying forget the boundaries for a moment. I have a daughter with a deformed body and crooked smile and a dark mind who will never run and play with other children. She is hurting so badly. I am hurting so badly. Can't you for once forget our labels?

And Jesus, mouth open, suddenly taken aback, finds himself muttering something about it not being right to take children's food and toss it to the dogs.

Now you have to understand the import behind those words. Jews, unlike the Gentiles, never let dogs inside the house. If you wanted to feed them you had to take the family dinner food, get up, walk over to the window and toss it outside to them. So Jesus is saying, you want me to do that? You want me to take inside food, meant for us, for Israel, and walk over and give it to outsiders like you?

The woman sees the point but still begs him to have a wider vision than that. He can surely reach further than that, see further than that, can't he? Can't he?

Jesus presses his lips. He pauses. The woman is right. He may be a Jew, but he is also Lord. Finally he says, "Oh woman, you got me there. Great is your faith"—with that "Oh" implying, "I see what you're saying now." And so the daughter lived, and the mother lived, and Jesus, who, as Luke told us in his gospel, grew in wisdom, age, and grace, learned to see his mission wider than what he first thought. That's something to think about.

A dramatic and colorful story but we're not quite through with it yet. Let's go back to the woman, the loud-mouthed, persistent woman. What drove her so? What made her cross boundaries? What fired her passion? It was her daughter, of course. She is consumed by her love, by her mission. She is a mother. Her mission is her daughter. Her demon-filled daughter is going to die or endure a living death, and if this Jewish messiah can help, then, by God, he's going to! Little things like nationality and ethnic rivalry are not going to stand in her way. This woman has faith all right, but faith in the need to have things right.

I can still see this woman today. I can still hear her today. She is every parent who screams at their demon-filled children, "I'm on my way to church but before I go, I want you to know that I'm never going to stop. You think you can sulk and avoid me and I will go away. Let me tell you something. I am never going away and you can never run far enough to get away from me until you change your ways. Now pull yourself together and get some help!"

Yes, this woman of the gospel lives. This woman is a tigress who will humble herself to plead for her child, shout out to God, call him to account, and see that justice is done. She has a fierce faith, an indomitable hope, and a love that won't let up. She is every parent, teacher, mentor, and friend who challenges those they care about and who shouts after God's mercy and help. And that's also something to think about.

So—now I have an idea. Remain seated as I proclaim the gospel once more in a modern version. But this time, close your eyes, if you will, set the scene, put yourself in it, and listen anew.

At that time Jesus went into foreign territory, and suddenly out of nowhere a disheveled native woman ran out to him and shouted, "You, Jew, Son of David that you are, have pity on me, for I have a tormented daughter and my heart is breaking!" And she sobbed.

Jesus didn't answer. He just stood there trying to take it all in. His disciples, however, always ready to take charge, told Jesus to tell her to get lost. So Jesus said to the woman, "Sorry, I'm spoken for. I was sent only to the house of Israel."

She now fell on her knees and said in a softer voice, "Sir, help me, please, if not as a Jew then as a messenger of God's mercy." But he said, holding himself tall, "No, I don't think so. I'm not going to take what belongs to my people and toss it to dogs like you."

A nasty retort was on her lips, but, thinking of her daughter writhing and screaming in agony, she gritted her teeth and only said meekly, "Yes, but even dogs like me will take scraps. Surely you can cross lines when my daughter is hurting so, can't you?" And Jesus sighed as he thought to himself, "She is right. This is my Father's will." Aloud he said, "Oh woman who taught me who I am, your persistent faith in what is right has made both you and your daughter whole. Go in peace."

And she with joyful tears stood up and bowed to him. He with a knowing smile bowed to her. And they departed.

32. Hospitality

When I used to go around giving talks to parishes, I would ask the people to play a word association game. I asked them to shout out, without thinking about it, what immediately comes to mind when the name of their parish is mentioned.

For example, St. Theresa's: the response might be, "great choir." St. Joe's: "won the state basketball tournament." Sacred Heart: "best bingo around." St. Robert's: "great school." St. Alphonse: "deadly dull." And so it goes. What word comes to mind when your parish is mentioned? Think. Whatever the word, one that would be most desired, most pleasing for most parishioners to hear, I think, is the word, "hospitality." Wherever one's parish is mentioned, it would be great if people associated it with hospitality.

Basic hospitality issues from the celebrant, lectors, cantors, ushers, the congregation. In 2004 an article appeared in *America* magazine entitled, "Hospitality at Church." Students were asked to attend Mass and services in many different parishes and to rank their experiences. Much to the surprise of the instructor, the twenty-year-olds' experiences of "Church" were profoundly affected by simple hospitality, that is, whether it was offered to them. They rated highly such experiences as being greeted at the door, people moving over so they could be seated in the pew, parishioners visiting with one another before and after the liturgy, and parishioners simply acknowledging them.

The great preacher Tom Long tells of a case when this was not done. He says that he grew up in a small rural church of ordinary folk in Georgia. One Sunday morning while they were at worship, a rather shabby stranger appeared, walking in the side door. Probably one of the many drifters who rode the rails. The stranger walked in and walked past the preacher who was giving the sermon. The congregation looked at him, and he looked back at them. The preacher even stopped his sermon and stared at the man. The man did not take a seat, nor was he offered one. He spoke not a word, and no one spoke to him. He simply looked across the congregation, paused for a few moments, and walked out the opposite door.

But after church that day the people gathered around one of the big oaks outside church and discussed what had happened. They did this for several weeks. They never knew who the stranger was, but they sensed that God had put before them some kind of moral test and they had flunked. God had shown hospitality to them, and they had failed to show hospitality to the stranger.

Too bad, Long adds, that the people had not heard of the ancient second-century Christian treatise that taught that if a stranger enters your house where the Eucharist is being celebrated and there is nowhere for the stranger to sit, the bishop who is presiding at the Eucharist is to get up and sit on the floor, so that the stranger may be welcomed in the name of Christ. That's hospitality.

That story reminds me of a similar one I heard about a Catholic church where a quite shabby, hippie kind of young man walked into Sunday Mass and walked straight down the center aisle and sat down before the sanctuary. Everyone, including the pastor, was understandably distracted and then annoyed. Someone had to remove that young man.

But who? Finally, Ed, a senior usher, old and bent, started down the aisle. Everyone could hear his cane striking the marble floor. Old Ed would put that man in his place and in no uncertain terms ask him to leave; and maybe Ed would even brandish his cane. The congregation waited, as did the pastor, as Old Ed, cane stroke after cane stroke, seemed to take forever to reach the young man. Finally he did, and the congregation held its breath. He stood over him a moment, then Ed bent over, laid down his cane, and, with great effort, sat beside the stranger and put his arm around him. There was a long silence, and then Mass continued. At the end of the Mass the pastor returned to the pulpit and said to the congregation. "This morning, very few will remember the sermon I preached, but we will all remember the sermon we saw."

All this underscores basic parish hospitality, a starting point. But, with today's gospel in mind, we learn from Jesus that hospitality not only embraces each other on-site, but also the stranger off-site: "When you hold a banquet, invite the poor, the crippled, the lame." People you don't know, as in: "Lord, when did we see you hungry or thirsty or a stranger or sick or in prison and did not take care of you?" Then the Lord will say to them, "Truly I tell you, just as you did not do it to one of the least of these, you did not do it to me."

Therefore, a parish that has hospitality embraces the stranger and makes visitors feel welcome—not just the ones who come our way, but all those in need wherever they are: embracing them through our food and clothing drives, perhaps twinning with a parish in a third-world country, or participating in the diocesan Martin House project, which builds affordable housing with the poor.

A parish has deep hospitality when, collectively, it never forgets that 24,000 people die everyday from malnutrition, and it tries to help where it can. A parish has deep hospitality when it remembers that the biblical command to "love your neighbor as yourself" appears in only one place in the Hebrew Bible, while the command to love the stranger appears in more than 30 places. A parish that has hospitality remembers how Mother Teresa, when invited to receive the Nobel Prize in 1979, honored the biblical tradition by insisting that the ceremonial banquet be cancelled and asking that the $6,000 cost for the banquet be donated to the poor in Calcutta. The money saved on that one banquet would help her to feed hundreds for a year. The parish that has hospitality recalls the mystic who said, "If I am hungry, it is a biological problem; if my brother is hungry, it is a spiritual problem."

In short, the parish of noted hospitality is not only welcoming to visitors and strangers on its doorstep but is ever mindful of Jesus' instruction to consider the poor, the crippled, the lame, the blind, and the stranger beyond that doorstep—those who can't repay.

The parish whose hospitality is apparent when parishioners and visitors get together and is known to reach out in works of charity beyond itself, is by every measure considered a good parish.

33. Ruth's Legacy

The book of Ruth was read during the week. Like the stories of Joseph and his colorful coat, and Job and his bad hair day, and the comic novella of Jonah the runaway prophet, the book of Ruth is basically a work of fiction, a short—only three pages—historical romance novel that, like the others I mentioned, was commonly circulated in the Middle East. And also like the others, the book of Ruth was basically pondering some of life's big questions.

The Joseph story deals with the unexpected reversal of fortune; Job, with the perennial question that still breaks backs: how can a good God permit evil or not do anything about it; Jonah, like Ruth, with how to treat outsiders. These stories weren't history. They were creative folktales of the Middle East that the Hebrews took over to try to figure out how to deal with these thorny matters. They didn't always come up with an answer, and they frequently changed their minds, but through their stories they struggled with big issues. That's why the Bible is more of a book of questions than of answers.

The book of Ruth is a classic woman's tale. A Hebrew couple, Naomi and Elimelech, migrate to the foreign land of Moab to avoid a famine back home. There they have two sons who marry local Moabite women. Elimelech dies and then, ten years later, the two sons die, leaving Naomi in that society defenseless without a man. One daughter-in-law, Orpah, decides stay put in Moab, but the other, Ruth, decides to go with her mother-in-law, who wants to return to her people at Bethlehem. Naomi protests but Ruth responds with those famous words, "Where you go I will go, where you lodge, I will lodge. Your people will be my people, your God will be my God."

As a clergyman who has witnessed many weddings I am always amused when the bride and groom select those words as their reading. They like

131

the "Where you go I will go, where you lodge I will lodge. Your people will be my people" sentiment, taking it to mean that they will be at one with their spouse, but never realizing that these words were spoken, not to a spouse, but to a mother-in-law! I can't image any groom publicly declaring to cherish and follow his mother-in-law!

Anyway, like a good story, things happen fast. Ruth and Naomi, poor and outcast, go back to the Bethlehem area. Since it was a humane custom when harvesting to let any corn or grain that fell off the wagon be left for poor people to gather, Ruth and Naomi find themselves following the farm wagons to get something to eat. In true soap opera style the owner, a fellow named Boaz, notices gorgeous Ruth and orders his men to let more than the usual amount of corn fall off the wagon. Old Naomi, like Mrs. Bennet in *Pride and Prejudice*, quickly sizes up the situation, smells a possible rich husband in the making, and advises Ruth in the art of seduction. Eventually it all works out, and Boaz and Ruth marry and live happily ever after. A made-for-television story.

But that's the surface story. The real issue the story subversively deals with is how one treats outsiders, especially one's enemies. At different times the Hebrews had different answers. Mostly the answer was hate: destroy your enemy. After the exile, for example, the leaders Ezra and Nehemiah, in a desperate need to regroup and emphasize a defeated people's identity as God's Chosen Ones, cruelly forced the men to divorce the foreign wives they loved. "Stick with your own" was the motto. But stories like Jonah and Ruth lingered in the background as a challenge to think outside that box.

By the time of Jesus, society was still an "us against them" affair. But Jesus the Jew starts to tap the old underground tradition. Could it be because the son of Ruth, the foreigner, became the grandfather of King David, from whom Jesus was descended? In other words, outsiders are in his genes. Anyway, Jesus begins his subversion. He openly eats with outcasts and sinners, for which he was roundly criticized. He dares to touch and cure the segregated, untouchable leper. He cures the son of the hated Roman occupier, the centurion; he spoke of his Father letting it rain on the just and unjust, said love of God and love of neighbor were two sides of the same coin, and, when asked "who is my neighbor," responded with a story about a good Samaritan rather than a good Jew. On Calvary he prays for his Roman executioners.

Here at last was something definitive for his followers, a new teaching. His disciples were to treat all equally. His disciple Paul, who urged us in today's reading, "Do not conform yourselves to this age," summed up the new rule by declaring, "There is no longer Jew or Greek, there is no longer slave or free, there is no longer male or female; for all of you are one in Christ Jesus."

That dealt a blow to categorizing a whole people. It dealt a blow to prejudice, segregation, ethnic cleansing, racism, and any other external line of measurement as a warrant for unequal treatment. Or, at least, it was supposed to. The fact is, as we know, many of the people who carry Jesus' name have had a hard time following his words and example.

Let me share three true memories.

In 1942, by order of President Franklin Roosevelt, nearly 120,000 people were forced into internment camps in rural Wyoming. There families lived in a single room in a barracks with no privacy. They earned 12 dollars a month repairing shoes or raising pigs. A barbed-wire fence circled the camp. Guards were everywhere. Tower searchlights constantly swept the camp. The charge against these men, women, and children? They were of Japanese descent, and Pearl Harbor had just happened. Never mind that two-thirds of them were American citizens. Using false intelligence, such as that the Japanese were communicating with enemy submarines, the government trampled their civil rights and imprisoned them because of their race. After the war, each survivor got 25 dollars and a train ticket. Most had no homes by this time. There was no job waiting. They faced discrimination. They even had trouble finding a grocery store that would take their money. Later President Reagan finally apologized on behalf of the nation for humiliating a people because of their nationality, saying that this is not what America is all about: to judge a whole people for the sins of a few.

My second story happened some twenty-five years later. On March 16, 1968, American soldiers, in an event that became known as the My Lai Massacre, killed some three to five hundred unarmed citizens, mostly children and women, of South Vietnam. When it finally came to light, some twenty-six soldiers were eventually charged with the horrendous crime, but only Lt. William Calley, a platoon leader, was convicted. As an aside, three U.S. soldiers who tried to halt the massacre and protect the wounded were later denounced by U.S. congressmen. These soldiers received hate mail, threats, and found mutilated animals on their doorsteps. It would take thirty years before they were honored for their efforts.

When it all came to light, having learned the lesson with the Japanese, the U.S. Government bent over backwards to assure the Vietnamese people that all Americans were not like that. Those soldiers represented an aberration. Most were dedicated and compassionate. In other words, don't blame a whole people for the crimes and sins of the few.

Finally, an Auschwitz survivor remembers: "I was just a boy when the Nazis put me, along with my family into a cattle car in a city in France and started us on the long journey to Auschwitz. We had no water and we had no food, but each night the train would stop and sit still for hours. Time and time again, after hours had passed, there would be German people who would sneak out of the forest, come up to the sides of the cattle cars and push in between the slats of the car small containers of water and bits of food. Their generosity kept me alive. What they did was done at a great risk. So—whenever I hear someone with a German accent, I say to myself, 'Could that be the child or grandchild of one of those who dared to help me in my time of need?' Then I smile at them."

Others who hear a German accent say all Germans are barbarians, just as all Irish are drunkards, all Italians are Mafia, all Orientals are evil, all Muslims are terrorists, all whites are trash, all blacks are lazy, all soldiers are cruel, all Americans are imperialists, and on and on. You name the label.

Jesus encourages us to make judgments about wicked and conniving individuals, but forbids us to brand a whole people as evil, inferior, or tainted because of the shameful deeds of a few. Where such labeling and prejudice exist, we are called to be like the soldiers who blew the whistle at My Lai— and we'll probably get the same treatment, but that's the cost of discipleship.

So that seemingly innocent soap opera called the book of Ruth, the story of the foreign Moabite outsider who became an ancestor of the Jew, Jesus, has opened a whole range of speculation and a whole moral code to live by.

Who would have thought it? But such is the power of the word of God.

34. *Variation of a Theme*

Twenty-Sixth Sunday in Ordinary Time A, Philippians 2:1–5

What one-liners and clever stories have in common—besides being funny or, like the gospel, being tricky—is that, quickly and imaginatively, in a few fanciful words, they capture the big mysteries of life. They exploit human truths that lie beneath the surface. That's why stories and catchy aphorisms are so wise and ring true.

Two drum-rollers: "When I die, I want to die like my grandfather who died peacefully in his sleep. Not screaming like all the passengers in his car." It takes time to get it, but after we laugh we sense the comic/tragic subplot of aging.

"We're having a raffle for a poor widow. Would you like to buy a ticket?" "I'm afraid not. Even if I won, my wife wouldn't let me keep her." Funny, but unspoken is the perennial challenge of marital fidelity.

Listen to this. As a crowded airliner is about to take off, the peace is shattered by a 5-year-old boy who picks that moment to throw a wild temper tantrum. No matter what his frustrated, embarrassed mother does to try to calm him down, the boy continues to scream furiously and kick the seats around him.

Suddenly, from the rear of the plane, an elderly man in the uniform of an Air Force general is seen slowly walking up the aisle. Stopping the flustered mother with an upraised hand, the white-haired, courtly, soft-spoken general leans down and, motioning toward his chest, whispers something into the boy's ear. Instantly, the boy calms down, gently takes his mother's hand, and quietly fastens his seat belt. All the other passengers burst into spontaneous applause.

As the general slowly makes his way back to his seat, one of the cabin attendants touches his sleeve. "Excuse me, general," she asks quietly, "but could I ask you what magic words you used on that little boy?" The old man smiles and confides, "I showed him my pilot's wings, service stars, and battle ribbons, and explained that they entitle me to throw one passenger out the plane door on any flight I choose."

We smile but the serious message is that when all else fails in life, try tough love.

Here's a life-truth I learned in third grade that captures truth:

Hearts, like doors, will open with ease
To very, very little keys,
And don't forget that two of these
Are "I thank you" and "If you please."

In a Father's Day column, the late humorist Erma Bombeck recalled:

One morning my father didn't get up and go to work. He went to the hospital and died the next day.

I hadn't thought that much about him before. He was just someone who left and came home and seemed glad to see everyone at night. He opened the jar of pickles when no one else could. He was the only one in the house who wasn't afraid to go into the basement by himself.

He cut himself shaving, but no one kissed it or got excited about it. It was understood when it rained, he got the car and brought it around to the door. When anyone was sick, he went out to get the prescription filled. He took lots of pictures...but he was never in them.

Whenever I played house, the mother doll had a lot to do. I never knew what to do with the daddy doll, so I had him say, "I'm going off to work now" and threw him under the bed.

The funeral was in our living room and lots of people came and brought all kinds of good food and cakes. We never had so much company before.

I went to my room and felt under the bed for the daddy doll. When I found him, I dusted him off and put him on my bed, He never did anything. I didn't know his leaving would hurt so.

And so she, like us, belatedly realized the truth of Jesus' saying, "The greatest among you will be your servant" (Matthew 23:11). Time to dust off the people we take for granted.

For you women, how about this:

Before I lay me down to sleep,
I pray for a man who's not a creep...
I pray he's rich and self-employed,
And when I spend, won't be annoyed.
Pull out my chair and hold my hand.
Massage my feet and help me stand.
Oh send a king to make me queen.
A man who loves to cook and clean,
I pray this man will love no other,
And relish visits with my mother.

A good chuckle but, underneath, the perennial battle of the sexes resonates here.

Remember Robert Fulghum's simple words of wisdom from *All I Really Need to Know I Learned in Kindergarten*?

Share everything.
Play fair.
Don't hit people.
Put things back where you found them.
Clean up your own mess.
Don't take things that aren't yours.
Say you're sorry when you hurt somebody.
Wash your hands before you eat.

Flush...
Hold hands and stick together.
Be aware of wonder.

What is that but today's epistle made simple? Remember what St. Paul wrote: "Do nothing out of selfishness or out of vainglory; rather humbly regard others as more important than yourselves...."

How about this funky pop culture take on a gospel teaching:

Rich or broke, saint or sinner,
Some are fat, some are thinner;
Brave or chicken, loud or quiet,
Some who sell, some who buy it;
Big or little, drunk or sober,
Blonde or dark, lazy, loafer;
Eager beavers, adolescent,
Bright or dull, effervescent,
Middle-aged or just beginners,
Tired loser, constant winners;
All the victims of the Fall,
Jesus loves them—one and all.

The New Testament mantra, "God is love" is wrapped up here.

Finally let's end with a version of the gospel. It's Ambrose Bierce's classic story, "An Occurrence at Owl Creek Bridge," a story so intriguing that subsequent ages have continued to retell it in many different forms.

It's a story of a man about to be hanged. Enemy soldiers march him out to a bridge across Owl Creek. They take a board and they place it so that half the board rests on the bridge and the other half extends over beyond the bridge. One of the soldiers stands on the half that rests on the bridge itself, and the condemned man is made to walk out and stand on the other half that's overhanging beyond the edge. Next, the man's legs and arms are tied. Then the rope is dropped down from the top of the bridge and put around the man's neck. When everything is ready, the commanding officer barks an order, the soldier steps off his board on the bridge; the condemned man's board gives way, and he plunges downward with the rope around his neck.

But something strange happens. The rope breaks, and the condemned man goes plummeting down to the river below. Down, down, down into the water he sinks. And as he does, he's aware that he's alive, and he struggles to free his hands and his feet, and, miraculously, he manages to untie himself.

Realizing that he has a second chance at life, the man begins to swim down the river. As he does he passes a tree branch floating in the water. He is struck at the beauty of the leaves on the branch. He marvels at the intricate pattern of the veins on the leaves. Then he sees a spider spinning a web, and he's struck by the beauty of the web and the tiny drops of water that are clinging to it like so many sparkling diamonds. He feels the wetness of the water on his body. He looks up and he sees the blueness of the sky. Never has the world looked so beautiful to him.

Suddenly the soldiers on the bridge begin to fire at the man. So he fights his way through a hail of bullets, passes a water snake, goes over a waterfall, and swims ashore totally exhausted. He drops to the sand and he rolls over. He looks upward and he sees a flower nearby, and he crawls over and he smells it. Everything is so beautiful, and it's so great to be alive.

Then a bullet whistles through the trees and the man leaps to his feet and begins to run. And he runs and he runs and he runs until he comes to a house with a white picket fence around it. And, mysteriously, the gate swings open. The man can't believe his eyes. He's back home, safe! He calls his wife's name. She comes running out of the house, arms outstretched to greet him. As he rushes forth to embrace her, he suddenly feels a searing pain in his neck, a white light flashes—and everything goes black. He is dead.

Yes, he had imagined the entire story during the time between falling through the bridge and the noose breaking his neck. He imagined that he had gotten a second chance at life, a life that he suddenly saw in a different way, a life that he suddenly saw through new eyes. For the first time, he had seen the world for what it was—a beautiful place. For the first time, he saw life for what it was. He saw the signs of hope that he had missed.

The hidden gospel message? Unlike in the gospel, he never got the chance to change his no to yes.

35. Wellsprings

Although some people immediately politicized the terrible massacre in Tucson, Arizona, by chalking it up to the vicious rhetoric of conservative right-wingers, the facts have shown that any political motive was entirely absent. The man, the shooter, had no political agenda. He was just plain insane.

But, as one perceptive letter writer in *The New York Times* (1/13/2011) wrote, "The real issue is not whether inflammatory political rhetoric caused the Tucson shooting. It's the fact that so many people initially assumed that it did." His point is that our daily, everyday atmosphere is so uncivil and so full of hate that people automatically think that way.

He's right, and that assumption has roots that go from Arizona to New Jersey. Listen: "Four 15-year-old teenage boys were arrested last week and charged with bias intimidation of their female bus driver after crowding around behind her on the ride home from school, making racial slurs, and praising the Klu Klux Klan." Thus began an editorial in my local paper. The editorial goes on to ask, "Where does this kind of hate come from? How is it learned, and who teaches it either directly or indirectly?"

Good question for Christians to ponder. We know that these teenagers were not born prejudiced or threatening; somewhere along the line they must have absorbed these attitudes. From where?

Let's turn to Florida. A community had been hard hit by one of those terrible hurricanes. Power was out, houses were flooded, roads were closed—we all know something of that. At the Red Cross station at the local middle school, a distraught African-American woman asked tearfully for six flashlight batteries.

"My kids are afraid of the dark," she explained.

"Sorry," came the answer. "Only two batteries to a family. However, if you have relatives living with you, you can have two more for each one."

The woman just stood there paralyzed, feeling helpless—when Ryan Abel, who is white, piped up: "I'm a relative."

"So am I," announced a young Chinese girl nearby.

The Red Cross worker handed the woman six batteries with a smile.

Two incidents, two entirely different attitudes, one stating that we are divided by color, race, and religion, and the other stating that we are united by compassion, concern, and charity; one as far as one can get from the teaching and example of Jesus, the other as close as one can get. If any of those boys were Christian, it would have been a crucifixion all over again.

There are many causes, I suppose, for prejudice, but surely the parents and their attitudes, their casual table talk and example have to be paramount. At least they're there first and have the privileged position of shaping values. It's beautiful when they do so in favor of Jesus. Allow me to illustrate.

Around Christmas time, a man turned nostalgic and wrote of his childhood memories. His father, a man of faith, was a florist in Philadelphia. At Christmas time, he taught his son how to make the wreaths, how to make them carefully and honestly, no corners cut, no putting profit before doing something right, and telling his son, "That's the way God would want you to live."

The man telling the story remembers once working in the back room and seeing Joe Sweeney, a steelworker, coming in, and how proud the man felt when he saw his father hand one of his wreaths to Joe. Then he overheard this conversation:

"I'm a little short," Joe said.

"Joe," his dad replied, "pay me when you can."

When his father returned to the back room, the son said, rather hurtfully, "You just gave a wreath away for nothing, and it was one of mine."

He said his father looked him in the eye and said, "You'll learn some day that it isn't the money that counts; in God's eyes, it's the people who count."

Once when he was older the son delivered flowers at Christmas time in his father's old Ford. "What do you want?" asked a sad voice at one house.

"Flowers, Ma'am."

She opened the door slowly, "Who sent them?'" She was about 70, bent over with gray, stringy hair.

"There's a card inside the envelope on the package," he said.

She asked him to put the poinsettia on the coffee table, and she opened the envelope and read the card. Her face brightened and she burst into tears.

"It's from my daughter in California. I haven't heard from her in nine years. Bless you, son. Bless you."

She limped over to a desk, opened a drawer, grabbed a $5 bill and handed to him.

He handed it back, "Please," he said, "use it to call your daughter." When he returned to the shop and told his father about the old woman, his father smiled, reached for his wallet, took out a $5 bill and gave it to him. The boy had learned his lesson well. His father taught him. It's hard to imagine him shouting racial slurs at anyone.

Do people talk like his dad anymore, saying that doing things right and honestly is the way God would want their children to live, that it's people, not money, that counts? Do we give those kinds of life lessons as a normal gospel way of growing up?

There has to be a reason why two boys turned out differently, one belittling a woman in order to separate people into categories, another handing back a $5 bill in order to connect a mother and daughter. There has to be a reason why a white man and an oriental woman claimed relationship with a black woman, and why four white teenagers refused a relationship with a black woman.

The reason usually is the people in our lives, the ones who shaped us and taught us by how they lived. I wonder what the home life of those boys was.

Whatever, we're talking Jesus here. We're not talking about believing in him—anybody can do that. That takes no sweat—but following him; you know, the healthy one who touched untouchable lepers, the master who ate with outcast outcasts, the preacher who told tales about a good Samaritan, the prisoner who forgave his enemies, and the Jew who cured the Roman soldier's son. Yes, that one.

Let's pray for those teenagers and the people involved in the Tucson tragedy. But, while we're at it, let's look to ourselves gathered as we are right now as baptized Christians in a Christian church and ask ourselves if being a Christian makes any difference.

Now, in a few moments we will all stand and declare what we believe. That will be the easy part.

36. Hereafter

THIRTY-SECOND SUNDAY IN ORDINARY TIME, C, LUKE 20:27–38

Today's readings are about people dying and living again, about, if you will, the afterlife. The notion is not one we talk about a lot, although recently we have the challenging film called *Hereafter*. That's the title, as some of you know, of the current Clint Eastwood movie starring Matt Damon. It's about the character he plays named George who can communicate with the dead.

The movie has nifty special effects and even though the movie engagingly affirms the existence of an afterlife, it does stumble. For example, it steers clear of any specific religious beliefs, skirts the relationship between behavior and consequences, and even fudges on the existence of God.

Whatever, the movie *Hereafter* does bring up the topic of the hereafter, a topic that figures in our gospel today about the seven brothers who died, and it raises the question: do we believe in the hereafter? Many profess not to. The secular world proclaims that what you see is what you get: that is, no God, no afterlife, no spirit world. Still, these secular folk, for all their loud talk, can't get the possibility of the supernatural out of their minds or imaginations. Look at how our media is saturated with vampires—they're practically a cottage industry!—and wolf men, alien creatures, plasma beings, magic rays, glowing eyes, the living dead, poltergeists, invisible spirits, and on and on.

It remains a fascination exploited by people who profess out loud that they don't believe in the supernatural. I think all these extraterrestrial creatures are a covert way for these vocal secularists to sneak the spirit world in through the back door. They really can't quite get it out of their system. Actually, surveys show that most people have mystical experiences, times when they sense that there is "Something More" than what they see,

"Something More" being in capital letters, Something More meaning Some One More.

A striking sunset can trigger such experiences. So can a child falling asleep in one's lap, a lovely meadow, a feeling of the presence of someone you've loved and lost. The surveys also show that most people don't tell anyone about these common experiences. But they know what they experienced. Among such people is a man named Professor Paul Meyers. Paul works at the University of Portland's health center in Oregon. In an article in the University's magazine he writes, "One day I was at a conference of health care professionals when the speaker asked if anyone present had ever been visited by a dead relative. No one moved. Then a few hands inched upward, and everyone began to squirm. But the hands in the air kept multiplying until the vast majority of people in the room held a hand in the air."

He was not surprised. It was as he expected. Many people—sound, rational, sensible people—have such experiences. He knows that because, as a health professional, he's heard many such stories from patients, relatives, and friends over the years. He shares some of them. Listen: three men were walking a trail in Yellowstone National Park, fly rods in hand. Suddenly, one stopped and said, "There's my dad coming down the trail!" The other men stopped also. No one spoke. A hawk sailed over. The wind combed through the pines. The man's father had been dead for many years. He had often taken his sons fishing in Yellowstone as the boys were growing up.

Paul Meyers goes on to cite a man named George who had been in a war and never quite came home. He was an edgy man, especially harsh to his uncle Johnny. One day Johnny died from rheumatic fever. George was wracked with guilt. On the day of the funeral, as the family trooped back into the kitchen after Johnny's funeral, the phone rang. George answered it. There was a long silence as he listened to the speaker at the other end of the line. George hung up the phone and fell into a kitchen chair, slack-jawed. "That was Johnny," he said. "He told me he forgave me, and everything was fine between us, and that I shouldn't feel so guilty." To the day he died George swore that it was Johnny on the phone that day.

Finally, a girl was asleep in her college dorm room. She felt a pressure on her stomach and chest and shoulder, pressing down with enough force to wake her. She sat up and saw her grandfather at the foot of the bed. He had died a month before. "I love you," he said. "Don't worry about a thing. Everything is going to be just fine." She felt a great peace and confidence and reassurance and fell back to sleep.

Those are the sorts of stories Meyers heard from all kinds of well-balanced people. He comments: "For all of my years of training as a scientist and clinician, I have had experiences that I cannot explain away in sensible fashion, and I have come to the conclusion that sensible explanations only block the gift you may receive."

Along these lines, one of the most remarkable stories in the annals of American religious history happened not far from us. During an illness in the mid 1800s, the Rev. William Tennent, Jr., pastor of the famous Old Tennent Presbyterian Church in Manalapan, New Jersey, fell into a coma so deep that his family assumed he had died. Funeral preparations were underway when a physician discovered a warm spot under one arm and insisted that the funeral be delayed. But after William showed no other signs of life, the family decided that the funeral should go on. Shortly thereafter, his brother Gilbert entered his brother's room and saw the doctor there, moistening William's tongue with oil. Thinking he was force-feeding him, he began to argue with the doctor when suddenly his brother opened his eyes, groaned, and then sank back into his coma again.

Well, they nursed him back to health. After a period of amnesia, William began speaking about what he had experienced. He recalled meeting "a superior being" who guided him to a place where "an innumerable host of happy beings" were. William wanted to remain in this company but his guide informed him that he had to return to earth. An interesting story.

Back to Professor Meyers, who concludes his reflection by quoting Thornton Wilder's last words in his classic novel *The Bridge of San Luis Rey*: "There is a land of the living and a land of the dead and the bridge is love, the only survival, the only meaning." What Wilder is saying is that the great intangible, love, is impervious to change or decay. It transcends what the senses can see. Love is the connective key to a world beyond our sight but not beyond our hearts, and sometimes those we love and who love us let us know they've crossed the bridge.

We Catholics, who, shortly, will recite in the Creed that we believe in "the resurrection of the dead and the life of the world to come," have long known and celebrated these truths. All Saints and All Souls days are our collective way of expressing our belief that there is more to this world than meets the eye and that any contact between the worlds is no surprise.

37. Doubt

THIRTY-SECOND SUNDAY IN ORDINARY TIME, C,
2 THESSALONIANS 2:16—3:5

In today's epistle, St. Paul writes, "Pray that we may be delivered from confused and evil men. For not everyone has faith." Well, yes, but not everyone who is faithless is confused or evil, especially those who are hanging onto faith by a shoestring, those who have doubts. Let's look into that, into doubt.

Once upon a time, long ago when I was child in Catholic grammar school, my classmates and I were taught to have a strong faith and have nothing to do with doubt. We were reminded of the Thomas story—Dirty Doubting Thomas he became in our minds—and warned against the Devil's ploys to get us to doubt the truths we were taught.

Most days, as we all grew up, we fervently believed. Other days the ground seemed to slip beneath our feet, especially as time went on and successive breakthroughs in scientific understanding began to eat away at religious certainty. The biblical flood story was found in other ancient collections. Evolution proved the world was more than 6,000 years old—billions of years, in fact. Scholars doubted Moses existed. Miracles had natural explanations. Limbo, like St. Christopher, slipped out of sight and—horrors!—not all priests were holy. And how can a good God permit so much evil?

People got bolder and began to voice their doubts—not just celebrity atheists, but even church people. Other ordinary people simply kept their doubts to themselves and wondered if they were hypocrites when they went to church but really didn't believe.

And there, in that word, I found, was the trouble. The word I'm referring to is "believe."

Somewhere, early on in Christianity, in an effort to combat heresy, the word shifted meaning. The word "believe" comes from an old German word originally meaning "to commit to." To believe in Jesus meant to commit to him and his teaching and way of life. In fact, in its early years Christianity was referred to as "the Way"—that is, a way of life, a way of seeing reality as Jesus saw it, of living as Jesus lived and taught.

But, as I said, when heresies popped up, the word "believe" was radically changed and came to mean the acceptance of certain intellectual propositions. The true believer became one who believed the right things, right doctrine—you know, the Apostles' Creed, the Ten Commandments, the Precepts of the Church, and so on. In a word, a believer was someone who was orthodox, someone who conformed to institutional teaching.

So, by this standard, the Corleones of *The Godfather* fame were good Catholics because they were believers. They believed every article of the Creed, every precept of the Church. They never wavered, never denied an article of faith. Church officials, who would never challenge them for their murderous way of life, would have instantly taken them to task for publicly denying the Trinity. That would make them "unbelievers," and they would have to be excommunicated, cut off from the community of believers, lest they lead them astray.

But once you understand that belief is about commitment and practice, the justice and mercy of Jesus, and not about a set of propositions, then it makes it easier to handle doubt, which, of itself, is not a bad thing, since it is a reminder of our limitations as human beings to understand everything and is a necessary and needed critique of the arrogance of being certain. I hate to give him credit, but snide Voltaire was right when he said, "Doubt is not a pleasant condition, but certainty is absurd." And the Church has been absurd at times.

This woman struggling with doubt tells us how she handles it: "I no longer silently quizzed myself on the Creed in church on Sundays. Belief was about commitment and practice, not about a set of propositions with which to agree to disagree. Faith is the accumulation of habits that are celebrated, reinforced through rituals…it is more like craftwork than a process of reasoning; often repetitive, simple tasks done again and again. Kindness, friendliness, the attempt to be generous, the desire to enrich, ease, and aid the lives of others, the attempt to be patient." That's belief. That's faith.

You should know that it is this kind of practical, living, committed faith that has intrigued a new wave of avowed atheists who lately have begun to give grudging praise to religion as commitment and not as creed.

One atheist, for example, writes, "One can be left cold by the doctrines of the Christian Trinity...and yet at the same time be interested in the ways in which religions deliver sermons, promote morality, engender a spirit of community, make use of art and architecture, inspire travels, train minds, and encourage gratitude at the beauty of spring....The error of modern atheism has been to overlook how many aspects of the faiths remain relevant even after their central tenets have been dismissed."

Edward O. Wilson, a famous Harvard biologist and atheist, argues that religion offered a competitive advantage to early societies, for it bolstered social order and helped bind a tribe together. He writes, "Organized religions preside over the rites of passage, from birth to maturity, from marriage to death," adding, "beliefs in immortality and ultimate divine justice give priceless comfort, and they steel resolution and bravery in difficult times. For millennia, organized religions have been the source of the best in the creative arts."

Another atheist professor cites research showing that a fear of God may make a society more ethical and harmonious. He cites one study that found that people were less likely to cheat if they were first given a puzzle that prompted thoughts of God. He says, "The very ritual practices that the New Atheists dismiss as costly, inefficient, and irrational turn out to be a solution to one of the hardest problems humans face: cooperation without kinship."

Finally, this atheist says wistfully: "My entire life has been one long search for faith. I haven't found it. I do not believe in God. Having said that, which should lift an eyebrow or two, I want you to know that I love the idea of God. I love piety. Without it, you lead a life unmoored, in a state of isolation. You are a tiny speck in a vast universe. I'm jealous, frankly. I feel as though I've missed out on the greatest thing that can happen to a person—faith in God. It must be wonderful."

Beautifully put.

Let's summarize by turning to *The New York Times* Op-Ed columnist

Nicholas Kristof, who has called our attention to these trends. He says: "The latest wave of respectful atheist writing strikes me as a healthy step toward nuance. I've reported on some of the worst of religion...yet I've also been awed by nuns and priests risking their lives in war zones. And many studies found that religious people donate more money and volunteer more time to charity than the nonreligious....The new wave is skeptical but acknowledges stunning achievements, from Notre Dame Cathedral to networks of soup kitchens run by houses of worship across America...."

What are we to make of all this? What are we to conclude? We are to conclude that doubt is not incompatible with true religion, and that the best place to work out one's doubts or live with them is not outside but inside a community of faith, one that shares rituals, encourages cooperation, and translates good words into better deeds in the name of Jesus.

So for the Thomases and budding atheists among us here this morning, thank you for your presence. You've brought your doubts to the right place. Doubts may agitate the mind but they still leave the heart open to commit to Jesus and the good things he taught.

FEASTS &
OCCASIONS

38. New Year's (Solemnity of Mary)

LUKE 2:16–21

2012 ... can it be? Seems like only yesterday that the world was panicky that it was going to end in the year 2000. But, here it is, for better or for worse. Let's ease into it with a prayer: "Dear God: my prayer for 2012 is for a fat bank account and a thin body. Please don't mix them up like you did last year. Amen."

O.K., a smile is a good way to start. As for resolutions, how about sharpening your brain for 2012?

Johnny's mother has three children. The first child was named April, the second child was named May. What was the third child's name? Johnny, of course.

Before Mt. Everest was discovered, what was the highest mountain in the world? Mt. Everest; it just wasn't discovered yet.

In California, you cannot take a picture of a man with a wooden leg. Why not? You can't take pictures with a wooden leg. You need a camera.

If you were running a race and you passed the person in second place, what place would you be in? You would be in second place. Well, you passed the person in second place, not first.

OK, time to move deeper. One of baseball legend Satchel Paige's maxims is "Sometimes I sits and thinks, and sometimes I just sits." Today's gospel tells us that's exactly what Mary did. She reflected on and treasured many things in her heart. She carved out sacred space in her life to sort things out. Back then she was lucky. In our super-hyper, gadget-addicted world, that is exceedingly hard to do: to carve out sacred space, to sort things out, to have time to think, pray, contemplate, so that we might discover our place in this world and what God might want of us for the future, for this New Year.

This future is more important than we think. We often talk about how the past made us what we are, how it conditioned us to live a certain way, and so on. But that's not altogether true. What is more true is that it really is the future that makes us who we are. Yes, the future we want, the future we desire, the future we commit ourselves to—that's what determines what and who we are more than anything that happened to us yesterday or the day before.

If someday in the future we want to be a 15-minute celebrity for its own sake, very rich no matter what it takes, powerful without morals, to dominate without compassion, then these future goals will slowly but surely determine who we are or what we will become.

We peg such people whose future has been realized like that but whose hearts have not. We say things like, "He is very rich, handsome, and charming, but keep away from him, for he uses people and throws them away." Or: "She is beautiful and popular but she is also a foul-mouthed gossip who destroys people's lives." These people are lionized and have realized their future but it didn't include kindness or charity. They became successful doers but failed beings.

So, time to play Mary's role and ponder: what about our future? That is, not only what do we want to do in 2012 but what do we want to be, to become on the way to doing? Out of many possibilities I suggest two New Year's resolutions that may realize a better future. They are "retool" and "recalculate."

By retool, I mean, retool our words. Our homes, streets, airwaves, and public squares are full of nasty words. The F-word, for example, is now mainstream as men and women, boys and girls use it in normal conversation. The word appears in a book title that is No. 1 on *The New York Times* best-seller list and in the title of a Grammy-winning song. It's an equal opportunity vulgarity and a boring one at that. Non-stop obscenities pollute our society and drop the bar so low that many people can't speak a sentence without them, indicating not only a limited vocabulary but a limited sensitivity.

There are other words that insult, put down, and demean, and there are words left unsaid that should be said. And that is a shame, for words are powerful. Has your day or night ever been spoiled by a disparaging word from someone close to you? Has a note or letter or email ever left you limp, sick in body and spirit, made you cry? If someone says to us, "You look wonderful!" we perk up and smile. If someone says, "You look terrible," we shrink into sullenness. The doctor calls to give us the result of our biopsy. The word "positive" can strike terror in our hearts. The word "negative" can fill us with an elation that sends us floating up to the ceiling. Two simple words—positive, negative—yet look what they can do to us. Words are powerful.

On the other hand, think of the words that inspire, lift up our spirits, encourage us, words like "I love you," or "It's all right, I'm here"; "You're such a special person"; "We'll lick this together"; "You look nice today"; "That was a good job." We soar.

There are so many times when we desperately need words of affirmation and encouragement. The world is so mean-spirited—listen to Bill Maher, our politicians, bullies; and look at Facebook, Twitter, and the blogs—and can carry the most vicious, the most vile and hateful, even pornographic words. Don't be a part of that for 2012. Your calling, your goal is to be an encourager. And not just because you want to be a nice person, but because you are a Christian, because your calling and mine is to bring the healing and peace of Jesus Christ to others. So, resolution number one: in the name of Jesus, retool your language.

The second resolution is taken from our GPS world: recalculate. An example will serve: in 1821 a young lawyer named Thaddeus Stevens took on the case of a slave owner whose female slave, named Charity Butler, had run away. Stevens won the case, and Butler was returned to her slave owner. Case won. Another victory for the lawyer. Another fat paycheck. Another bit of fame. Stevens should have been elated. But he wasn't. The case gnawed at him. He knew he had won an unjust case, and his conscience would not give him peace.

So, in our language, he recalculated. He became an advocate against slavery and went on to serve seven terms in Congress and was a driving force behind the 14th and 15th amendments to the Constitution, which guarantees equal protection under the law and gave slaves who had been set free the right to vote. Nearly 200 years later archaeologists digging up Thaddeus Stevens's property discovered a hidden passageway in his home likely used to help runaway slaves escape through the Underground Railroad.

Nobody knows the name of Thaddeus Stevens today—celebrities have taken over—but he is a man whose recalculated vision of a better future drove him on, defined him, and made him noble. We can—must—do the same. Recalculate our lives. Retool our words.

So, back to Mary: "And Mary kept all these things, reflecting on them in her heart." I hope you will do the same with the words I have spoken.

Have a blessed and holy New Year.

39. A Saint for July

It's summer and it's July, and the July 4th celebrations with their themes of patriotism, freedom, and the land of equal opportunity are still ringing in our ears. I thought that therefore it might be a good occasion to take some time out to add to our Catholic lore, our Catholic culture, our Catholic litany of saints, and introduce you to someone whose name, in the future, you will get to know. He's an American. He is also black. He is also a priest, the first recognized black priest in the United States. His name is Augustus, or Gus, Tolton.

Augustus was born on April 1, 1854, in Missouri, one of four children, and named after St. Augustine, the great bishop of North Africa. Of course, being born in that time and place meant that he and his siblings were all automatically born into slavery. Gus was a slave. The family they served were the Elliots, who were Catholic and, as was the custom, they had all their slaves baptized into the faith. (By the way, there are still Elliots living in the area.) When the Civil War broke out in 1861, Augustus' father, Peter, joined the Union Army, where he lost his life from dysentery.

When Augustus was seven, his mother took the children on a long and arduous trek to freedom by fleeing first to Hannibal and then crossing the Mississippi River. The trip was dangerous, including a frightful ride in a rowboat where they had to duck gunshots. They finally arrived at Quincy, Illinois, which was free territory, and where former slaves gave them safety and access to the Underground Railroad.

With his brother Charley, age 10, Augustus, age 9, went to work in a tobacco factory in Quincy making cigars. Picture a couple of black kids working some ten to twelve hours a day rolling cigars. (Unhappily, Charley would die young of pneumonia). Later Gus worked in a saddlery, and as a custodian and factory hand.

Fortunately, when they arrived at Quincy, the family was embraced by a local pastor, an American-Irish priest, Father Peter McGirr, who had come to America at age 15 during the Irish potato famine and therefore knew something of prejudice and loneliness. Augustus at first went to a segregated school, then to the all-white St. Boniface's parochial school. That set off a storm. The parents there were outraged. The pastor and sisters received threatening letters. Gus was called illegitimate because he had no father. It was intolerable.

It was Father McGirr who again came to the rescue. He took all the Tolton children into his school of St. Peter's. Many of his parishioners protested the presence of black students and made threatening noises, but the indomitable Fr. McGirr held fast. He preached fiery sermons on the expansiveness of Christianity to remind people what the gospel meant.

As he grew older, Augustus, always an intelligent and pious lad, began to feel the desire to become a priest. But the insurmountable fact was that the American seminaries were closed to him because he was black. So his parish priests managed to have him enrolled in a seminary abroad, the international Propaganda College in Rome, where students from every country and culture attended so that they could go back and evangelize their countries.

Augustus naturally thought he would be sent to Africa as a missionary when he finished his studies, but an enlightened cardinal at the college, knowing full well the resistance the new priest might receive, nevertheless felt that America needed a black priest. Because America was a democratic nation, as he had heard, he thought the people there might just give Augustus a chance to prove himself.

So Augustus was ordained on April 24, 1886, in the Basilica of St. John Lateran in Rome and returned to America. He came to New York and offered his First Mass on American soil at St. Benedict the Moor, a black parish church on Bleecker Street in New York City. The full and joyous congregation that day experienced the first American black priest offering Mass in their church. The next day he celebrated Mass for Religious sisters in Hoboken. He was then off to Quincy.

He was an associate for two years at St. Joseph's parish in Quincy, Illinois, where he quickly gained a reputation as a fine preacher—even to the point of drawing many of the German and Irish Catholics to the parish meant for blacks. He soon became "Good Father Gus" to many. It wasn't long before he was asked to speak at public gatherings, and his fame grew. Nor, unfortunately, was it long before racism and jealousy raised their ugly heads from both Catholic priests and even from envious black Protestant clergy. His enemies began to refer to his church as the "nigger church." The prejudice reached its peak with the arrival of a new pastor at the neighboring German parish. This pastor began openly to refer to him as the "nigger priest." The fact was, he was losing parishioners and income to Father Gus. Eventually, he used his connections to force Fr. Gus to minister only to blacks and to declare that any white donations belonged to white parishes.

Under all this pressure, Augustus moved from Quincy to Chicago in 1889, and there served as pastor of St. Joseph's. When that parish closed, he took up his duties in a black church called St. Augustine's Association, which met in the basement of the half-finished church of St. Mary's, which eventually became Chicago's first Negro parish, and Father Tolton became Chicago's first black pastor. The parishioners, of course, were thrilled. At last they had their own black pastor. This parish would become the center of black Catholic life in the city for more than 30 years.

Father Tolton continued to be in demand, and he wound up lecturing at many gatherings, speaking in places like Boston, New York, and Texas, and at the first Black Catholic Congress in Washington, D.C. The press, of course, played up the unique situation of a black American priest.

Sadly, it was not to last. In 1897, after returning from a diocesan retreat on an extremely hot day and while walking home from the train station, Father Gus had a heat stroke. He was rushed to Mercy hospital but he did not survive. Off and on he had always had some bouts of illness. He died that night at the age of 43. His body was brought back to Quincy, where he was buried in St. Peter's cemetery.

He had a large funeral, according to the newspapers, "four blocks long plus streetcars...." But even in death he apparently faced prejudice—even though it was remarkable that, back in 1897, he was allowed burial in a white cemetery at all, he was placed deep in the ground so that another, white, priest could be buried above him, and his inscription is on the backside of the large cross that marks the other priest's grave.

It took more than a century, but he was eventually recognized for his gifts and ministry. In the 2009-2010 Year for Priests, when Chicago was looking for some Chicago priest as a model, many thought of Fr. Tolton. The cardinal of Chicago seized on this suggestion and lost no time in setting in motion the process of Father Tolton's canonization. Back in Missouri a regional high school was built in his honor.

The little black Catholic boy had come a long way; from slave to future saint. So, by this time, had the Church. So he belongs to us and we to him. And in hot July, with freedom flags on every house, he's worth remembering.

40. The Guns of August

It is somewhat ironic that a month named after a great Roman emperor, Augustus, is filled with such a rare collection of some remarkable Catholic saints. Within these thirty-one days there are saints Bartholomew, an apostle of Jesus; John the Baptist and his martyrdom; the deacon Lawrence, broiled to death on a gridiron during a Roman persecution. There are Alphonsus Liguori, the founder of the Redemptorists; John Vianney from France, patron saint of priests; Stephen, a king of Hungry; the Spaniard, Dominic, founder of the Dominicans; Clare, friend of Francis of Assisi, after whom the Poor Clares are named.

There is Bernard, a celebrity monk of his time; Rose of Lima, Peru; Monica and her son, the great St. Augustine from Africa; a pope, Pius X; and, nearer our time, during World War II, Maximilian Kolbe of Poland, who heroically died in place of another prisoner; and an Austrian army recruit, a young husband and father, who refused to take the oath to Hitler.

Of the six lay people I just mentioned in our litany of saints, this morning I want to tell the story of that last one, the Austrian army recruit who refused to take an oath to Hitler and who was, as a consequence, killed for his faith. His name is Blessed Franz Jägerstätter—a good Austrian name—martyred in 1943.

Let me begin by saying straight away that Franz Jägerstätter would be voted the least likely to be on his way to canonization. His beginnings were not promising. He was born Franz Huber in 1907 in Radegund, Austria (not far from Mozart's or the Trapp family's beloved Salzburg), the illegitimate child of his mother, Rosalia. He knew poverty and hunger. His grandmother raised him at first, until his biological father was killed in World War I and his mother, in 1917, married Heinrich Jägerstätter, who adopted Franz.

As a young man, Franz was the Austrian version of Marlon Brando in the movie *The Wild One*, zooming around the countryside on his motorcycle. Franz was the natural leader of a gang, whose members were arrested for brawling in 1934. He had fathered an illegitimate child, a daughter, the year before. So far, not quite saint material. For three years he worked in the mines in another city and then returned to Radegund, where he became a farmer on the farmstead inherited from his stepfather. In 1936 he met and married a deeply religious woman, Franziska, who turned his life around. For their honeymoon they made a pilgrimage to Rome. They had three daughters. Now settled down, Franz lived his faith with quiet but intense conviction.

In 1938 things began to change dramatically. The Nazis were on the move. Franz—the only one in his village to do so—publicly opposed the German Anschluss, the annexation by Germany of his beloved Austria. He remained openly anti-Nazi and declared he could not fight in an evil war. With the actual arrival of the Nazis, he witnessed denunciations, the imprisonment of the clergy on trumped-up charges, and, most of all, the callous extermination of the mentally ill. He joined the third order of St. Francis, worked as the local parish sacristan, and was a daily communicant.

He was in the German army twice briefly, each time getting a deferment. His experience only served to conflict his conscience further as he became more and more convinced of the immorality of Hitler's war. Finally, he was called to active duty in 1943. He sought counsel from three priests and even his bishop, all of whom told him that his military service was compatible with Christianity. Even his attorney reminded him that other Catholics were serving in the army and took the oath to Hitler. Still, Franz just could not reconcile such advice with his conscience. Besides, he also knew in his heart that the priests and bishops would be arrested if they had said anything other than what the government permitted and—such was the climate of the times—that no priest or bishop could be sure that Franz himself was not a Nazi spy trying to entrap them.

Franz, knowing full well the consequences, lost no time in declaring himself a conscientious objector and was forthwith imprisoned at first in Linz in Austria and then later at Berlin, where, on August 9, 1943, he was sentenced to death for, in the technical jargon of the time, "undermining military morale." He was beheaded by the guillotine and cremated the following day. He was just 36 years old.

Two days before he died he had written to Franziska: "Dear wife and mother, I thank you once more from my heart for everything that you have done for me in my lifetime, for all the sacrifices that you have borne for me. I beg you to forgive me if I have hurt or offended you, just as I have forgiven everything.... My heartfelt greetings for my dear children. I will surely beg the dear God, if I am permitted to enter heaven soon, that he will set aside a little place in heaven for all of you."

At the time, his stance was regarded as foolish by his neighbors and roundly criticized by his fellow Catholics who had served in the military. Indeed, at first, the town fathers refused to put his name on a war memorial or give his widow a pension. Franz Jägerstätter would have slipped into oblivion, except for an author named Gordon Zahn, who, after the war, researching the subject of Catholic responses to Hitler, unearthed his story and put it into a book, *Solitary Witness*, and the world knew it had a hero. In one of those notable historical coincidences, Zahn's book influenced Daniel Ellsberg's decision to take a stand against the Vietnam War and bring the Pentagon Papers to public attention.

In 1946 Franz's ashes were reburied in his home town near a memorial now inscribed with his name and the names of almost sixty village men who died during their military service. He was beatified in Linz on October 26, 2007. The following year, on December 20, 2008, his widow and three daughters were introduced to Pope Benedict XVI in connection with the presentation of a new biography of Franz.

In one of his last letters he wrote, "Just as those who believe in the Nazi party tell themselves that their struggle is for survival, so must we too convince ourselves that our struggle is for the eternal Kingdom. But with this difference: we need no rifles or pistols for our battle, but instead, spiritual weapons—and the foremost of these is prayer...without God's help and grace, it would be impossible for us to preserve the Faith and be true to his commandments...."

In these days when so many of our leaders shift with every political wind, when our notion of tolerance means anything goes and therefore nothing really counts, it is refreshing to discover someone who clings to gospel principles to the point of laying down his life for truth.

Franz Jägerstätter—sinner, saint, husband, father, 36-year-old martyr—is hardly a household name among us. He's not one of our manufactured celebrities, but he's infinitely better worth knowing about, better worth imitating. Blessed Franz Jägerstätter, pray for us and our country.

41. Black History Month: The Slave and the Singer

Every February since 1976 the United States has celebrated Black History Month to commemorate the contributions of African Americans. Because we live in a pop culture, the usual roster highlights celebrities like Whoopi Goldberg or Oprah Winfrey or actors like Morgan Freeman or Sidney Poitier. Because we have come to church to step back from the pop culture for a bit, in honor of Black History Month we're going to look at two lesser-known African Americans, both of whom knew Jesus, and both of whom have enriched our lives. One is a slave and the other a singer.

Very few know the name of Pierre Toussaint, but if he is ever canonized as the first black American saint—which is a possibility—I tell you there will be dancing in the streets of New York from Harlem to Bedford Stuyvesant. For almost seven decades this black man attended New York's oldest church, St. Peter's, in downtown Manhattan. He was an immigrant. Here's his story.

Born into slavery in the French colony of Haiti in 1766, Toussaint was among the 800,000 slaves who made it easy for the French plantation owners to amass huge amounts of wealth from their coffee and sugar crops. But when the French revolution exploded and the slaves lashed out with their own uprising, many of the slave owners packed up and fled. John Berard du Pithon, Toussaint's master, fled to New York City with his wife, his sister, four slaves, and Toussaint.

When du Pithon fell on hard times in the city and eventually died, Toussaint stayed on with his master's family. For the next twenty years he supported them with the money that he earned as a hairdresser. And even beyond that, Toussaint and his wife, Juliette, who was also a slave, made their modest home a haven for orphaned black children, raised them, and eventually even found jobs for them. He also raised enough money through his wealthy customers for a special home for orphans that had been built by a priest, a place that helped those who needed food, medicine, or clothing. When, on her deathbed, his late master's wife arranged for his freedom, Toussaint dedicated the rest of his life, and much of his money, toward ransoming the freedom of other slaves. He also spent the lion's share of his time visiting and nursing those who had been struck down by yellow fever or cholera.

Pierre Toussaint died in New York City in 1853 at the age of 87. Both blacks and whites would readily agree that nothing seemed more personally important and critical to Toussaint than sharing joy by helping others, even his own slave masters.

In the eyes of the Vatican, miracles play no small part in the process of canonization, as you know. And there is already one instance where it seems a reality. A man in Haiti had been diagnosed in 1966 as having cancer in both the abdomen and lung. He had only about three months to live. The story goes that a local priest who had been counseling the patient at the time suggested that he pray to a fellow Haitian, Pierre Toussaint. While the patient continued to lose weight, hope, and the will to live, the prayers to Pierre Toussaint continued. And when finally the doctors routinely examined the patient on one particular day, they found, to their amazement, that there wasn't a trace of cancer anywhere in the man's body and there wasn't a shred of medical explanation for any of it. He was pronounced completely healthy.

As I said, whoever heard of Pierre Toussaint? His steadfast faith, his overflowing heart, his heroic care for his own people, his love of Jesus, are not topics for primetime news broadcasts that love murder and mayhem. But now we have heard of this black man, and it seems likely that one day millions of Catholics will be venerating Pierre Toussaint as the first black American saint by way of the streets of New York. Looking at him, it is easy to catch a glimpse of God, a mirror of what we ought to be.

Our next candidate was something of a soft celebrity. She too loved Jesus and sang of him—and only of him. She is the great gospel singer Mahalia Jackson. Born a hundred years ago in New Orleans, Little Halie, as she was known, grew up in a ramshackle, three-room house on Pitt Street that housed 13 people and a dog. Her father, who fathered other children as well, was a dockworker, and her mother a maid and laundress. Little Halie was born bow-legged, and the doctors wanted to correct the condition by surgery, but her aunt would not allow it. Her mother died when she was five, and her strict aunt raised her, forcing her and her siblings to work from sunup to sundown, often beating her if she didn't do her work right. Of course she and her siblings never had time to go to school.

Her one solace was that she loved to sing. She began to sing in the Baptist church where she was baptized. In 1926, when she was 16, she and her relatives moved to Chicago. At a service in her new church she sang in the congregation, was heard, and then coaxed to sing in the choir. She began touring with them and soon landed a job as soloist. She toured with a famous gospel band for fourteen years. She married a man named Ike Hockenhull in 1936, who saw that there was no money in gospel singing and urged her to sing secular songs, but Mahalia, as she was now called, would not and vowed she never would. And she never did. This tension and his gambling habit led to a divorce.

Mahalia signed on with Decca records. They soon let her go because there was no market for gospel music. She then signed on with the famous Apollo label, and her recording of "Move On Up a Little Higher" sold eight million records, a staggering number at the time, especially for a gospel recording. She toured Europe and sang in concert halls as well as churches. Her rendition of "Let the Power of the Holy Ghost Fall on Me" won the first place music prize in France, where she was dubbed the Angel of Peace. Her rendition of "Silent Night" on Denmark's national radio provoked more than 20,000 requests. She was now considered the greatest spiritual singer alive.

In 1950 this bow-legged, poverty-born, orphaned, school-less, abused black girl sang in Carnegie Hall. Eleven years later she sang at John F. Kennedy's inauguration. In 1963 she sang at the March on Washington, on the same stage from which Martin Luther King gave his famous "I Have a

Dream" address. She was known as "The Queen of Gospel." Harry Belafonte called her "the single most powerful black woman in the United States."

She died in 1972 from a combination of heart failure and diabetes complications. Thousands of people passed by in final tribute. She was considered, as Dick Gregory called her, "a moral force." In a world of shallow celebrities, that's a tribute to embrace.

So during Black History month or any history month, it's good to remember two people who started out in life with the odds against them but whose faith and love of Jesus made them larger than life. The slave and the singer have much to teach us.

42. A Reflection on Mary

Back in the heyday of TV's Bishop Fulton J. Sheen, America's famous premier religious preacher at the time (he's still replayed at times on EWTN), a signature Marian poem he frequently cited went like this:

> Lovely Lady, dressed in blue,
> Teach me how to pray!
> God was just your little Boy,
> Tell me what to say.

We aspiring young priests at the time had our own version:

> Lovely Lady dressed in green,
> Make me preach like Bishop Sheen!

Whether the prayer was answered or not is another matter. But the incident does serve to introduce our topic of Mary and also with a reference to a poem.

Who has not heard of Elizabeth Barrett Browning's famous poem that begins,

> How do I love thee?
> Let me count the ways.

On this feast of Mary I want to count the ways why we love her and why she has remained so persistent through the twenty-one centuries that we have been around as a people of God. In counting let us turn to the first record: Scripture.

The initial description we get from Scripture, particularly from St. Luke, is that Mary is the first disciple, the first recipient of the Good News. Luke makes this point by telling us that when the angel comes and asks Mary to become the mother of the messiah, she says "yes" and then remains loyal to that "yes." Mary, then, was the first believer in Jesus, the first follower, the first disciple. What an honor from God! For this, from the beginning, she earned a place of deep respect and honor in the early church community.

Second, in the gospel, Mary is revealed as someone who was a faithful disciple. She kept God's word with all her heart and that, most of all, endeared her to her son. I don't know if you remember that incident when Mary and her relatives were trying to see Jesus, who was in the full bloom of his public ministry, and there was a big mob around him. So they sent word through the mob, and they said, "Jesus, your mother and your relatives are here." And Jesus made this response: "But who is my mother, my father, my brother and sister? The one who keeps the will of God. That's my mother, and my brother, and my sister." And in effect what he was saying was that Mary's claim to greatness was not that she was his biological mother, but that she, above all, was faithful, even when it cost her.

Third, in Scripture she clearly walks our walk. She becomes a representative, the image, of all those people who hurt, who are silenced and exploited. Remember, Mary lived in occupied territory. She was segregated. She was a woman without power. She had to keep her mouth shut while Herod killed the innocent children of Bethlehem. She had to stand on the fringe of the crowd while she saw her son publicly humiliated, carrying the cross. She had to stand behind the soldiers' spears that formed a fence, and she could not get to her only son on the cross to give him some comfort. She was permitted nothing but a broken heart, endless tears, and at the moment of his death, a scream heard throughout the ages. And I think that's why people have always related to Mary. People can identify with her. Those who hurt, know loss, those who are oppressed, who cannot speak out loud and instead must suffer in silence look at Mary and see themselves.

Fourth, Mary is, like so many of us, a pilgrim in the dark. When the angel said, "You are to be the mother of God," she asked the question, "How can this be?" And how many people throughout the ages, including you and me, have often asked that time and time again? How can I tackle this challenge? How can I survive? How can I begin all over again? We're full of Mary's questions: How can this be? How can I carry on? How can I survive life? How can I get along? I don't know what I'm going to do. We are asking the questions Mary asked.

Fifth, Scripture says that Mary is the keeper of memories. Remember what St. Luke says? She didn't understand, but Mary treasured all these things in her heart. She is the keeper of memories. And that is important for her and for us. As the secular marauders and haters of truth come in and destroy books and monuments and names and the values we cherish, we need the wise to keep alive the memories of God's presence and the ancient stories of deliverance. We need our Marys who will tell over and over again the old stories of faith, stories that give us hope again. Mary, the memory-keeper, is sorely needed today.

Sixth, Mary is the God-bearer, as Advent reminds us, and that too is our role. She gave forth to the world the living Christ, and committed people through the ages have always identified with that role. They embrace it as their role too: to be a Christ bearer, to birth the Lord and give him to other people by word and example.

And finally, I think Mary persists because she is ours. She has, in fact, been given to us. Remember the scene on Calvary? Jesus is dying. There's his mother. "Who will take care of my mother when I'm gone?" So he turns to John, who represents all the Christian family, and says, "Son, behold thy mother." And he gives away his last, and his most precious possession. And we are the recipients of that. Jesus' mother is our mother. We are never alone. We have an advocate. We have a mother.

And so, in the last analysis, whether it's Our Lady of Guadalupe, our Lady of Lourdes, Our Lady of Fatima, or Our Lady of Medjugorje—you name it—behind the appearances, behind the shrines, behind the titles and festivities, is a very human woman—pilgrim, wife, mother, widow—who won't go away. There's not a tear or a smile of Mary's that we haven't experienced. There's not a question or a hurt or a pain or a suffering that we can't identify with. We love her because she is one of us. She loves us because her

Son gave us to her.

How do we love Mary? We have counted the ways—seven of them. After twenty-one centuries, we still can't get her out of our minds and hearts, and we still need her more than ever.

"All generations shall call me blessed," prophesied Mary to cousin Elizabeth, and she gave the reason why: "Because he who is mighty has done great things for me." The implication is that, through our Mother Mary's intercession, the Mighty One will also do great things for us.

43. Trust Dies In Brooklyn

(July, 2011)

The tragic killing and dismemberment of a lost 8-year-old Hasidic boy in Brooklyn is beyond numbing. The parents decided to let him be a "big boy" and walk from day camp to where he was to meet his mother. He got lost, trusted himself to a stranger, one of his own kind, and met his horrible death. The grief of his family is unimaginable. His parents must be struggling with guilt; his neighbors are reeling from shock; the country is appalled. But I want to tell you this: of all of the wrenching and searing losses here, I submit that the greatest, most profound, and most lasting loss that will affect that community and our country for decades and decades to come, is the loss of trust, for the boy was betrayed by one of his own kind.

Yes, if you think about it, trust is the worst thing that you can lose. Unfortunately, today the loss of trust cuts deeply everywhere, and that loss has profoundly changed society. In contrast, let me take you back for a minute to what it was like before trust disappeared. What I am about to tell you is true, not just a bit of nostalgia.

People of my age can remember what no one under forty can even imagine today: when we were kids, our mothers would throw us out of the house in the morning with the order to be sure to be back in time for dinner—an order you dared not ignore. Parents were caring then, but they had no compunction in sending us out on our own all day, because our world was peopled with adults we had known all our lives. In my neighborhood there was my father's bakery with all of the employees. On the same block was the butcher, Mr. Dunn; the fishman, Mr. MacCauley; the grocer, Mr. Donovan. Up the block was the tailor, Mr. Lo Castro; the barber, Mr. Genco—and all the neighborhood mothers. In a word, all over town, from

174

a kid's point of view, you had a large network of surrogate parents and spies, and when you got home you were consistently dumbfounded when your mother scolded you for walking the railroad tracks again. How did she know?

We spent the day playing in the streets—there was no TV or Twitter or organized sports. We made up our own games and rules: stickball, marbles, pick-up baseball with rocks for balls and T-shirts for bases, ring-a-leeveo, jack-knife, roller skating, playing cars or jacks, or riding our bikes the six miles to Farrington Lake to go skinny dipping. It surely had its flaws, but it was a community, and we were, by today's standards, unbelievably free. The whole world was our playground.

But then one day it all began to unravel. Walmart and the box stores came along and fatally undercut all the local merchants, leaving the neighborhood bereft of adults. The neighbors were soon warehoused into look-alike developments. Gated communities and security-wired homes sprang up. Mothers worked. Families began to split up. Prosperity beckoned elsewhere. The old neighborhoods disappeared, and strangers moved in, and you didn't know the people behind the counters in the stores anymore. It wasn't safe to go out alone. Children no longer walked to school. They had to be bused, even if for two or three blocks.

Trust simply evaporated. One's word, in a land of strangers, wasn't worth anything anymore. The old handshake to a deal or, what was called back then a "gentlemen's agreement," was no longer sufficient. There were empty social spaces. And one thing is as certain as death and taxes: once the old social connections no longer exist and a vacuum is formed, then, quick as a whoosh, the government steps in to fill the gap, and it has with a vengeance.

Now we no longer have 100 friendly eyes watching over our children. We have 1,000 neutral surveillance cameras and paid strangers. Now we are no longer a nation of gentlemen's agreement handshakes. We are, significantly, a nation of lawyers where even best friends sign contracts. Hey, you never know. We no longer have the social pressures of a close-knit community to regulate behavior. We have ever-multiplying rules and law enforcement. In the era of routine divorce and fatherless families, betrayed children expose themselves on Facebook to get attention. Today is the era of the helicopter mothers who hover over their kids and keep in constant cell-phone contact. No one today would think of letting a child below teen age out on his or her own.

People make prenuptial agreements because they can't be sure of staying together. This is the age of marital betrayal as Arnold Schwarzenegger, John Edwards, Tiger Woods, and a host of senators and Hollywood celebrities remind us. This is the age that, in order to gain his 100-billion-dollar Facebook empire, Mark Zuckerberg betrayed his best friend. All of which, in short, means that this is the age of distrust.

Anyone here who is divorced, has had an errant spouse, has been betrayed by a child, friend, employer, a company, knows the wound it inflicts and how very hard it is to trust again. Nothing is as corrosive as betrayal. It is life's worse sin. It festers for a long, long time and changes the way we live.

Think, if you will, of our classic betrayer. We're all familiar with Judas and his garden visit. And we all remember Jesus' words, "Friend, do you betray the Son of Man with a kiss?" But we read that so abstractedly. Think of the pain of your own instances of being betrayed. Think of the pain, the shock, the awful disappointment. Now, with that in mind, go back and re-hear Jesus' words spoken with deep hurt as, with tears welling up in his eyes, he says, "Judas, of all the things you could have done—pointing, signing, whatever—you, one of my own kind, used the friendship kiss to betray me? Oh, Judas, how could you?"

No wonder Dante put Judas in the lowest pit of hell.

There is no sin that lingers so long, poisons hearts so deeply, and changes a community of trust so profoundly as betrayal. What happened in Brooklyn last week is what has happened to our country. That close-knit community that existed on trust, that knew each other, was confident of protection, and ready for help when needed has now been betrayed by one of their own. Things will never again be the same in Brooklyn. You can be sure of that.

And yet. Yet, having said all of this, I must insist that as Christians we are called to trust and to rebuild it where it has failed. And how do we do this? Two words: be moral. If that sounds simplistic and something of a letdown, let me assure you that it will not be committees or government programs that will restore trust. It will be people like you, committed to the moral life Jesus taught us, committed to forgiveness and reconciliation, who will rebuild trust.

One of my favorite movies is *To Kill a Mockingbird*. My favorite scene is the one in the courtroom where Atticus Finch, in a deeply prejudiced South, is defending a black man accused of rape. His children, Scout and Jed, had snuck up into the balcony among the black people who were there attending the trial. At the end of one day of the trial, all were going home. Atticus Finch was among the last to leave. As he began to move toward the door under the balcony, all the black people stood up in silence as a sign of respect. The black minister reached down and tapped Scout on the shoulder and said to her, "Miss Scout. Stand up! Your daddy is passing!"

And I think those are the best movie words ever spoken. Imagine, really imagine, those words being spoken of you. Imagine people trusting your word. Imagine living in such a way that people would stand up when you passed by because there is an integrity about you or, as we might say, the Spirit of Jesus is within you. Yet, that is our calling as Christians.

Let us pray for the family of Leiby Kletzky, and for the wounded Hasidic community of Brooklyn seeking to rebuild trust. Let us pray for our country. But, above all, to restore trust, let our words be true and our actions be faithful to the gospel.

44. *Trust Revisited*

These days in our weekday readings we have been listening to the foundational myths of Israel. Written between 300 and 400 B.C., and drawing from fragments of old records, folklore, and ancient traditions, plus their own spin, the biblical writers told the story of how a group of nomads—their ancestors, almost a thousand years before them—became a people. Such foundational myths are critically important. They provide beginnings, how this or that people are different from all others. Foundational myths provide cohesion and identity. This is what makes us who we are, this is where we came from, this is what we aspire to be. Foundational myths are ideal standards that measure how we are doing as the people we profess to be.

For ancient Israel, it was all about unexpected choice. Yahweh chose them. So as to never, ever forget this undeserved calling as God's Chosen Ones, they were bound by ritual, law, and the 10 Commandments. They were solemnly covenanted to justice and compassion. They were to keep holy the Sabbath, honor their parents, refrain from murder, adultery, and theft, and celebrate Passover, when, each year, their foundational story would be repeated precisely to remind them how they are different and to call them back to their ideals if they have strayed.

America also has its foundational myths: its wars of freedom, the American Revolution, the Civil War, the Federalist Papers, the Founding Fathers, a democratic government, fairness, and Johnny Appleseed, Paul Bunyan, and Betsy Ross. Unlike all others, we are a nation of equal opportunity, a free press, religious freedom, justice, a land of laws that apply to all across the board. Our ideals are enshrined in our "sacred scripture," the Constitution, and carved on our public buildings and concretized in our institutions.

But just as Israel sinned and forgot who they were, so have we. Today, at this time in our history, we suffer from severe amnesia. As a result, we are a seriously soul-sick country. We have forgotten who we are as rampant individualism—a disastrous notion of freedom that means I am free to do whatever I want—has swallowed up the common good. We have become a society of self-serving individuals who have fractured community and subverted our institutions. As a result, all the polls show that our level of trust in our once-admired institutions is at an all-time historical low. Never have so many Americans distrusted so many in power.

Let's start with the press. Polls show that people distrust the press because of its selective reporting, partisan slants, and open biases. Confidence is down to 28%. Remember back in 2010 when Shirley Sherrod, a member of the Agriculture Department, was outed as a racist because, according to the media, she supposedly denied a white farmer assistance? She was quickly fired by the Department, dropped as damaged goods by the White House and the NAACP, and vilified by the press. Until, it turned out, her remarks, caught on video, had been selectively edited to portray the opposite of what she meant. The media, in its usual competitive rush for scandal, having ignored basic journalistic guidelines, was caught with egg on its collective face. The recent Rupert Murdoch newspaper scandal of hacking private and government phones, paying bribes, and compromising Scotland Yard—soon to be a book, movie and mini-series you can be sure—reminds us of how bad things have gotten and why.

Education is gravely tarnished. Public education is riddled with bloated bureaucracy, low test scores, and endemic cheating scandals—think, for example, of Georgia, where, in July of 2011, investigators uncovered the biggest cheating scandal ever in a public school district. One investigator said, "I ran out of synonyms for cheating." Pennsylvania, Rhode Island, New Jersey, and other states are under investigation because widespread cases have surfaced of supervisors, principals, and teachers—the ones who are supposed to be models of honesty and integrity to their students—conspiring with the students to cheat on tests in the race to illegally raise scores and get federal money. Some teachers have even held "changing parties" to erase and correct students' answers.

Then there's the man who caused quite a stir when he wrote a revealing article in the prestigious journal *The Chronicle of Higher Education*, detailing how students (and some professors) in blue-ribbon colleges and universities all around the country hire his company to write their term papers. The students, he wrote, are too lazy or incapable of writing a coherent sentence, much less a paragraph. He cites a case of one university student who paid him handsomely to do her research work, emailed him instructions in what can only be described as a third-grade-level spelling and composition, and got her masters degree. She is now out there somewhere as an inept teacher or nurse or counselor with her fraudulently ghost-written degree but still basically unable to read, write, or put together a paragraph adequately, and he, with his "profit first" mentality, continues shamelessly seeding society with dishonest and ill-prepared graduates. No wonder we've lost trust.

Politics. What can we say about politics that hasn't already been said? There are, of course, good politicians but the old joke just won't go away. You know: politicians really aren't so bad; it's the 90 percent who give the other ten percent a bad name. Confidence in politicians is down to a dismal 12%. Best-sellers like *Reckless Endangerment* chronicle the devious machinations of the people who caused the worst economic meltdown in our history, a meltdown that to this day impacts all of us and will for decades and decades to come.

The book reveals the maneuverings, the old boys' cozy network of congressmen, bankers, and CEOs, the cheating and lies and backroom deals that earned the politicians millions of dollars. Not one of these politicians to this day has been criminally charged for such "reckless endangerment," even though they wreaked untold harm on the nation. In fact, not only have they gone on to even more lucrative government jobs but the current administration has decided not to prosecute them, saying it would cause too much economic disturbance.

Corporations control Congress with their endless lobbying money. General Electric, the world's biggest corporation, pays no taxes while its CEO advises the president.

Sports is tainted as Olympic committees are bribed to choose certain cities. Drugs and steroids plague players who now have all kinds of asterisks next to their names in the record books. Soccer can't seem to get out from under game-fixing scandals—think South Korea, where dozens of players have been indicted this past week (July, 27, 2011). Think of organized crime and its foothold in international sports.

Privacy is a thing of the past. It no longer exists as hackers break into Sony, AT&T, the Pentagon, and Lockheed Martin. One of the fastest growing businesses on the Internet is the business of spying on consumers as tracking technology grows ever more sophisticated. Every time we tap a computer key we are watched, profiled, and sold to some corporation, and eventually we receive targeted ads. Even Google, which is touted as giving us free and uninhibited access to all the knowledge there is, is personalized, and the answer we get is different from someone else who taps in the same word so we never move outside our circle. As one expert put it, "We're getting a lot of bonding but very little bridging."

And, finally, as for Church, that old bedrock standby of moral guidance and integrity, think of the Anglicans divided over gay marriage or the Catholic clergy sexual abuse scandals. Would you trust any of them? In the mid-1980s, confidence in organized religion was 90% or above. Today it stands at half that.

This is a catalog of once revered institutions that, according to the polls, we distrust, and it's no joy to say it out loud, no joy at all that every public and private institution we know—church, law, government, industry, corporations education, sports—has betrayed us. They are so full of self-serving corruption, often legal corruption, and the "profit first" mentality that, outside of the military, which still enjoys high standing, we have a massive and corrosive loss of trust. And that's because we have strayed far from our ideals. And not just as Americans, but as Christians.

The answer to restoring trust is the same as it was for ancient Israel: remember. Review and rededicate ourselves to our foundational story. We here who are Catholic need to return to our basics, which means the gospels. Forget, for the moment, parish, diocese, Church, and law. Just look at and review Jesus' charter program, which includes such things as forgiving your enemies and praying for those who persecute you; that there's more than ourselves to consider and measure life by; and to feed the hungry, visit the sick, give drink to the thirsty and aid to the poor.

Jesus asks us to remember that we do not live by profit alone. Anyone listening? What gain is there, he asks, to cheat to get ahead or to betray your family and friends, to buy your college degree or to pillage the taxpayer for private gain if in the process you lose your own soul, your sense of self, your status as a child of God? He reminds us that those who selfishly hug their lives to themselves will wind up losing them, but those who lose their lives for his sake will find them. Remember, he says, I have chosen you, chosen you to be the salt of the earth, a light for others to see by.

Imagine if we remembered all this. Like the sun to the night, the wind to the dark cloud, trust, at last, would be restored.

Trust begins with us, with remembering who Jesus is and remembering who we are.

45. *Opening the Box*

Feast of the Body and Blood of Christ

It may interest you to know that today's liturgical feast of the Body and Blood of Jesus Christ is a late one. It was established in the 13th century. Question: why, after 1100 years, did the Church feel it necessary to do this? A parable will explain why.

Once upon a time there was a very gracious and very wealthy man who always threw a dinner party once a month for his close friends. These were times of wonderful food and vintage wine, a time of joy, great intimacy and sharing. Well, it so happened that on one occasion a few of his closest friends got sick at the same time and were unable to attend.

The man felt bad but nevertheless he wanted them to have a memento of the celebration they missed so he took a bottle of his best wine from the table and put it in a special ornate box and set it on the sideboard where it could be seen. He knew his friends would see it, open the box, and enjoy the wine knowing that they had not been forgotten. So he went to his servant and told him, "Pierre, be careful of that box and make sure that you treat it with respect because what's in there will gladden the hearts of my friends and they will always think of me."

The servant wasn't quite sure what the master meant, but, being of rigid mind, he took his words too literally so that every time he passed the box, he bowed to it. Eventually the bowing became a habit. Well, it so happened that that very week the master suddenly died, but he had often expressed his wish that his friends would continue those monthly meals in his memory, and so they did. When they arrived in good spirits at the next gathering the servant pointed out to the jovial friends the special box. They were intrigued, but they couldn't help but notice how the servant bowed each time he passed it. Unsure why he was doing this, it wasn't long before they too began to bow to the box before they sat down to dinner. For some reason—perhaps a sense of awe—none of them ever asked what was in the beautiful box.

As time went on, that box, sitting there silently on the sideboard for all to see, had a depressing effect. The meals began to grow less and less joyous and more and more quiet, more solemn, to the point where, finally, instead of celebrating being together as friends, they began to eat in silence and to gaze with respect at the box never, ever knowing that a bottle of the best wine, meant to be happily shared among them in the wealthy man's name, was inside unopened and unused.

End of parable. That's what happened to the Eucharist. In earlier times people had a very close and intimate relationship with this sacrament. It was, after all, a shared meal reflective of the intimate Last Supper. They would even take home some fragments for consumption by the family during the week. Some, even children, would bring the sacred Bread hidden on their persons to Christians in jail. But by the thirteenth century, all that history had been forgotten. By that time, the Eucharist, in its ornate tabernacle-box, still sitting there, had become an awesome and remote mystery, something to be bowed to and approached with fear and trembling and then only very rarely and by very specially chosen people. The people felt they were not worthy.

So the Eucharist became something hidden inside the box or to be looked at with bowed heads from afar—such as when the priest elevated the host in Mass—and that was all. All this, of course, was a far cry from the generous and intimate fellowship meals Jesus shared with the poor and the unworthy—so much so that the Pharisees complained that he ate with publicans and sinners. It was a far cry from the Last Supper, where there were only rough fishermen present when Jesus broke bread and shared wine. The bar for approaching Jesus was obviously set pretty low. So, centuries later, why were people staying away?

The Church slowly began to realize this sad state of affairs and finally had to legislate that people receive the Eucharist at least once a year and to establish feasts like this one we're celebrating today—the Body and Blood of Christ—in the hopes that the people would remember its meaning and

Jesus' desire to be near us and, so to speak, unlock the box.

So we are here today to remember. There are lots of things we could remember about the Eucharist, but let us focus on two key words: unity and mission.

Unity. In this regard, I call your attention to something quite unnoticed but profound that happens at Mass. Before he holds up the host and the chalice and says "Behold the Lamb of God," the priest breaks off a small piece of the host and drops it into the chalice. Why does he do that? He does it because it's a custom that goes back to the old papal Masses when a piece of host from the previous papal Mass was placed in the chalice to signify continuity with the Mass that went before. Even more, on Sundays and feast days the pope would send a small piece of the host he had to the other churches in Rome.

It was a gesture that signified unity: all ate the same Eucharistic bread. All were bound by a common faith. All were united in one church. So if you happen to notice my dropping a piece of the large host into the chalice—and I'll be deliberate about it today—think what you are meant to think when you see it: we are connected with all those throughout the world who this day are celebrating the Eucharist whether openly in cathedrals or secretly, at the peril of their lives, in internment camps or private homes—and this is happening more and more today as Christians are daily being severely persecuted in many lands. We are connected to one another through this Mass. Yes, here all are united in one global faith, one Lord. We belong to something larger than ourselves. We are brothers and sisters to all those who this day break bread in the name of the Lord. It's a powerful thought.

Mission. "Do this in memory of me" are words always said aloud at every Mass. Question: what should we do in Jesus' memory? Meet in assembly and celebrate this ancient ritual of course, but it goes deeper than that, much deeper.

Remember that before the words "Do this in memory of me" are these words: "This is my body given for you...my blood shed for you." That's what we should do in Jesus' memory: As he has given his body and blood for us, so we should give our body and blood for others—in his memory. That is to say, justice, mercy, and sacrifice should characterize those who have received these gifts from Christ himself. That's our mission: to be sent out from here bearing the gifts of faith, hope, and love.

The Eucharist is unity and mission. Unity says we are connected to those Christians in China, Yemen, Iraq, and Africa who today celebrate Mass in secret and in terror. Mission says we are sent, sent to share what we have celebrated. The parting words say it all: "The Mass is ended, go in peace." That word, "Mass" is the Latin word for "mission." Therefore, when we leave here, in a very real sense our Mass just begins.

46. Saints and Celebrities

ALL SAINTS

The media recently has been filled with the news of the "Barefoot Bandit"—the teenager who eluded authorities for so long, who cheated, lied, carried arms, stole, and caused hardship to so many. But, as one woman on TV said, he should go free because "he's so cute." His mother had other ideas. This is America, so, cashing in on his celebrity status, she immediately called in a pulp writer in the hopes of penning a best-seller and perhaps a television mini-series. The networks are still trying to get him for an interview. He's hot news, a hot item, a celebrity. While legally he can't profit from his crimes, the movie and publishing companies that have bought his story, can and will. There's a hungry public out there that adores a cute criminal no matter how badly he has hurt others.

Saints and celebrities. They're worlds apart. James Danaher, a professor of philosophy at Nyack College in New York, notes some of the differences. He writes: "Today the celebrity has replaced the saint. Go to any bookstore and you will notice celebrities rather than saints author books that purport to instruct us in the Christian life. Publishers know that in order to sell a lot of books, the author has to be identifiable by a great many people. Consequently, television preachers, sports stars, and every other imaginable celebrity are the ones from whom we take our spiritual direction. Sadly, their spiritual authority comes from their celebrity rather than their saintliness. This is our fault as much as it is the fault of our culture. Indeed, what we recognize and revere about a person is their celebrity status. We somehow attribute to them not only a greater identity but a greater authority as well."

Then he goes on to remind us that the celebrity is the very opposite of the saint. The celebrity draws his or her identity from the notoriety that

187

masses of people provide and who therefore employs armies of public relations people to keep them before the public eye. The saint, on the other hand, simply draws his or her identity from God. Unlike the celebrities and their wannabes who stand or fall by the adulation of a fawning world, the saint, immune to such deceptions and distractions, is anchored to God alone, and that is the secret of their inner peace. The saint is also very aware of sin, especially his or her own, but more aware of God's forgiveness and love. The celebrity endlessly seeks a bigger venue, a bigger screen, while the saint seeks the true humility that deflects pride.

Danaher sums it up: "When all else is stripped away we are no more than God's creation—God's beloved daughters and sons. The way we get to that core, and our true identity is always a way of descent. In contrast to the ladder of success that our culture tells us we should climb, the saint's journey is downward. Indeed, we enter heaven as we descend into the littleness of the children who are aware of nothing but their father's love. This will be our heavenly state, but the saint, unlike the rest of us, desires to live as close as possible to that state now."

Now it's time to make these prosaic words live. And since, in our time, Mexico is often in our news for blame and crime and drug associations, let's focus on a Mexican you should know but probably don't. That's because he's not a celebrity but a saint.

In November, 2010, a report on religious freedom revealed that seven out of 10 people in the world today are unable to freely live out their faith. It also found that Christianity is the most persecuted religion in the world with at least 200 million suffering from discrimination. Times, it seems, haven't changed much, so I ask you to go back to the 1900s in Mexico when the government launched a fierce persecution of the Catholic Church. This is where our story of a brave priest begins. His name is Miguel Pro.

Miguel Pro was born in 1891 in Guadalupe, Mexico. He was a precocious, high-spirited, risk-taking child. He was quite close to his older sister, and when she entered the convent he began to feel a call to become a priest. But that would wait. There were girls and the expected career of managing his father's successful business to entice him. Eventually, like Francis of Assisi, he gave it all up and entered the Jesuit novitiate in Mexico when he was 20. He was there until 1914, when it became intolerable to remain there because, four years before, the government had unleashed a tidal wave of persecution against the Catholic Church, and it was becoming more and more severe. Accordingly, along with other Jesuit seminarians, Miguel had to flee to the United States to a Jesuit house in California, and from there, in 1915, he was sent to a seminary in Spain where he remained to continue his preparation for the priesthood. He was ordained in Belgium in 1925.

Miguel frequently suffered from severe stomach problems and underwent several operations. Still his health did not improve, and so his superiors felt that it would be better for him to return to Mexico in spite of the ongoing persecution there. He returned in the summer of 1926. Restrictions against the Catholic Church had grown worse. Catholics were not allowed to teach in schools. Public worship was forbidden outside of churches, religious organizations could not own property, clergy and religious were forbidden to wear their Roman collars or habits in public, and priests who criticized the government were subject to five years imprisonment. Sound familiar? Since the churches were closed, Miguel went into hiding to secretly minister to the Mexican Catholics both spiritually and physically, especially the poor. Hunted by the secret police, like Sherlock Holmes he donned many disguises. Sometimes he was a beggar, sometimes a police officer (so he could bring Communion to death-row Catholics), sometimes a businessman.

Eventually he became a wanted man when he and his brother Roberto were falsely accused of a bomb attempt against the Mexican president, even though one who was involved in the attempt testified that Miguel and Roberto had no part in it. Nevertheless the brothers were betrayed. Roberto was spared, but Miguel, because he was a Catholic priest, was sentenced to death by firing squad, without any legal process. On November 23, 1927, at the firing range, he stretched out his arms in the form of a cross, forgave his about-to-be executioners, refused the blindfold, and died shouting, "Long live Christ the King!"

The president had the execution photographed and spread the pictures on the nation's front pages as a warning to others. The pictures had quite the opposite effect. They rallied the opposition. We can still view those poignant photographs. We can see Miguel kneeling in prayer before his execution. We can see him standing against the fence with his arms outstretched.

We can see a saint.

He was beatified in 1988 by Pope John Paul II, who, ironically, 54 years after Miguel Pro's execution, visited Mexico. I say ironically because the anti-Catholic laws were still on the books, and the pope in all of his public papal garb was technically forbidden to enter the country. But this time he was welcomed by the president and wildly cheered by the people.

We know Oprah, Homer Simpson, Adam Sandler, Betty White, Ben Stein, Barbie and Ken, and the rest of the pantheon of celebrities—they are the air we breathe. Surrounded by such celebrities it's time we should be familiar with some saints and strive to become one.

47. Father's Day: St. Dad

There are the calendar saints and then there are the ordinary everyday ones who live among us. Today I want to showcase one unsung and underappreciated group—our dads! Yes, I know it's a bold statement—calling dads saints—for they are not in favor everywhere. Dads are pummeled in the popular press as selfish, mean-spirited, chauvinist slobs. The popular magazines even ask if their gender is needed any longer. "Are Men Necessary?" is a headline reflecting the rise of single mothers and the modern technologies that appear to make men obsolete.

But it's time to take a look at what some don't see, don't want to see: the power, the influence, and, yes, even the holiness, of dads. To prove my point I turn to the late Tim Russert, the former Washington bureau chief of NBC News. Before his unexpected and sudden death, he wrote a book about his father called *Big Russ & Me*. It was a huge success and soon became number one on *The New York Times* best-seller list. This book about his father clearly struck a chord all across America. Tim says that he received close to sixty thousand letters and emails, and that most of the letters described a father's sacrifice, fortitude, and perseverance. They told of his advice and guidance; or gave examples of his kindness, generosity, love, and, yes, wisdom. Many of the letters were unforgettable. Moreover, Russert notes, these letters and stories—which he included in a new book, *Wisdom of the Fathers*—have two striking things in common.

First, he says, the letters he received were overwhelmingly positive, even though there was the occasional dissenting voice telling of a bad father. No, in exceedingly large numbers his correspondents admired their fathers and deeply cherished their memories. The second big theme that comes across in these letters, Russert says, is that the most precious things a father can provide are time, attention, and love. "For about six months I read hundreds of emails and letters every day, but I can't recall a single one that said, 'My father gave me every material thing I wanted,' or, 'What I remember most about my dad is the new TV he bought me.'" What we remember about our fathers, Russert says, "has little or nothing to do with material objects. We remember the time they gave us—whether indirectly (through hard work) or in more conventional ways—time spent providing advice, telling a bedtime story, or simply showing up for a recital, a spelling bee, or an athletic event."

So, here are some random sample letters from his book *Wisdom of Our Fathers*. Listen to them and savor them and think of your own father. This man writes:

One thing I'll never forget about my father—a hard-as-nails, tough-love man who fought in two world wars and a war in Africa during the twenties—was the single tear running down his cheek the day he dropped me off at Fort Dix on my way to Vietnam, and the one hug that made up for twenty-two years of no hugging. Only he could understand what the coming year had in store for me. He couldn't even share his sorrow with my mother. Because of her weak heart we told her I was going to a missile base in Guam. It seemed as if all the years of absence from each other's lives came together at that moment in New Jersey. We finally shared a bond no one else in my family could ever understand, father to son, man to man, soldier to soldier.

Another:

As a young child, I sometimes stuttered. Once, when I was six and our family was traveling in the car, I was trying to tell my parents something and couldn't get the words out. Stuttering confused me, which caused me to stutter even more. Although this didn't happen very often, it was painful for my parents to witness. That day, while my dad was driving, he calmly reached into the backseat and pulled me closer to him. Then he put his arm around my shoulders and patted my right arm. I remember feeling a sense of immediate calm that allowed me to get the words out.

This one wrote:

> I loved my dad very much, but I really didn't know him. My two brothers and I were put in an orphanage at a very young age because he couldn't take care of us. We were allowed visitors once a month, and I remember sitting on the front steps, my eyes glued on that long driveway, hoping that my dad would show up. And he did. He lived in Louisville, six miles away, and he walked six miles to visit us because he couldn't afford the bus fare. But he always brought some kind of little toy. He was buried in Shepherdsville, Kentucky. I am seventy-three now, but someday I hope to go there and see his grave. To this day I can't talk about my dad without getting choked up.

This one wrote:

> A few weeks after Dad was buried, I was going through his personal effects. I opened his wallet, where I found a dollar and a couple of pictures of his four granddaughters. I pulled out his driver's license and out fell a tag like the ones you get on your Christmas gifts. I looked at it closely and, on the back, written in my mother's hand, was a note that said, "He tried to write his name and he wanted to ask you, 'When are you coming home, Daddy?'" This man whom I used to think I could never satisfy, had carried around for forty-seven years a note from his wife and two-year-old son from Christmas, 1944. I learned from this that a father's love is an enduring thing. Sometimes, it's hard for children to see and sometimes it's harder for fathers to show, but that love is always there.

Another writes that, in the summer of 1968,

> I had just graduated from high school in Brooklyn and was eagerly awaiting the start of a college career at Brooklyn College in September. I got a summer job doing clerical work at a shipping company and made sixty dollars a week before taxes. When I told my father about the job, he was excited for me and added that he wanted me to contribute fifteen dollars a week for the household expenses. I was angry at him for asking me to give up some of my hard-earned money, but I complied with his request every week. The week before I

started college, he handed me a large envelope that contained all the money I had given him over the summer. "I wasn't interested in your money," he told me. "I just wanted to teach you a little responsibility." And he did.

And a few short ones:

My dad taught me to tie my shoes, to cross the street, to get an education, and to believe in my country, my God, and my family. I never had to look far for my hero. He was just across the living room, sitting in his favorite chair, reading the newspaper and watching the nightly news. Dad's been gone three years now, but I still think of him every day, the way he would laugh at a joke so hard that he'd start to cry, or how, when we were little, he'd get up in the morning, come down for breakfast and remind us to say good morning to Mr. Sun. All these years later, I finally realized he was the sun.

And this:

A couple of years ago, I called to congratulate my parents on their fifty-third wedding anniversary. And I complimented them on how much their marriage had meant to their children. As I was shedding a tear, Dad said, "That's a load of baloney. The deal between your mother and me was that whoever left first had to take all eight of you!"

Another light note:

When we were about ten and twelve, my brother and I decided it was time to start smoking. But where would we hide the cigarettes? We found a loose board in the attic. Just the place, we thought. After all, nobody would smell smoke coming from the attic. Two sons of a volunteer fireman smoking in the attic! Dumb and dumber! One evening, we decided it was time for a break in homework and a well-earned smoke, but much to our surprise—and horror—the loose floorboard was nailed shut. Nothing was ever said or needed to be said. And we never smoked cigarettes again.

Let me end with one that says it all:

I was visiting my parents a few years after my mother's health started failing, when my dad had completely taken over her care and the house. I was up early and heard them talking. I didn't want to disturb the moment, and I tried not to listen, but I overheard my mother tell Dad that she was sorry she was such a poor companion these days. She wanted to be traveling and doing things together, as they had often discussed. There was silence and then Dad said, in a choked voice, "Don't you know I just want to be in the same room with you?"

I was struck by the simplicity and love in that remark... I loved my parents for the example of their relationship. My mother died several years ago, Dad is still alive, but he is suffering from some dementia. He lives with me now, and I have come to understand the simplicity and importance of being in the same room with him.

If their children found something special in their fathers, if through them they caught a glimpse of what God might be like, then who is to say they were not saints?

Let me end by citing another author, Philip Yancey. In his book *Disappointment with God*, he relates a touching story from his own life.

One time on a visit to his mother—who had been widowed years earlier, in the month of Philip's first birthday—they spent the afternoon together looking through a box of old photos. A certain picture of him as an eight-month-old baby caught his eye. Tattered and bent, it looked too banged up to be worth keeping, so he asked her why, with so many other better pictures of him at the same age, she had kept this one. Yancey writes, "My mother explained to me that she had kept the photo as a memento, because during my father's illness it had been fastened to his iron lung."

During the last four months of his life, Yancey's father lay on his back, completely paralyzed by polio at the age of twenty-four, encased from the neck down in a huge, cylindrical breathing unit. With his two young sons banned from the hospital due to the severity of his illness, he had asked his wife for pictures of her and of their two boys. Because he was unable to move even his head, the photos had to be jammed between metal knobs so that they hung within view above him—the only thing he could see. The last four months of his life were spent looking at the faces he loved.

Philip Yancey writes,

> I have often thought of that crumpled photo, for it is one of the few links connecting me to the stranger who was my father. Someone I have no memory of, no sensory knowledge of, spent all day, every day thinking of me, devoting himself to me, loving me. The emotions I felt when my mother showed me the crumpled photo were the very same emotions I felt one February night in a college dorm room when I first believed in a God of love. Someone like my father is there, I realized. Someone is there every day thinking of me, loving me. It was a startling feeling of wild hope, a feeling so new and overwhelming that it seemed fully worth risking my life on.

Saint Dad. It fits.

48. Thanksgiving

LUKE 15:1–7

A few years ago, an American and a British journalist were discussing Thanksgiving on a British radio program. The American asked if Thanksgiving was celebrated in the United Kingdom. "Yes," the British journalist replied, "but we celebrate it on the 6th of September."

"Why then?" asked the American.

"That's when you chaps left," the Brit answered good-naturedly.

Well, it is true that Thanksgiving is celebrated as a national holiday primarily in the U.S. and Canada (in Canada, it is celebrated in October), two former British colonies. Thanksgiving in the U.S. is usually traced to 1621 when a Pilgrim leader, William Bradford, proclaimed a day of feasting to commemorate the first harvest after a long year of suffering. What you may not know is that, as the colonies grew more prosperous, the people forgot all about Thanksgiving and the meaning it held for their ancestors. As a result, for generations Thanksgiving was celebrated sporadically, if at all, with no set date.

Then in 1822 Sarah Hale, a young widow from New Hampshire—she who gave us the nursery rhyme, "Mary had a Little Lamb"—decided to revive this important celebration. Sarah, a mother of five children and an editor of a women's magazine, began a 40-year campaign of writing editorials and letters to governors and presidents to get Thanksgiving officially recognized as a national holiday. Three Presidents turned her down. Her obsession became a reality, however. In 1863, President Abraham Lincoln proclaimed the last Thursday in November as an annual celebration of Thanksgiving.

What is interesting is that of all the presidents it should have been Lincoln who responded to Sarah's request. His own life was at very low ebb at the time. The country was literally falling apart, and Lincoln's political future looked bleak. Many of the members of his own cabinet openly despised him and joked about him in public. His wife had been investigated as a possible traitor—a process that Lincoln personally found to be bitterly wounding. In the face of such personal and national circumstances, Lincoln's call for a day of prayer would have made sense. But Thanksgiving? At a time like that? What must this man, who apparently had little to be thankful for, have been thinking of?

Anyway, he did establish the day, and we are here to give thanks. Giving thanks reminds us how blessed we are. Yet, I think today we're very much in the mindset of Abe Lincoln: how can we give thanks with all that's going on?

On the personal level, there are those among us who have lost family and friends who will not be here to share the Thanksgiving meal with us this year. The empty place will bring tears. I think especially of the rash of teenage suicides this year.

We are physically sick, perhaps seriously so, or have someone who is, and that weighs on our mind. Will I—will they—be here for next Thanksgiving?

Our relationships may be under strain, our marriage on the rocks, our jobs shaky—or we are among the nation's 10% plus who have lost them—and so Thanksgiving and Christmas will be leaner this year. We feel the burden of rising taxes, the national debt. We worry how we will make out financially, how our children will survive, how the next two generations will shoulder the burdens we are leaving them.

On the national level, our country is waging two endless wars as the casualties mount. We are at the mercy of terrorists. We think of the all-too-common headlines about people marching into schools and businesses and killing others. Too many gangs in place of families. So many of our leaders are self serving, if not outright dishonest, and have deeply betrayed us. We have a historically low opinion of our politicians and Congress. Our nation seems to be suffering from a deep soul sickness, unattached from any deep spiritual vision or meaning or anchor.

We have never been so polarized. We seem adrift. Like Lincoln we are beset from all sides.

Yet, like a beleaguered Lincoln, we are asked to give thanks this week. Why was he able to do it? I suggest he tapped two sources.

The first comes from the reflections of an anonymous author who wrote:

If you woke up this morning and were able to hear the birds sing, use your vocal cords to utter human sounds, walk to the breakfast table on two good legs, and read the newspaper with two good eyes...you are more blessed than millions of those who could not do these simple things.

If you have never experienced the danger of battle, the loneliness of imprisonment, the agony of torture, or the pangs of starvation...you are ahead of 500 million people in the world.

If you can attend a church meeting without fear of harassment, arrest, torture...you are more blessed than three billion people in the world.

If you have food in the refrigerator, clothes on your back, a roof overhead, and a place to sleep...you are richer than 75% of this world.

If you have money in the bank, in your wallet, and spare change in a dish some place...you are among the top 8% of the world's wealthy.

If you are over thirty and either of your parents is still alive, you are very rare. Over a billion people are orphans by then.

If you hold up your head with a smile on your face and are truly thankful... you are blessed because the majority can, but most do not.

Perhaps, that's the kind of thing Lincoln saw among the misery. Perhaps, therefore, like Lincoln, we must look past our troubles to appreciate the deeper truths we have just mentioned and give thanks for them.

The second source of motivation for giving thanks, looking for the moment beyond the heartaches and headlines, is to remember that the only house to make the papers is the one that burned down. The other five hundred in your neighborhood are not newsworthy. Which is to say, to re-member and remember deeply the everyday, ordinary heroisms—and they are countless—that pass quite unnoticed and unheralded but which are absolutely necessary to gentle our lives, comfort our hearts, and secure our place in this tumultuous world. You know, the love, the service, the care, the subtly planted seeds of faith, hope, and love that someone puts quietly there every day that make a difference.

It's all summed up in this old reflection. Listen:

When you thought I wasn't looking, I saw you hang my first painting on the refrigerator, and I wanted to paint another one.

When you thought I wasn't looking, I saw you feed a stray cat and I thought it was good to be kind to animals.

When you thought I wasn't looking I saw you make my favorite cake just for me and I knew that little things are special things.

When you thought I wasn't looking, I heard you say a prayer, and I believed that there is a God I could always talk to.

When you thought I wasn't looking, I saw tears come from your eyes, and I learned that sometimes things hurt but it's all right to cry.

When you thought I wasn't looking, I saw that you cared, and I wanted to be everything that I could be.

When you thought I wasn't looking, I looked—and wanted to say thanks for all the things I saw when you thought I wasn't looking.

Today, when they think we're not looking, someone will guide the dis-abled, nurse the sick, take food to the grieving, wash clothes, fix a meal, visit the homebound, put a flower on the table, decorate a house, do an honest day's work, buy a gift for Christmas, tell a story to a wide-eyed child, fix a toy, mend a broken heart, work for peace and justice, bless the world, and include us in their prayers. No fanfare. No cameras. No headlines. But while they—millions and millions of them—thought we were not looking, today we take time to look, and so we say thanks for these people.

Friends, these are difficult and scary times. Like President Lincoln we are sorely conflicted personally and nationally, and there seems little reason to celebrate Thanksgiving.

But for a few moments I have tried to lift up your heads and hearts and give you a vision of two good reasons to be thankful: first, for all of our troubles, we are still blessed in many ways compared to the rest of the world and, second, we have countless, selfless, quiet, taken-for-granted, out-of-the-corner-of-eyes heroes who, day in and day out, tirelessly shape our faith, rekindle our hope, and show us how to love. They are our promise of a better future.

For these admirable riches, O God, we do give thanks.

49. Introductions to the Passiontide Readings

[This chapter is a potpourri of introductions to the Passiontide readings, particularly the Passion itself. I have never given a homily, however brief, after the reading of the Passion. I want to let it stand as is, with its words settling into the hearts of the congregation. They don't need a ferverino or, worse, a rehash of what they just heard and spoke. Let the moment marinate. Instead I have always shared a few preparatory words before the reading of the Passion.

The following, then, are snippets of brief homiletic introductions for those times when a full homily is not called for or may be inappropriate because the event speaks so fully of itself that it needs no long commentary.]

I. He Rode On

Gloria Swanson was one of Hollywood's top actresses from the 1920s to the 1930s. She was quite ambitious. Early in her career, Swanson was quoted as saying, "I have gone through enough of being a nobody. I have decided that when I am a star, I will be every inch and every moment the star! Everybody from the studio gate man to the highest executive will know it." And Swanson made sure of that. Before returning from a trip to France, Gloria Swanson sent a telegram to her film studio informing them that she expected a grand welcome when she arrived in California. To quote the telegram: "Arriving with the Marquis tomorrow morning. Stop. Please arrange ovation." The studio knew enough not to argue with Swanson. An ovation was duly arranged.

Welcome to this celebration of Palm Sunday. Today we celebrate Jesus' triumphant entry into Jerusalem and the events surrounding his Passion.

Jesus didn't have to arrange his own ovation when he entered Jerusalem. Word about him had been spreading throughout the countryside. Healer, teacher, leader—he was becoming quite a celebrity as Holy Week begins. Actually, too much of a celebrity to suit the entrenched, seething bureaucracy, and so, even as the crowd waves its palm branches and shouts its hosannas, the shadow of a cross looms in the background. But he rode on.

As he did, he was not fooled by the crowd's adulation. He knew that public opinion is a fickle thing. What would these people be shouting this time next week? He knew. But he rode on.

He heard the whispers in his ear, "You've got to give the public what it wants. Judea was always a thorn in the side of the Romans. Just say a few negative things about Caesar. That will raise your numbers at least a dozen points. Make the people a few extravagant promises. No one expects you to keep them." He heard these flatterers. He ignored them. He rode on.

He knew what really lay ahead for him. And he did not welcome it. Rejection, pain, death was not the cup he would have chosen for himself. He had no martyr complex. He did not willingly seek to die. But he rode on.

He rode on looking into the faces of people around him, at the crowds who would shout hosanna one moment and crucify him the next. But he rode on.

He felt deep disappointment with his disciples—one of whom would betray him, his most trusted who would deny him, and the three closest to him who could not even stay awake while he agonized. But he rode on.

Why? Because he loved us enough not to let our double-tongued words and betraying sins shackle us forever. He had said it all in happier times: "Greater love than this has no one than to lay down his life for his friends." With that love burning in his heart, he rode on.

Let us now pick up on his journey and, together, with sincere and penitent hearts, join in the reading of the Passion.

II. The Church of St. Peter and all Cowards

At this time, even for all of its danger, some people still travel to the Holy

Land to trace the steps of Jesus on his way to Calvary—the route called the *Via Dolorosa*: the street full of sorrows.

I want briefly to call to your mind one church on the pilgrimage, the Church of Saint Savior. To the locals, it has a nickname. Cunningly, they call it the "Church of Saint Peter and All Cowards." The reason is that, if you step outside the church, you're standing in what once was the courtyard of the house of the high priest. At this place Simon Peter, who had followed his dear friend from the Garden of Gethsemane, also found himself on trial.

The judge was not the high priest but a common household maid and the bystanders gathered in the courtyard. There Peter three times denied that he even knew Jesus and attempted to completely disassociate himself from the prisoner before the judge inside. Peter, as we know, lied and gave false testimony. Then, as a rooster crowed, Peter remembered how Jesus prophesied his cowardly betrayal, and Peter fled the courtyard sobbing in grief.

Peter's courtyard happens every day when you and I are called on to give testimony regarding our relationship to Jesus and his teachings. While we seldom verbally deny him or his way of life, we often choose an even more cowardly position: silence. While we will not be executed for witnessing to our beliefs, we fear another type of dying: the painful death of being socially scorned and rejected by our friends. So we stand, far too often, with Peter and the other cowards. Too many times, by our silence or outright agreement with evil, we deny our consciences and our Lord.

Well, today, at any rate, among friends who are here to worship with us, we can publicly proclaim out loud our faith in Jesus and enter into the story of his Passion, a story that, in so many ways, is our story. So let us begin. Please stand.

III. *Thought Starters*

On Palm Sunday, April 9, 1865, Confederate General Robert E. Lee surrendered to Ulysses S. Grant, General of the Union Army, at the village of Appomattox Court House, Virginia. This surrender ended the bloodiest war ever fought on American soil. State against state, brother against brother; it was a conflict that literally tore our nation apart. But that Palm Sunday, the nation rejoiced.

Five days later—Good Friday, April 14, 1865—President Abraham Lincoln was shot and mortally wounded by John Wilkes Booth in Ford's Theatre—Lincoln: who wrote the Emancipation Proclamation, who gave us the immortal Gettysburg Address.

On Palm Sunday the war ended. Triumph. On Good Friday, Abraham Lincoln became the first U.S. president to be assassinated. Tragedy.

Today we start our most holy week of such contrasts. Today we wave palms. Friday we wave fists. Today we shout hosanna. Friday we shout, "Crucify him!" We are asked to savor our triumphs, our virtues, our genuine goodness and our failures, our moral compromises, our betrayals.

So in a moment we shall take our parts in the drama we call the reading of the Passion to find ourselves there among the good guys, the bad guys, and the on-the-fence ones who are neither good nor bad, hot nor cold, just unwilling or unable to make a commitment.

If we are good, we are to confirm and deepen that goodness as we watch Jesus, full of love, give himself for us. If we are compromised, we are to promise repentance and a renewal of our lives. If we are playing both sides of the field, we are at last to get off the fence and make a commitment to Jesus and determine to make our motto that cliché, "What would Jesus do?" "What would someone who did not spare himself out of love for me do were he in my place?"

So, now that we have our roles, let us stand and take our parts in the Passion Play.

+   +   +

In 1942 the first American troops are marching into London during the conflict known as World War II. The people of London are cheering the American soldiers. The friendly reception exhilarates the young soldiers. They sing as they march. Suddenly the troops turn into a main street and a strange hush falls over the scene. The happy songs die on their lips. They are looking for the first time upon an area in London that has been blown to bits. They see the great wounds on the city inflicted by falling bombs. They suddenly realize the city has suffered terribly. In these young soldiers' hearts, one moment, celebration; the next, great sadness.

Welcome to Holy Week. Welcome to the triumph and the tragedy of the six days preceding Easter. That's the kind of world we live in. One moment we are on top of the world, believing that nothing can go wrong. And then suddenly, literally, all hell breaks loose. That, as they say, is life. But so is the steady love of God that overcomes all things.

+   +   +

The Greek author Plutarch describes how kings are supposed to enter a city. He tells about one Roman general, Aemilius Paulus, who won a decisive victory over the Macedonians. When Aemilius returned to Rome, his triumphant procession lasted three days.

The first day was dedicated to displaying all the artwork that Aemilius and his army had plundered. The second day was devoted to all the Macedonian weapons they had captured. The third day began with the rest of the plunder—borne by 250 oxen, whose horns were covered in gold. This included more than 17,000 pounds of gold coins. Then came the captured and humiliated king of Macedonia and his extended family. Finally, Aemilius himself entered Rome, mounted on a magnificent chariot. Aemilius wore a purple robe, interwoven with gold. He carried his laurels in his right hand. He was accompanied by a large choir singing hymns, praising the military accomplishments of the great Aemilius. That, my friends, is how a king enters a city.

But the King of Kings? He entered riding on a lowly donkey. If he had consulted his political advisors, they would have been aghast. What was he up to? Leaders are supposed to project strength and power. Palm Sunday makes us ask, "Is this a new kind of leader?" Let us read together as we uncover the answer.

+   +   +

Fleming Rutledge in her book *The Bible and The New York Times* tells the story of a woman in her church who would not come to church on Palm Sunday. [Evidently, in their church they enacted the scene in Pilate's courtyard on Palm Sunday.]

This woman couldn't stand being asked to shout, "Crucify him! Crucify him!" "I just can't do it," the woman explained. Rutledge says, "I always felt very sad for her. She had missed the whole point. She could have come to church every other Sunday of the year and she still would have missed the whole point…It was very important to her to think of herself as one of the righteous. She could not confront her own darkness. How sad this is. If she but knew it, there is great power in the act of repentance."

Can we confront our own darkness? Can we confront our need for repentance? Would we welcome Christ into our world? For, you see, Christ, the real Christ, comes as a disturber, an unsettler, almost as an anarchist. Think of the things we value. Status. Power. Money. Image. How does it all square with this humble figure riding on a donkey?

Not very well, does it? Look at our popular heroes. I'm thinking about the action-type movies preferred by most males. How do the heroes of these movies spend their time? Blowing things up. Avenging past wrongs. Asserting their dominance over their foes. Again, reconcile these images with that humble figure riding on a donkey.

+   +   +

A few years ago Pastor Javier Viera and his wife, Marianne, wandered into the New-York Historical Society to see an exhibit that had been recommended to them by a friend. The exhibit was titled "Without Sanctuary." It was an array of photographs and postcards that had been collected by a collector, James Allen. These photographs and postcards were of lynchings that had taken place throughout the United States. The exhibit is hard to talk about on Palm Sunday—picture after picture of a limp body hanging from the end of a rope. The images were grotesque and disturbing, says Viera.

"However, what was most disturbing about these photographs," says Viera, "was not the bodies of the victims. In each picture was a gathering of ordinary people who came to watch the atrocities take place. The lynching was a social event. People dressed up for the occasion…"

"It was clear that these lynchings were a cultural phenomenon. They were events not to be missed. In [one] picture, as a body is hanging from the noose…you can see in the background a man smoking a cigar with a broad smile on his face. Others are sipping beer, gossiping, smiling, and laughing. A couple flirts and enjoys a romantic moment. Little boys beam with broad smiles, seemingly filled with pride to be part of such an auspicious gathering…

"Something else was more troublesome yet than the fine, upstanding people in these pictures. The images of these events had not only been documented on film," says Viera, "they were also turned into postcards. They were cherished mementos to be mailed to family and friends…."

OK, you and I are repulsed by these images. What I want to remind you is that these are not images from Rome 2,000 years ago. These are images from America less than 100 years ago. A hundred years later are we still among the crowd shouting, "Crucify him!"?

50. On My Fifty-Fifth Anniversary

So…Let me briefly tell you something about myself. Briefly indeed as I will tantalize you by letting the details go for another time and other circumstances where a Manhattan and a good dinner will unseal my lips.

One of six children, I was born in Jamesburg, went to Sacred Heart School in New Brunswick, two years of high school at St. Peter's in New Brunswick, then to the minor seminary, St. Charles in Catonsville, Maryland, where, after a week, I was expelled, and in a panic grabbed a third year at Seton Hall Prep. Then I reapplied to the seminary and went back expecting to be a senior, but instead was put on trial and ignominiously made to go back and repeat the 9th grade with all the freshmen, consigned the following year to a small, special remedial class for slow students and pushed through, with the result that I never graduated high school and I have no high school diploma or any degrees.

There are the bare facts, and maybe I should stop there, but I'll go on with a few more items plus an early story and an early embarrassment. I was ordained a priest in 1955, and the bishop sent me to, at that time, a very little rural place in the boondocks called New Monmouth, which is part of Middletown, with a wonderful pastor, Father Bob Bulman. It was a great place to start the priesthood. There was just one little incident when I first arrived. Hence the following story, which I've told before, though where I can't remember.

The first week there, I had to drive into the little village, if you can call it that, called "Wasserman's Junction"—consisting of a general store, a barber shop, and a small liquor store—to get some things, and I couldn't find a parking place. The only one left was in front of the liquor store. So I parked there and went about my business. Well, it seems there were two elderly sisters who lived nearby and who were the self-appointed watchdogs of the town. Before long, word had got around the parish that the new young priest had a "drinking problem." Me, who has a glass of wine now and then and a very occasional Manhattan,

Well eventually I was able to trace the rumor to its source . So, about two weeks later—Father Bulman warned me not to do this but I did it anyway since I saw his heart was not in the warning—I drove to the junction and parked my car in front of the sisters' house, locked it, walked home, and left it there overnight. I never heard any more rumors from them again.

After wonderful years there, I was sent to St. Joe's in Keyport, one of my more colorful assignments. Now the embarrassment story. While there, a young couple, Maria and Alberto, came to see me. Excitable, she was distraught because she could not have a baby and came to cry and weep and ask my earnest prayers—which I just as earnestly promised. About six months later the town was having its annual Memorial Day parade and I, as the young curate, was invited to be on the platform with the local dignitaries to offer a final prayer. As one of the ladies groups came marching by, who should be marching among them but Maria, and not only Maria, but a very pregnant Maria. Looking up she saw me on the platform and—excitedly pointing to her very extended womb, in a voice that could be heard all over Monmouth county—she shouted, "Thanks to you, Father Bausch!"

But at Keyport I also had one of those aha! experiences. Back then—we're talking early '60s—there was a new lay movement for married couples called the CFA, Christian Family Action [CFM, Christian Family Movement in most dioceses.] Participants met monthly using a guidebook to study the gospel, following the three movements of Observe, Judge, and Act. It was, as I said, an early lay movement. I was invited to be their young chaplain and, because it was a lay movement, I was not allowed to speak until the meeting was all over. I remember that they made me sit on my hands because if I can't use my hands I can't talk [last three words are mouthed].

I was never so humiliated and humbled in my life. Not because I had to sit on my hands but because, forced to be silent for two hours, I had to listen, really listen, to their stories of how, day after day, they struggled to be good Christians. Month after month I listened to them struggling inwardly with shady practices at the companies at which they worked, the politics of the workplace, the compromises they were forced to make, the fear of losing their jobs, difficulties with children—school, rebellion, drugs—trying to make ends meet, hardly ever getting a vacation, trying not to lose faith in hard times, struggles with prayer, not feeling God's presence, doubts.

And slowly I began to realize what a privileged, innocent life I led. Gradually I began to realize with some guilt that I would always have a job, no matter how poorly I performed. I had no accountability to the people. I could go home that night and get a full night's sleep with no colicky baby or sick child to attend all night. I would take my scheduled vacations and not have to pinch pennies. In short, I began to realize that these people were the saints on the frontline. I began to feel I was not worthy of them. I knew in my heart I was incapable of their heroism.

By the time it was over, I knew I had found my priesthood's core: that they, the laity, would teach me, not the other way around. I gained a profound sense of reverence and respect for their lives and gifts, and when I became pastor I made it clear to the people from day one that I was there to promote and call forth the gifts and charisms they already had, to teach them who they were as a People of God, to support and learn from them, to make them aware that this was their parish. I was temporary and would leave some day but they were permanent, for in every sense, they were the local church. I was sent there to serve, to remind them who they were. I never failed to consult them. The Keyport experience had defined my priesthood.

After Keyport came Maple Shade, the very last parish in the diocese near Camden: being sent there was a punishment for something I had written in a magazine that the people in the chancery found offensive. They originally had wanted to throw me out of the diocese but finally decided on exile. Turned out to be a good place.

Then on to St. Benedict's in Holmdel with the great Father Bill Anderson and, finally, to Colts Neck, where I spent 22 very happy and creative years as pastor sprinkled with annual summonses to the chancery carpet.

There, that's enough to tease you with! And then, all of a sudden, I realized I was old enough to retire! And I said to myself, "Where did the years go? They went by just as fast as I spoke these words, and I knew they went by fast because, when I would go to a class reunion, all my classmates had gotten so old they didn't recognize me!

Well, if the saying is true—and I can vouch that it is—that "inside of every old man is a young man asking what happened," I tell you this: through my store-bought glasses, looking past my liver-marked hands, ignoring for the moment the eight decades plus of life and pondering 55 years of priesthood, the answer is clear: grace happened. How else to explain God's writing straight with the crooked lines of my life? I look at these hands with their arthritic crooked fingers—symbol of all of my imperfections, shortcomings, and sins—and marvel as I think of all the children over whom they poured the baptismal waters. I think of over a half century plus of signing the cross over repentant sinners, pressing the healing oils on the foreheads of the sick, offering the sacred Host to nourish the yearnings of pilgrims, joining other hands in matrimony, holding the hands of those in excruciating pain or grief or despair and, not the least of which, gesticulating to urge on the homiletic word, the point in the classroom, the lecture, the conferences—thousands and thousands of them—or to tap the keys that eventually morphed into books.

It all becomes a symbol of an undeservedly graced priesthood. And this is in spite of, at times, a singularly ungraced leadership and shameful scandals such as the one we are going through now. But in this regard I readily recall the words of another octogenarian, the late Jesuit, Father Walter Burghardt:

"In the course of a half century" he wrote,

> I have seen more Church corruption than you have read of. I have tasted it. I have been reasonably corrupt myself. And yet, I love the Church, this living, pulsing, sinning people of God with a crucifying passion. Why? For all the Christian hate, I experience here a community of love. For all the institutional idiocy, I find here a tradition of reason. For all the individual repression, I breathe here an air of freedom. In an age so inhuman, I touch here tears of compassion. In a world so grim and humorless, I share her rich

joy and earthy laughter. In the midst of death, I hear here an incomparable stress on life. For all the apparent absence of God, I sense here the real presence of Christ.

I say "amen" to that, adding once more that for me that real presence has always and most powerfully resided in the people: their faith, their trust, their heroism that often put me to shame.

Enough: let me end with a dialogue I read years ago—when and where I can't remember—but it says it all:

And the Lord said GO
And I said, who me?
And he said Yes, you.

And I said,
But I'm not ready yet,
And there is company coming
And I can't leave my family.
You know that there is no one to take my place.
And he said, You're stalling.
And the Lord said GO.

I said
But I don't want to.
And he said
I didn't ask if you wanted to.

And I said,
Listen, I'm not that kind of person
To get involved in arguments.
Besides, my family won't like it.
And what will the neighbors think?
And he said, Baloney.

And yet a third time the Lord said GO

And I said, Do I have to?
And he said, Do you love me?

And I said, Look, I'm scared.
People are going to hate me
And cut me to pieces.
And I can't take it all by myself.
And he said,
Where do you think I'll be?
And the Lord said GO
And I sighed,
Here I am… send me.

Fifty-five years ago he sent
and fifty-five years ago I went
and here I am not yet spent
with the help of a lot of friends.

Thank you.

FUNERAL
HOMILIES

51. Jackie May

JOHN 11:32-45

An ancient rabbi, the Baal Shem-Tov, one day was standing on a hill with his students when they noticed foreign troops invading their town. From their vantage point they were able to see all of the horror and violence of the attack. The rabbi looked up to heaven and cried out, "Oh, if only I were God!"

A student asked, "But Master, if you were God, what would you do differently?" The rabbi answered him, "If I were God, I would do nothing differently. But if I were God, I would understand."

From time immemorial, among all people, from scholars to simpletons, from kings to peasants, if there is anything that defies understanding and makes people disbelieve in God, it is human suffering. Everyone bangs his or head on that one, from the sharp challenge this Jewish woman of the gospel, Mary, gave to the Rabbi Jesus—if you had been here (you can catch the implied sarcasm), you who are so mighty, my brother would not have died—to the latest parent who learns of her small daughter's abduction and death.

How can a good God permit such evil? Does he exist? If he does, is he powerless? We hate such unanswered questions. We scientific-minded, practical, digital Americans have no tolerance for mystery. We don't understand.

The only thing we can do with mystery is to turn it around and around and around like the facets of a diamond and contemplate it and check its angles. I tried to do that with Jackie May. She was exceptionally bright, as many of you know: a schoolteacher for thirty years with two Masters and working for a doctorate, with a wonderful future ahead of her and her family.

And then one day over a dozen years ago, with the suddenness of a 9/11 attack, while working out at the Atlantic Club, she had a brain aneurism. And from that point on, the talent and gifts that her family and friends knew were compressed, as it were, into a body that was mostly immobile.

Subsequently, for twelve years, alert, brilliant, answering with ease the TV quiz show questions, she lay mostly paralyzed in the nursing home. Twelve long years, visited by a faithful husband and children and exceptionally kind neighbors and parishioners from St. Mary's.

One has to have a profound faith to see more than tragedy here. But there have in fact been wise people who have teased us to look beyond such tragedy—to grace.

I think, for example, of someone we remembered on the first day of this month of October, St. Thérèse, "The Little Flower," the talented consumptive Carmelite nun who died at 24. What a waste. But, as the world was to learn, hidden away in a convent, unknown, chronically sick, she spun a path of holiness from plumbing the grace discovered in the small details of humdrum.

But more than that, Thérèse had a canny sense of what we would call today "mystical ecology," that is to say, a deep sense that we are all connected to each other and the planet, not only physically and genetically, but spiritually; she knew that what she did in that remote convent had global reverberations. She had the modern understanding that we affect one another spiritually every bit a much as a toxic spill in China will physically affect Cuba.

We ourselves unconsciously embrace this understanding on a small scale whenever we ask someone, as we prepare for surgery, to pray for us. We concede a power we all have to cross time and space and touch one another for better or for worse. Sensing this truth, in what must appear to outsiders a strange irony at best or a joke at worst, the Catholic Church got around to making this recluse, Thérèse, the patroness of the worldwide foreign missions.

It was the Church's way of affirming the Mystical Body, the Communion of Saints, the Halloween, All Saints, and All Souls the Christian world is about to celebrate—which is to say and declare that she who never left the convent brought graces to countless others.

She was a global, spiritual influence. No wonder such diverse people as the beat poet of the '60s Jack Kerouac, the artist Andy Warhol, and the unwed mother and communist turned Catholic, Dorothy Day, held her in high esteem.

+   +   +

You see where this is leading. I always got the impression when I visited Jackie that I was entering a convent-like situation, that she, with her faith, was spreading countless blessings to people she would never know. That while others, understandably, saw only total waste, I knew I saw something deeper: a gifted woman in a Carmelite-like cell at CareOne making a difference. And that puts the whole thing in a different perspective.

If there is mystery, it lies not just in a good God powerless before evil but a good God who draws good out of evil. And it's a goodness with ripples, with tributaries.

Think of all the people, like so many of you here, like her family, who have been forced to grow beyond their self concerns and reach into the depths of compassion, comfort, and care because of this woman. Think of the monotonous heroism of her husband and neighbors, who, year after year, read to, spoke to, and gave comfort and presence to her, who ministered to her.

And even as Mary of the gospel complained, "If you had been here my brother would never have died," Jesus, who cried and was as troubled as she was, was right when he said to her sister, "Did I not assure you that if you believed you would see the glory of God?" And then he followed up, saying, "Untie Lazarus and set him free."

And so he has said about Jackie, and so he has done for her. Untie her. Take off the paralysis, the tubes, the hospital bed, the medications, the support systems. Let her go free, free at last to see those she has touched, those she has saved, those she has graced from her solitary bed.

Jackie May is free, uninhibited, passing to join tomorrow's All Hallows—all holy—eve and the next day's All Saints. She has left us to be rejoined in a different way. She knows the liberating love of God and will continue her presence, her intercession.

We extend our sympathy to Ken and the family as we marvel at what, once again, the grieving Rabbi has done: he has lifted up the lowly, given release to the hopeless, freedom to the bound and life, eternal life, to the dying.

May we embrace the comfort of that wisdom. May she rest in peace. Amen.

52. Zaira D'Avella, Growing Older, Growing Great

LUKE 2: 25–35

A professional storyteller by the name of Dan Yashinsky relates that he was telling stories at a downtown arts center when a restless group of kids stomped in. They were ten-year-olds from a Catholic school in a new housing development. In they came munching potato chips and blowing bubble gum, clearly not in a listening mood. Since it was close to Halloween, Yashinsky wisely lit a candle, turned off the lights, and started telling ghost stories, and it wasn't long before they were hooked.

He wound up telling them one of those summer camp scary stories where, you know, the narrator's voice gets quieter and quieter until the moment when the ghost grabs the poor victim, and then he raises his voice loudly and says something like "I gotcha!" and the kids scream and jump into one another's laps. Which is exactly what happened.

Well, when the lights came on the children lined up to leave, talking excitedly about their shocking experience Yashinsky noticed one girl standing quietly, holding something around her neck. He asked her if she liked the stories, and she said, "Oh, yes, but when you told the last one I didn't jump."

"I noticed," he said. "How come?"

"Because when I knew it was going to be scary, I held the Blessed Virgin

220

Mary." She showed him the medal she was still holding. "You should get one, too."

"I'm not sure I should, " he answered. "I'm Jewish."

"That's okay, " she said sagely. "Get a Jewish one."

Then he makes this appropriate comment: "Writing my book about storytelling as an art and way of life, I have often remembered the girl's good counsel. When you know something scary is coming, you must find and hold onto your own source of reassurance and wisdom. You must have a steady beacon to guide you through perilous waters."

You can see where I'm going with this story. With it, I've already said something important and something significant about the life and meaning of Zaira D'Avella, a woman who had her scary moments from the very beginning, but who survived because she held on to her source of reassurance and wisdom: her faith. And then, as her family well knows, she in turn became a steady charismatic beacon to guide others.

Let's go back. In her journey from Manhattan to Brooklyn to Freehold and, spiritually, to Colts Neck, her life was challenging. Her mother died when she was less than two years old, and her father and sisters raised her. She was a sickly child, often seriously so, but, in a preview of what was to come, each time she survived, and each time, as it turned out, the traumas added another layer of depth and greatness to her soul.

Stephen tells me that, at three, Zaira even had a vision of her mother, who directed her to the doctor who saved her. Later when she grew up she frequently had dreams about her loved ones and cherished the messages they gave her. So it was obvious that, from the start, this was a special child. No wonder she grew into such an extraordinary, visionary adult.

Life was not over. Like Mary, whose Advent season this is, who heard old Simeon predict that a sword would pierce her heart, and who found out what he meant some thirty years later as she transitioned from the sweet mother with sweet infant to the distressed pietà with a dead son cradled in her arms. And so it would be with Zaira.

She also lost a son, Bernard, to cancer. He was only 24. I remember it all so well. I remember in my early years visiting Bernard at home. I remember having his funeral at St. Mary's, never dreaming I would be here today for his mother's. That sad time was probably the time when I first got to know

Zaira and the family well, and I sensed right off, like so many others, that I was dealing with an unusual person. She still had remaining her beloved children, Richard and Denise, of course. And then—how could I not mention it?—there was the light of her life for 60 years, her husband, Bernard. She absorbed his love of the opera, reprised his favorite childhood foods, kept alive his family roots. She loved him, and her one big concern at the end was that she was not going to be here to take care of him.

As she moved though the years, she became, as we say, a senior citizen or an elder, or, as I like to think of it, a prophet. To me she clearly became like old Simeon of our gospel. As he was in the Temple day and night so Zaira was in the temple of prayer—she was a very prayerful person—and the temple of good works bearing witness to the manifestation of God.

Characteristically, this wounded healer became a member of Compassionate Friends, an organization of those who lost children. She became a hospice volunteer and a member of the parish Lazarus ministry. And although she herself battled cancer twice—in 1991 and 1997—that didn't stop her from traveling, being a member of the Monmouth county Family Division and the Child Placement Review Board, or, above all, from cherishing and nurturing her husband and family whom she adored—and, I gathered, vice versa. Yes, as old Simeon took the child Jesus in his arms, so Zaira took her family and friends into her arms—literally. Like the prophet, she blessed people with her hugs. Many people. All kinds of people.

I was always amazed to find her always so upbeat, so positive even when I knew she was battling cancer. The last time I saw her—I visited her at the house several months ago—she was as usual: gregarious, positive, joyful, her usual happy self, confident that once more she would beat the disease. I was amazed and humbled at her attitude, her faith, her hope, her love. Departing after the obligatory hug, as I drove away I wondered who had comforted whom.

I was glad that she migrated to St. Mary's. She was a force, a connector of persons, colorful and cheerful. She was wife, mother, grandmother, pilgrim, parishioner, lover of people and lover of nature—and, above all, a faith-filled prophet.

Zaira is a legacy to embrace, and since I opened with a story, let me end with one to explain what I mean. It's a story about a musician who also had an unusual name: Bonnee Hoy. Bonnee was a gifted composer who died in the prime of her life. At her memorial service, a friend told of a mockingbird that used to sung regularly outside Bonnee's bedroom window on summer nights. Bonnee would stand at the window peering into the darkness, listening intently, and marveling at the beautiful songs the mockingbird sang. Being a musician, Bonnee decided to respond musically. So she whistled the first four notes of Beethoven's fifth symphony. With amazing quickness, the mockingbird learned those four notes and sang them back to Bonnee. Then for a time, the bird disappeared. But one night, toward the end of her life, when Bonnee was very sick, the bird returned. And, in the midst of its serenade it sang the first four notes of Beethoven's fifth several times.

The friend then paused and said these powerful words. He said, "Think of that! Somewhere out there in this big wide world there is a mockingbird who sings Beethoven because of Bonnee."

And I say, think of that! Generations of family and friends will sing songs, pass on memories, find comfort and new strength, new virtue, new hope because of Zaira D'Avella. They will know that when something scary is coming, they will have a steady beacon to guide them through perilous waters: the life and legacy of this special woman.

So, to the family and friends, for whom this will be a sad Christmas, I say, think of Zaira as she is now. She is like Simeon with a smile on her face and joy in her heart. After a long apprenticeship of love and service, after a long battle with sickness, she is at last, looking into the face of Christ—with Bernard at his side.

She has forever made her own the words of Simeon: "Master, now can dismiss your servant in peace for at last my eyes have seen your salvation."

53. Michael Savoia

A Reading of the Holy Gospel According to Matthew and John.

At that time, on one occasion Jesus asked his disciples, "Who do people say that I am?" And they said, "Some say John the Baptist, but others Elijah, and still others Jeremiah or one of the prophets." Jesus said to them, "But who do you say that I am?" Simon Peter answered, "You are the Anointed One, the Son of the living God." (Matthew 16:13–16)

On another occasion, after many of his disciples turned their backs on him, Jesus asked the twelve, "Do you also wish to go away?" Again it was Simon Peter who answered him, "Lord, to whom shall we go? You have the words of eternal life." (John 6:66)

Finally, after the resurrection, when they were all on the shore of the Sea of Tiberias, after the disciples had finished breakfast, Jesus asked Simon Peter, "Simon, son of John, do you love me more than these?" Peter said to him, "Yes, Lord, you know that I love you." Jesus said, "Feed my sheep." (John 21:15)

The gospel of the Lord.

The Homily
For three reasons I want to start off with a story. First, it buys me time to

compose myself for this difficult task, for I knew and loved this gentle man, this gentleman. Second, the story is an Italian folktale my mother brought from the old country, and how could I not tell an Italian folktale to catch the spirit of someone named Michael Savoia, son of Philomena and Santo from Staten Island, no less? Besides, it will keep the kids' attention for a while. And third, it's really a covert gospel story, and therefore it contains a truth about this man's life.

The story goes like this. Angelo was a fisherman who hated fish. He hated their sight, smell, and taste but he had a family to support. In his little village, about the only job he could find was fishing. To make matters worse, his boss, Luigi Carrini, was mean-spirited. Everything Angelo did was wrong.

One day, as Angelo hauled in a large catch, he saw a beautiful fish, its scales multicolored, its eyes almost turquoise. Angelo could not have such an animal killed, so he tossed it back. The fish began to swim away but then it stopped, looked back at him with those beautiful eyes, and nodded.

"Angelo!" It was Luigi, who had witnessed the whole scene. "I won't let you throw away my profits. You're fired!"

Dejected, Angelo wandered around, afraid to go home with his news. That evening, he stood on a cliff above the gloomy sea, looked down at the waves crashing on the rocks, and wept. Suddenly there was a chill in the air. Someone was watching him. It was an old hag dressed in black, all skin and bones. It was Death.

"Angelo, go ahead. Jump. It won't hurt."

"No, I can't."

Death decided to bargain. "Angelo, I can give you something so valuable you'll never have to fish again. I can give you a cow with an endless supply of milk. You can sell the milk to feed your family."

"And how would I earn this cow?" Angelo asked.

"Meet me here one year from now. I'll ask you three questions. If you can answer them, you may keep the cow."

And if I answer wrong?"

"You'll have to come with me."

Angelo, so tired of life, agreed. The woman disappeared and there stood the cow. When Angelo arrived home, his family was delighted. They filled pail after pail with milk. More pails were borrowed from the astonished neighbors. Soon the family was thriving.

One year later, Angelo waited on the cliff. Sensing someone behind him, he turned, expecting Death. Instead there stood a beautiful lady, her dress rainbow colored, her eyes almost turquoise. Those eyes suddenly looked at something behind Angelo. It was Death in her black robe, all skin and bones and gliding toward him.

"Angelo, are you ready for your three questions?"

"Yes, he is," quickly interrupted the beautiful lady, "and that was your first question."

Death, taken aback, was angry. "Angelo," she said, "are you going to let this woman speak for you?"

"Yes he is. That was your second question," shot back the beautiful lady.

Death pointed a finger at the woman. "Who are you anyway?"

"I am queen of the ocean with a debt to repay. That was your third question. Death, you have no business with this young man."

Death vanished, and Angelo found himself alone with a bright full moon shining down on him.

Thus my tale about death and three questions that only the Italians could foil so cleverly. Now I want to suggest that just as these three questions from the Queen of the Ocean upstaged death for Angelo, so three questions from the King of Heaven, Jesus, have done the same for Michael. These three questions from Jesus, found in the gospels, not surprisingly, deal with faith, hope, and love.

First Jesus question: "Who do you say that I am?" Jesus asked this question, you may recall, of his apostles. Their answers varied. Some said the prophets of old, others Elijah. It was Peter who got it right: "You are the Anointed One of God."

Michael believed that. He was genuinely a man of deep religious conviction. He and Marie would faithfully make their journey from Red Bank to be here with us. His religion meant a great deal to him. It sustained him in good times and in bad, in sickness and in health, and he had both in these past difficult months. But he never faltered. He, like Peter, gave the right answer and so thwarted despair and subverted death.

Second Jesus question: "Will you also go away?" Jesus asked this one of his apostles at a time when so many people were scandalized by him and had left him. Again, it was Peter who said, "Lord, to whom shall we go? You have the words of everlasting life."

"Will you also go away?" Like all of us, Michael was unnerved by the open wound of the scandals in his Church, but just as he had serious criticisms of his country but never for a moment considered moving to Cuba, or in a bad year leaving his beloved Yankees for the Red Sox, so too he never thought of moving away from the faith. Instead, on the contrary, like the candle that says to the darkness, "I beg to differ," Michael Savoia begged to differ. Yes, this gentle man with the slight smile engraved on his face, decided rather to bring light and beauty to a dark world. And he did—lastingly and generously, as we know. You can see it in his personal integrity, the marvelous architectural buildings he designed, his wonderful watercolors, his stunning photography.

His creative fingerprints are all over his many projects, not the least of which are these very buildings. His heartprints are all over his service to others, such as the parish council and the social and liturgical committees. Michael, in his own way, was a true Renaissance man determined to share his gifts, and we are all the richer for them. His bright life once more countered Dark Death.

Third and final Jesus question: "Simon, son of John, do you love me?" And when Peter, answered "Yes, you know that I do," Jesus replied, "Then feed my sheep."

Michael said everyday with his life that he indeed did love Jesus, and he fed others with love. He showed it in the way, for example, he loved Marie, his childhood sweetheart and wife of 57 years, and his children, Michael Anthony, Michele, Marie Louise, Mark Francis, and Matthew, and their spouses and grandchildren, Ryan, Mark, Miles, Marcus, Christine, Sara, Michael, and great grandchild, Lorenzo. He showed his love for Jesus in his love for his many friends, and I am proud to count myself among them as I suddenly recall wistfully that it wasn't that long ago that Mike, Marie, and I shared lunch at the shore.

So Michael Savoia proved his love a hundred different ways in word and charitable deed, and so answered the "do you love me?" question in the affirmative.

The bottom line is this: as a result of his answers, Death has no business with this man. Oh, yes, it confronted and claimed him for a while but finally had to release him and surrender him to Jesus, and now—believe this—the bright full moon of God's love shines upon him. All is beauty. All is truth. All is love.

54. Bill Barth and the Little Tin Box

JOHN 11:21–27

This week the nation has been focusing on memories, one in particular: the memory of 9/11 ten years ago. Old horrors and old heroisms were duly resurrected, noted, and celebrated as we were reminded that we live differently now because of these memories. We'll always remember 9/11. It will always define us as a nation.

Memories are powerful, and it is memories that have brought us here today. To tell us why, let me recall for you a favorite story of mine, Ed Hayes' wonderful tale called "The Little Tin Box." It's a story about an elderly couple who had just lost their farm and saw all their life's accumulation auctioned off. After the day was over and everyone had left, Tom and Mary are alone in their empty house with nothing but the kitchen table and chairs and the old bed upstairs—they were to be picked up in the morning. They sat down at the table and placed the only thing they had left on it: a tin box that had almost been sold by accident till Tom hastily retrieved it. Let's pick up the story here.

Mary was the first to speak. "They almost sold your little tin box."

"Yeah, that was close wasn't it?" said Tom, as he slowly opened the lid of the box. To the average eye the box appeared to be empty, but in reality it was filled almost to the top. The old battered tin box was filled with memories. Mary opened a suitcase and removed a small tin box that could have been a twin to Tom's. Slowly, one after another, they took out memories from their tin boxes and passed them to each other. One memory would awaken another one or be the leader of an entire parade of memories. "Remember the first night we stayed here after we were married …or when Dick came home from the Army…or that Christmas day in the 50s when we and the kids were snowbound?"…Their little tin boxes held memories that went back to their early childhoods.

These small tin boxes were what made Tom and Mary the richest people in the county. Early in life they had learned a great secret from Tom's grandfather. "The purpose of any possession," the old man had said, "is to make memories! The only purpose of money—only purpose—is to make memories. Things and possessions only rust and age, but memories, Tommy, memories are like fine wine…. They grow in value with time." Now that the farm sale and auction had completely dispossessed them of their belongings, they knew the wisdom of what grandfather had said to them….

Yes, it is wisdom like this displayed in this story that has brought us here today, a wisdom embodied in the life of Bill Barth. Ever since Bill died, family and friends have been recalling and sharing memories of him, plumbing the depth of the man, savoring his legacy through memory. As an old friend, I want to add my own memories. For example, you may not know this, but on this very day, September 13th, in this very church, 36 years ago, I witnessed Kathy and Bob's marriage. It's their anniversary today, the day Kathy remembers her father walking her down the aisle where he now rests.

As for Bill, his memory box includes the memories of him as a Marine, and more than that, as the proud recipient of the Purple Heart. Think of that. Then there was his 34-year supervisor's job at Fort Monmouth's Department of Engineering, his volunteering for the Colts Neck Fire Company. There was his fidelity to St. Mary's parish. I can still picture them coming in those front doors every Sunday.

But there was, I was to learn, even more to this quiet, steadfast man with the dry sense of humor. I remember very well going to the Barth house for lunch one day and being mightily impressed to learn that Bill had made all the furniture in the house. Bill, it turned out to my surprise, was an expert craftsman, and he would see a high-end cabinet or table or bedstead in a catalogue and reproduce them exactly. I couldn't get over the professionalism and the beauty of his work.

But that's a weak spot with me. I confess that I've always had a great awe of and admiration for those who can craft beautiful things. That's why one of my favorite TV programs is *This Old House*. I marvel at the talent and integrity of those gifted people creating a room, the lines of a ceiling, an elegant doorway or roofline, plumbing that works, lights that shine, landscaping that takes your breath away. Every bit as much as a renaissance painter, prizewinning author, or a renowned musician, these knowledgeable experts produce stunning truth and beauty and proclaim the integrity of their craft.

Bill, I saw, was one of those artists, those beauty-makers, and so instantly I took to him. I admired his gift, his talent—and that brings me to my second memory about Bill that has fallen into parish lore. Bill was in the hospital (Riverview, I think) with a heart problem when I went to visit him. He was weak and recovering and I, with some sense of shame—though not too much—took advantage of his weakness and told him that we were building a spiritual center. In it was to be a chapel, and I just happened to have with me a sketch I drew up of an altar. The altar was to be different— a slab atop a tree trunk—and I needed an artist, a gifted carpenter, and would he build it for the parish?

We would pay him, of course, but there were no models, no plans. Could he create such an altar? Would he? He was, as I counted on, too weak to say no. But in the worst of times he would have said yes. He got better, and he did build the altar—from scratch, from a tree he felled himself (why was I not surprised?)—and last night in the spiritual center chapel his body was respectfully and gratefully placed before the altar he made. It is his memorial. Every time we see that altar, we will remember him.

+   +   +

Anne, Kathy, Cindy, Patricia—children and grandchildren—all these things and more are in your husband's, your father's, tin box. It's full of precious memories deeply coated with faith, hope, and love. Like fine wine they will get better, more comforting, with age. Cherish them. Learn wisdom from them.

And now at last we have come to the part where we place two final memories into the box before the lid is put back on forever. The first is the full memory of these days: the shock, the grief, the love, the stories, the wake, the friends, this Mass, the burial. The second is the best and most enduring memory, one that embraces and validates all the others—the memory of another carpenter of long ago who said to all of us, "I am the resurrection and the life. He who believes in me, though he should die, will come to life. Do you believe this?"

Bill believed, and so today, that Carpenter has turned to Bill and embraced him, saying, "Come, let us carpenters talk of faith, family, and furniture. Enter into the joy of the Lord."

The
SERIES

55. An Excursus on the Series

Although not always feasible, it is sometimes very effective to give serial homilies, homilies that can stand alone but collectively are connected to an overall theme. This gives us a chance to focus and develop a point that will be remembered by sheer repetition. This kind of serial homilies can be done for a calendar month or connected to a liturgical season (Advent, Lent, or Easter) with its natural timeframe, or it can simply be an artificial arrangement of any kind. Of course, to make any series work, all weekend homilists must be on the same page. When I was pastor, this was not a problem because I and the weekend help were assigned the same Masses for a month and we would alternate months. This arrangement did give a wonderful chance to build up and expand a central thought (not to mention, the relief it gave to those who might otherwise have felt entrapped by having the same homilist all the time—"Monsignor always takes the seven!") Also, as I wrote in the preface, in connection with the serial homilies, it is absolutely necessary, as a powerful evangelizing opportunity as well as a practical strategy, to coordinate the series with the parish bulletin by including in it pertinent resources—for example, posting a timely excerpt, further reading suggestions, or (if appropriate) accessible retreat houses, spiritual directors, groups, or programs.

There are three series in this section. By far the longest is the first series on technology and the Christian, which seems appropriate for the season of Lent. The titles I chose for the five Sundays of Lent are:

Cell phones and Cars;

The Dives Syndrome;

Alien Voices;

Trivial Pursuits;

 iPod and I, God.

To this Lenten series I have appended the homily "Fatal Attraction." It's about Internet pornography. I realize that the Lenten Sundays have run out but I have included it only because of its logical affinity with the overall topic. It may, of course, be separated or used in another context. Sometimes these homilies are a little longer than normal and even perhaps a bit edgy. Sometimes I sense that I inadvertently slipped into the lecture mode, something I didn't want to do, especially given my limited knowledge. The reader will have to make adjustments. The reader, of course, can easily transpose the topic and translate the Lenten references to another time and context.

The topic of technology, I admit, is a vast one and (full disclosure), being of another day and age, I am quite limited in my approach and experience. Younger digital natives will be far more adept and will rightly improve and correct me. Moreover, the technology of the Internet and iPhone and smart phone and all the rest grows exponentially every day. In addition, there are large philosophical and social ramifications that only Bill Gates can fathom. Since I could not cover all of the exotic social and technical issues in the series, I have included here some random thoughts and resources that the more technically savvy homilists can mine. Others can just skip the long section that follows and go to the homilies.

Random Thoughts on Technology

Facebook is currently the second most popular Website on earth after Google. Facebook has 500 million users—400 million of whom spend more than an hour on the site per day—and the company continues to grow.

In a recent column for *The Wall Street Journal* Peggy Noonan claimed that in the Facebook age people will share anything about themselves and, as a result, most of what is shared is fabricated or only half-true. "An odd thing is that when privacy is done away with people don't become more authentic, they become less so. What replaces what used not to be said is something that must be said and is usually a lie" (Quoted by Anna Nussbaum Keating, *America*. November 22, 2010, p. 19). In fact, Facebook gathers tons of personal information on people, including their email addresses, current locations, sexual preferences, social network, finances, buying habits, friends, politics, and so on. (See "The Selling of You," *The Wall Street Journal*, April 7-8. 2011, Review Section.)

+   +   +

The homilist might note and comment on the irony that our culture of distraction has unwittingly spawned its twin, a culture of work, in which cell and smart phones, email, and Blackberries have created work around the clock. People are unable to disconnect from the demands of the workplace, even on vacation. You see them on the beach with their laptops and spreadsheets. You have people awakening to check emails, chatting on a cell phone while eating and traveling, bringing their work home to put in a 16- or 17-hour actual workday—all of which would have perplexed our grandparents who, once they shut the door on the factory or shop, were relieved and could look forward to their time.

The new technologies were supposed to lessen our workloads. When the computer got into the workplace in the early 1980s it was expected and solemnly announced that it would lead to the paperless office and a four-day work week. Instead, as we know, computers have created even more paper and a seven-day work week. So too, email was supposed to free us from extraneous phone calls and letters. Instead it has filled our lives with even more superfluous communication.

Once more, the result is that we have become so work-busy, so over-connected, so chronically distracted, so focused on the 2-inch screen or laptop, so incessantly media stimulated, so hectored by commercials, so herded to pursue more and more the things we think we need, that we have become disconnected from one another, our families, our communities, and our God. In short, to put it mildly, modern society is not friendly to the interior life, and that's a powerful homiletic thought to build on.

+   +   +

On a more ominous note, the first thing every computer user should know is that there is no privacy. The user should have a very large sign pasted atop his or her computer saying, "REMEMBER: YOU ARE BEING RECORDED, FILED & MARKETED." The moment you tap the first key, no matter what protections you think you have, someone is watching, recording, and filing. There is no privacy. One of the fastest growing businesses is spying on consumers. Lotame Solutions, Inc., BlueKai, and others install hundreds of pieces of tracking technology onto computers. Systems like Yahoo collect fees by placing targeted advertisements on websites. The technology is such that computers can follow the eye and facial movements of people, giving them data on which ads attract their attention.

+   +   +

One of the most intriguing and influential books of the last century was George Orwell's futuristic novel *1984*, which has proved to be remarkably prescient. In this novel everyone is under complete surveillance by the authorities, mainly by video screens. Watching over this totalitarian state was an enigmatic dictator called Big Brother. The people are constantly reminded that "Big Brother is watching you."

We are a nation of countless security and surveillance cameras, body imaging, and facial identity. Let's not forget Google Earth, where you can go online and peer into your neighbor's back yard.

There was a news report several years ago that Israeli scientists are now marketing a microchip that, implanted under the skin, will protect film stars and millionaires from kidnappers. The chip emits a signal detectable by satellite to help rescuers determine a victim's approximate location. Originally the chip was developed to track Israeli secret-service agents abroad. The $5,000 chip doesn't even require batteries. It runs solely on the neurophysiological energy generated within the human body.

Since this report was published there has been an explosion of interest in this technology. Farmers keep tabs on the health and safety of their cows and other livestock with such chips. But the use of such devices to monitor human beings is almost limitless. Already there is a monitoring bracelet for Alzheimer patients, so that families can use GPS systems to help find loved ones who might have wandered off.

In no time parents might want to monitor the whereabouts of their children via satellite. Why not have a chip implanted? Pet owners are already using such technology. The list of benign applications is growing every day. Why not have implanted a secure form of identification that would allow us to go through airports without waiting in line, a "glorified bar code" in one's fingertips that would allow us to be scanned in the check-out lane of the supermarket, so we wouldn't even have to present a credit card? These things are currently being considered. The list of possible uses grows longer with each passing day. Big Brother is watching.

+   +   +

Malevolent spies are known as hackers. In 2011, hackers posted twenty minutes of porn on Sesame Street's YouTube channel before it was caught. More widely they have attacked the websites of Sony, the United States Senate, the CIA, PBS, Citigroup, Lockheed Martin, law enforcement agencies, and others. They have stolen names, email addresses, and passwords of millions of users and published them online. They have compromised the data of more than 22 million people. If they can do all that to large corporations and governments, imagine how easily, if they had a mind to, they can invade your computer and its data. Legitimate collectors of data do have a mind to, and they do, and they sell the information to advertisers.

There are something like five hundred companies that are able to track every move you make on the Internet, mining the raw material of the Web and selling it to marketers—that you are overweight, have diabetes, have missed a car payment or two, read historical novels, support Republicans, use a cordless power drill, shop at Costco, and spend a lot of time on airplanes is not only known to people other than yourself, it is of great monetary value to them as well. So too where you are and where you have been, as we recently learned when it was revealed that both Apple and Google have been tracking mobile phone and tablet users and storing that information as well. ("Mind Control

& the Internet" by Sue Halpen, *New York Review*, June 23, 2011, pp. 34-35)

An article in *The Wall Street Journal* (Oct. 18, 2010) showed how tens of thousands of Facebook users, even those who set their profiles to be completely private, have been unknowingly transmitting information through their "apps" or applications to interested parties. Again, there is no more privacy.

So, sneaking in a religious note, in the old days preachers used to whip people into line by reminding them that they are always under the all-seeing eye of God. In my childhood parish church, in fact, there was at the apex of the nave this single huge eye in a triangle emanating rays that powerfully (and scarily) brought this truth home. Today, the Eye of God has been replaced by Google. I suppose some creative homilist can warn the digital natives that "If Google doesn't get you, God will!"

+   +   +

And, speaking of Google: There is this fiction about the liberating glory of the free Internet. The fiction says grandly that now at last the whole world can be harmoniously connected, and we can call up infinite information via Google amid the joys of infinite diversity. The reality is quite different. What most people don't know is that the search process has become what they call "personalized."

> Most of us assume that when we google a term, we all see the same results— the ones that the company's famous Page Rank algorithm suggests are the most authoritative based on other pages' links.., [but instead] now you get the results that Google's algorithm suggests is better for you in particular and someone else may see something entirely different. In other words, there is no standard Google anymore. (Eli Pariser, *The Filter Bubble: What the Internet Is Hiding from You*, Viking, 2011.)

What Pariser is saying is that, because every Internet user is non-stop monitored every time he or she uses the computer, a profile emerges, one collected by full-time professional companies that log your interests, choices, and biases and easily deduce your politics, tastes, and preferences. As a result, you get the answer that Google suggests is best for you. Someone else of a different profile will get a different result. Now, personalization has its advantages. With so much information available it makes sense for websites to filter it using information about us, our interests, and our friends. On the other hand, the Internet's potential and promise precisely to break down social barriers between people whom we might not otherwise know or connect with is compromised. The bottom line is that we are cut off from different opinions and conflicting points of view even though we think we're receiving "objective" answers, while all the time we are receiving "personalized" ones. In short, we are being indoctrinated with our own ideas. As Pariser neatly puts it, "We're getting a lot of bonding but very little bridging."

But there's more. Once Google started accepting advertising, then the floodgates were open for consumer profiling as well.

Write the word "blender" in an email, and the next set of ads you are likely to see will be for Waring and Oster. Search for information on bipolar disease, and drugs ads will pop up when you're reading baseball scores. Use Google Translate to read an abstract of a journal article and an ad for Spanish translation software will appear when you are using an online English dictionary.

We're targeted, and, to repeat, we are all profiled down to our toenails. We are being manipulated and are not as free as we think. Imagine the power this gives to the major corporations that run the world or to totalitarian governments. Concerning the latter read the following.

The Internet has been touted as a great force for emancipation—think of the "Arab Spring"—but others (see *The Net Delusion* by Evgeny Morozov) see it as decidedly ambiguous, having much power for good, such as the sharing of knowledge; and for evil, such as the authoritarian and corporate manipulation and monopoly of digital space, the funding of nationalistic and pro-government bloggers promoting authoritarian regimes. This danger grows as governments become more digitally adaptive and corporations and their propaganda—called advertising—can change attitudes and lifestyles at a whim and produce monolithic societies. (Did you know that Hugo Chavez is a gifted tweeter?)

Take the history of radio and television. They were once thought to be a way to expand free speech and broaden democracy with diverse voices. But, to the contrary, they soon became monopolies dominated by big business. So too, today. The industry structure, corporate advertising power and interests, determine what we hear and see.

> In essence Wu [a social commentator] is concerned that large corporations—AT&T, Comcast, Verizion, Apple, and perhaps Google—may be on the verge of carving the Internet into an oligopoly, gradually shutting off equal and free access, much as RCA did to radio and the Bell System did to telephony (p. 24, *The New York Times Sunday Review*, "The Internet: For Better or for Worse," by Steve Coll, April 17, 2011).

+   +   +

And now, finally, for some scary sci-fi stuff. The blending of men and machines, a kind of Cyborg entity—long the scenario of science fiction—seems to be at the door. At Brown University, for example, scientists have successfully tested what they call brain-computer interface (BCI), which allowed a paralyzed woman to move a cursor just by thinking. There are other examples of thinking provoking actions. The short of it is that we are quickly becoming able to connect directly to the Internet via a neural implant and, human nature being what it is, it won't be long before repair gives way to enhancement (think steroids in sports) as (rich) parents implant their kids to succeed.

There are scientists like the renowned Stuart Wolf who can imagine that before too long we will be wearing a headband that feeds directly into the brain that lets us, among other things, talk without speaking, see around corners, and drive by thinking.

> As early as 2000 Sony began to work on a patented way to beam video games directly into the brain using ultrasound to modify and create sensory images for an immersive, thoroughly inescapable gaming experience. More recently, computer scientists at the Freie University in Berlin got a jump on Stuart Wolf's vision of a car operated solely by thought. (Sue Halpern, p. 35)

And while we're in the sci-fi mood, how about Cyberwar? Secretary of Defense Leon Panetta has listed it as a top priority of concern. As *The Economist* put it,

> The computer and the Internet have transformed economics and given Western armies great advantages, such as the ability to send remotely piloted aircraft across the world to gather intelligence and attack targets. But the spread of digital technology comes at a cost: it exposes armies and societies to digital attack...Modern societies are ever more reliant on computer systems linked to the internet, giving enemies more avenues of attack. If power stations, refineries, banks, and air-traffic-control systems were brought down, people would lose their lives. (July 3, 2010, p. 11)

+   +   +

It might be a nice homiletic point to reveal that many of the hi-tech gurus send their children to schools that do not allow computers—people like the chief technology officer of eBay and employees of Silicon Valley giants like Google, Apple, Yahoo, and Hewlett-Packard. They deliberately send their kids to these schools that use pens, paper, blackboard, chalk, and workbooks and where not a computer is to be found anywhere. These schools even frown on computer use at home (*The New York Times*, October 24, 2011, Technology section). The super-tech parents feel kids learn better and deeper with simple hands-on approaches.

+   +   +

Well, leaving aside these provocatively rich topics and the fact that one of the earliest adoptions of Internet technology was the pornography business, which has topped out at 13.1 billion a year, all this is too rich for me, and I defer to those who might find the data interesting enough to create a powerful homily (or conference). As for me, I work with the everyday social-spiritual issues suggested by these more mundane news items:

• In a survey (Osterman Research for a software company), 33% of the respondents admitted to hiding from friends and family in order to check email on vacation.

- There are retreats that specialize in "digital detox," where gadget-addicted participants have to check in their digital devices or leave them at home.
- One pastor forbade his workers to get on Facebook. His counseling finds more and more marital problems, including infidelity, as people are now reigniting old passions and connecting with people who should stay in the past. "Married couples are getting on Facebook, and what happens can end up in my office."

Finally this report: Loren Rosenberg who was struck by a car while attempting to cross a busy Utah street said her eyes were glued to her Black-Berry. Rosenberg is suing Google, blaming the Google Maps service she was accessing at the time of her accident. It told her to walk along state Route 224, never warning her of high-speed traffic or the absence of sidewalks.

Every silver lining has a cloud.

+   +   +

Let me end this section on the digital world with a personal whimsy. I have a friend who writes light verse ("All light verse./It could be worse.") and, on the subject of the digital world I, as a certified nerd, wrote to him:

Poet, tell me this:
Would:

Hester Prynne
Be online?
Princess Grace
Cyberspace?
Old King Lear
On the air?

Uriah Heep
Heed the beep?

Percy Shelley
Watch the Telly?

And, furthermore, if provoked, would:
Wilbur Wright
Megabyte?

Uncle Tom
RAM the ROM?

John G. Fiske
Flop the disk?

Robert Stack
Whack the Mac?

Johann Strauss
Kill the mouse?

or simply would

Seigel, ("Bugsy")
Pull the plugsy?

+   +   +

There's all kinds of books that are germane to this topic. Two very good ones are:

Hamlet's Blackberry: Building a Good Life in the Digital Age by William Powers. This covers the material in these homilies, only much better and more engagingly.

The Googlization of Everything (and Why We Should Worry) by Silva Vaidhyanathan

And if you want to go deeper read the extraordinary article, "Selling our Souls" by Andrew Bacevich in *Commonweal* magazine, August 12, 2011. If you want some updated material check out the special issue in *The New York Times'* Science Times section, titled "The Future of Computing," December 6, 2010.

Our Sunday Visitor, by the way, puts out an annual edition of *OSV's Guide to the Internet* that is very helpful to believers.

The Confession Series

Everyone knows hardly anyone goes to confession anymore. Some Catholics never go. Everyone has his or her reasons for this situation. In a heavily therapeutic society a sense of sin has been dimmed. In an "anything goes" society, the definition of sin has been subverted. In a diverse society sin is relative and one person's vice is another's virtue. In a religiously confused society—to use a very "hot" example: gay marriage, vigorously forbidden for two centuries, is now morally embraced—sin is matter of raising human consciousness. Hang in there: things will change.

These four homilies on confession, preached to the choir, are mild, and they beg for the homilist's own refinements. They are designed to widen the congregation's understanding of why we have confession the way we do to begin with and the implications of community in one's moral life. They are not hortatory but simply informative. It is hoped that they might lead the listeners to an appreciation of the wisdom that repentance and the regular examination of conscience can be the tools of advancing the spiritual life.

These homilies can be used anytime or, perhaps more topically, for the first four Sundays of Lent.

The Church

Finally there are two related homilies on the Church and the parish. They are designed to widen the theological imagination of the average parishioner.

56. Cell Phones and Cars

It's Lent again, and it brings up my childhood memories of us kids trying to outdo one another by piously promising to give up spinach, school, and studying. But even with the joking aside, as kids we understood this "giving up" concept was not just a negative letting go but a positive thing, that is, a making room for the more valuable things we had been crowding out with things less valuable and even sometimes things that were morally constipating.

The laundry list of these morally constipating things has changed throughout the years, and each age has its new culprits. To perk up your attention let me list one for our time: the cell phone. Go back to October 13, 1983, when hundreds of people including reporters, gathered at Soldiers Field in Chicago to witness the first cell phone call from a car when an executive from Ameritech phoned the great-grandson of Alexander Graham Bell, who was living in Germany. The rest, as they say, is history, as the cell phone has built itself into a 150 billion dollar industry.

But, even back then, some alarms were raised by engineer Martin Cooper, called the father of the cell phone, who noticed the danger of the distracted driver, but his concerns fell on deaf ears as greedy eyes saw all that potential cash. Others noticed too, but as another engineer put it at the time, "If you're an engineer, you don't want to outlaw the great technology you've been working on…If you're a marketing person, you don't want to outlaw the thing you've been trying to sell. If you're a CEO, you don't want to outlaw the thing that's been making a lot of money"—the classic excuses of the morally shortsighted.

Another researcher brought his concerns about the growing evidence concerning the dangers of cell phone use while driving to his supervisor and was told, "Why would we want to know about that?" "The message was clear," the researcher said, adding, "Obviously, learning about distractions would not be very helpful to the overall business model." And there you have it, once more, all up and down the line: the triumph of greed over morality—everyone, each step of the way, putting profit over people with disastrous results. And the dollar sign people are not through yet.

A news item from *The New York Times* in January, 2010, has this opening paragraph: "To the dismay of safety advocates already worried about driver distraction, automakers and high-tech companies have found a new place to put sophisticated Internet-connected computers: the front seat." In October, 2011, it was reported that, despite a four-year national campaign against distracted driving, a majority of parents admitted to being distracted by cell phones and other devices—even while teaching their children to drive!

The article shows, again, how giants like Intel and Google, seeing vast profits before them, are bringing the power of the PC to the car with 10-inch screens above the gearshift showing hi-definition videos, 3-D maps, and Web pages—in short, "infotainment systems," as they call them—where the driver can scan a map while the passenger next to him can watch a movie. All this, right in your own car as you drive, making the car with its reclining seats, radio, CD, built-in phone, navigation systems, back-seat televisions, and bars more and more like self-contained living quarters, causing one wit to say he was going to sell his home and live in his car.

The car makers are piously saying that they are simply giving customers, used to smart phones and the Internet, what they want, even though a Virginia Tech Transportation Institute researcher makes the commonsense observation that motorists obviously face a much greater risk when looking at a screen. As common sense tells everyone else also, all this adds up to the distracted driver, and we already know that the distracted driver, the cell phone driver, has caused injury and death.

In 2003 motorists talking on cell phones caused 2,600 fatal accidents—that is, they killed 2,600 people: men, women, little children—and 570,000 injury accidents. In 2008, the figures showed that nearly 6,000 people died in crashes involving a distracted driver, and more than half a million were injured. These figures would be higher, but a front page article in

The New York Times (7/21/09) shows how the "U.S. withheld data on cell phone driving risks" because of "concerns about offending Congress" and the suspicion of the cell phone industry's pressure. The most recent report from the National Safety Council finds that most of the 1.4 million annual crashes are caused by cell phone conversations, and 200,000 are blamed on text messaging.

And you may recall that, in July of 2010, two students visiting Philadelphia from Hungary died while the Ride the Ducks sightseeing boat on which they were passengers was plowed over by a barge in the middle of the Delaware River. The barge commander was on his cell phone while piloting the boat and was also doing Internet searches on a laptop computer. Using a cell phone while driving, whether it's hand-held or hands-free, delays a driver's reactions as much as having a blood alcohol concentration at the legal limit of .08 percent.

Then there is the distracted pedestrian, the walking cell phone user. We see them all the time—it's we ourselves—walking along the streets, crossing the roads, talking on cell phones. Some letters to the editor take them on.

One person wrote, "I'm so glad that pedestrians who phone and text while crossing streets are getting some attention! As a daily driver to and from work in the Bronx, I often see pedestrians with phones glued to their ears crossing even heavily trafficked streets like the Grand Concourse against the light. Some don't even seem to hear the cars that are honking at them."

This lady writes, "I am a disabled woman who walks with the aid of two canes. Just recently, I was leaving my local train station, and a man, talking excitedly on the cell phone, kicked one of my canes as he rushed past. I bobbed badly, but managed not to fall. I found the man outside the station still talking. I tapped him on the shoulder several times, and when he took no notice, I yelled, "You kicked my cane and I nearly fell!" His irritated response? "I can't talk now. Can't you see I'm on the phone?"

Aside from the rudeness of those who talk incessantly and often loudly at the supermarkets and theaters and walking along the streets, and apart from the fact that it is illegal to drive while talking on the cell phone, there obviously is the moral issue here.

And that, of course, is why we make it a topic for a Lenten homily. Again, it is not just illegal to talk on the cell phone while driving. It is immoral. It is a sin. It is a sin because it puts people in mortal danger, because driving while phoning hurt or crippled nearly 600,000 people and killed 2,600 seven years ago and there must be many, many more today. Maybe that's why Oprah started a crusade against driving while on the cell phone and why on the back of New Jersey's windshield inspection stickers are printed the words in bold letters, "put the phone down." In 2011, a federal agency was calling for a ban on cell phone use by drivers, and the United Nations Secretary General called for an end to a "culture of multitasking" behind the wheel.

Finally—and frighteningly—there is what is called "distracted doctoring." Studies reveal doctors and nurses more focused on the screen than on the patient. Technology has had a truly significant positive impact on medicine, but its abuse is scary. There are revelations of a neurosurgeon making personal calls during an operation and a nurse checking airfares during surgery. Half of technicians running bypass machines admit texting during the procedure. In fact, 55 percent of the technicians who monitored bypass surgery admitted that they had talked on cell phones during surgery, and half said they had texted while in surgery, One medical malpractice lawyer is suing on behalf of a patient who was left partly paralyzed after surgery because his doctor was using a wireless headset to talk on his cell phone, making personal calls to family and business associates during the operation. These are not callous or indifferent people. Most are young, raised on electronic gadgets that are as "natural" to them as wearing shoes. They are simply oblivious to the dangers of distraction, just as we are when we phone or text and drive.

Those of us who are fans of the old *Law and Order* series on television are familiar with the phrase, "reckless endangerment." To put in motion reckless endangerment, to cause potential harm and death to others is a God issue, a moral issue, a conscience issue, and maybe we moderns have to confess that to God. It's not a new sin. It's an old sin violating an old commandment: "Thou shalt not kill," "Thou shalt not mortally endanger your neighbor." If we disobey these commandments, we become no better than the executives who pushed aside the early warnings and ignored the death toll as they added up their profits.

For us who are good people, it's not a matter of deliberate malice—of course not—but a matter of awareness, awareness of the stewardship we have for creation, God's creatures, and our fellow human beings. It is an awareness of the gospel imperative to live the moral life, to love our neighbor as ourselves.

Technology has blessed our lives in many, many ways but it also carries with it new responsibilities. For those of us who follow Jesus, his proclamation of "Love your neighbor as yourself" must be a guideline on how to work within those responsibilities.

So, for Lent our examination of conscience—not to mention our Lenten resolutions—might focus on the responsible use of the cell phone and to see it, not just as a pleasant gift and a wonderful convenience, but also as a moral issue. If it is sinful to endanger people, it is virtuous to protect them.

57. The Dives Syndrome

A New Yorker writes (and try to visualize his story):

The other day I was walking through a park in the City. Racing across Union Square to an appointment, I stumbled on a pair of grungy young men. One was playing an accordion, the other a violin. Their music was a sprightly, lively, intricate, intoxicating type of Eastern European folk music. Mesmerized, I stopped to listen to the furious melodies and rising and falling rhythms. A little crowd gathered about, and I noticed that we were in the middle of the weekly open-air farmers' market, with vendors carefully laying out fresh fruits, vegetables, and flowering plants for all to see.

As I listened to these two skinny guys, one with long dreadlocks, the other sporting a scraggly beard, I smelled something unusual—fresh peaches—from behind me. What a glorious moment: the music, the sunshine, the crowd, the shoppers at the market, and the smell of ripe peaches.

Just then someone cut through the rest of the crowd: a woman punching her BlackBerry and listening to her iPod. She knifed through us and rushed away. She had missed the entire experience, since she was entirely absorbed in her own world.

This story—this all too familiar story—reminds us that, for all of the marvels and benefits of technology, there is, if we are not careful, a great human loss. We are losing contact with each other and our world. It's a proven fact. This is called the Dives Syndrone. It's named after the familiar gospel parable about the rich man, Dives, and the poor man, Lazarus. Lazarus, you will recall, was lying at Dives' McMansion door starving and begging for crusts of bread while the dogs licked his sores—and all the while, Dives, a good man in many ways—we get no gospel indication that he was venal or wicked—never even saw him.

In short, Dives wasn't a bad man. He wasn't mean or cruel. It's just that, living in his own world, he looked right past Lazarus. He literally didn't see him. Lazarus was simply outside of his awareness, his vision, his consciousness, his interests. Living comfortably and innocently in his isolated splendor, relating to his own inner circle, absorbed with his own gadgets, Dives just didn't notice Lazarus. This kind of extreme self-absorption that blinds us to others is called the Dives Syndrome, and this spiritual disease is one of the hidden hazards of technology.

It's like the old Sufi tale of a man who was obsessed with gold. Every day he would go to the marketplace and gaze with envy at the gold seller, the man who bought and sold the precious metal, with a sturdy guard by his side. One day he could no longer contain himself and ran headlong to the gold seller's table and scooped up all the gold. The guard quickly caught him, and when they threw him in jail the guard shook his head and said, "How could you be so stupid? Didn't you see me standing right next to the table?" The man sadly replied, "I saw only the gold." People can become defined by their gadgets and learn to see only the virtual world that they construct. They disconnect from the real world and, what's more, from those they profess to love.

A case in point. There was recently a front page article from *The New York Times* (August 10, 2009) entitled, "Breakfast Can Wait: the Day's First Stop Is Online." It tells of a family of four—a mother, father, and two teenage sons. Not long ago, they had breakfast and ate together and chatted. Today, the first thing they do is check online. The mother is quoted as saying, "Things I thought were unacceptable a few years ago are now commonplace in my house, like all four of us starting the day on four computers in four separate rooms." How sad. Sounds like something from *The Twilight Zone* but it's all too familiar.

The sons sleep with their phone next to their beds so they start the day with text messages, and the father sends texts to his sons to wake them up. The father says, "I could always walk upstairs, but they always answer their texts." Notice: one more human contact replaced by an electronic one. The article continues: "Families that used to fight over the shower or the newspapers tussle over access to the lone household computer or about whether they should be using gadgets at all, instead of communicating with one another."

I remember a father telling me how he would drive his preteen daughter to school each day on his way to work and how he would enjoy their chats. Now, ever since she got a cell phone, as soon as she gets in the car she is texting her girlfriends. No more conversation. I cowardly resisted suggesting the obvious: declare the car a cell-phone-laptop-free space. You're the parent. I couldn't help recalling the Kaiser Communications study that found that young people did in fact use less media in homes with firm rules, like no television during meals and no television in the bedroom or with limits on media times.

Here's a mother who confesses that ever since she got her 14-year-old daughter a laptop for her birthday, she has missed the school bus three times and went from walking the family dog for 20 minutes each morning to only briefly letting the dog outside. Parents who are addicted themselves or unsure also contribute to the disconnect in family life. What do the surveys say? American parents spend 40% less time with their children than they did 50 years ago.

Another mother named Susan Maushart wrote a book with the long title, *The Winter of Our Discontent: How Three Totally Wired Teenagers (and a Mother Who Slept with her iPhone) Pulled the Plug on Their Technology and Lived to Tell the Tale.* What made her write her book was when she looked up to see her kids, ages 14, 15, and 17, and "all I could see were the backs of people's heads because they were interacting with their screens. It was the prime time of their teenage years—that last moment when we were all going to be together under one roof. I felt sick at the pit of my stomach that this was all going to dwindle away." So they all unplugged for six months and reunited as a family. Still another mother comments, "I worry for the kids that they won't know what it's like to share a story, to look people in the eyes—to know that sharing a space with someone is all about connecting and not with the technological device."

Is all this just social commentary? Is there a religious message for Lent here? Obviously, yes. We are becoming addicted to and captive to, our machines. We are creating our own self-enclosed world and are spending less and less time in face-to-face contact even with those we profess to love. No wonder a major magazine, *The Atlantic*, featured on its cover the bold headline in May of 2012, "Is Facebook Making Us Lonely?" We are losing the art of empathy, of unmediated conversation and communication, of a sense of the human family and its needs, of our own family, and that is a large moral issue. And maybe a Lenten practice should be to discipline the cell phoning and texting, confining them to certain hours and making house rules of a TV- and cell-phone-free dinner and family time before we forget how to communicate one on one, face to face, heart to heart. Remember also that the Internet can go both ways. I think, for example, of the free email newsletter called the "Huff-Post Family Dinner Downloads" that draws from events of the day to create mealtime conversation starters between parents and children.

Let me end with a neat poem that says it all:

In the house
Of Mr. and Mrs. Spouse
He and She
Would watch TV
And never a word
Between them was spoken
Until one day
The set was broken.

Then, "How do you do?"
Said He to She.
"I don't believe we've met."
Spouse is my name,
What's yours?" he asked.
"Why, mine's the same!"
Said She to He.
"Do you suppose we could be…?"

But the set came suddenly right about
And they never did find out.

Lent is time to find out.

58. Alien Voices

Teens and children of today are digital natives. They have been born into a world that always had computers, cell phones, and the Internet. With electronic books, virtual worlds, GPS navigation systems, and so forth, there is hardly anything in their lives that is not digital or electronic. There is literally no place where they can't be and aren't plugged in. The smart phone has become a virtual amulet, an object to be held, caressed, and attended to. No wonder devotees of Apple's iPhone call it the Jesus Phone. If you think I'm exaggerating the ubiquity of the digital, listen to this. For about $300.00 you can buy a pair of pants fitted with an Egokast LCD screen belt buckle. Just pop in an SD (secure signal) memory card with your favorite flick and you're set. There are also Geek jeans that have a full-sized working keyboard and wireless mouse and speakers, all stitched into the denim and all of which connect to your computer via wireless USB. Then, the pièce de resistance, there are bikini swimsuits that feature photovoltaic strips built into the fabric, so that the wearer soaks up the sun as do those little solar panels, enough to charge an iPod Shuffle and a full day's beach music. I've made my point. Technology has absorbed their world to a point where it's really hard to distinguish what is real from what is artificial.

Our children excel at technology. The digital world is truly their home. It is, as we said, where they were born and raised. What should be no surprise to anyone is the study [2010] by the Kaiser Family Foundation that reports that "The average young American now spends practically every waking minute—except for the time in school—using a smart phone, computer, television, or other electronic device" (*The New York Times*, January 26, 2010).

Yes, teens and pre-teens—and again I quote from the Kaiser study— "spend more than ten hours a day with such devices. And because so many of them are multitasking—say, surfing the Internet while listening to music—they pack in nearly eleven hours of media content in that time." That's a lot of time. The Kaiser study, by the way, also found, unsurprisingly, that heavy media use has some serious negatives including behavior problems, lower grades, and that there is a definite correlation between screen time and obesity.

Teens are psychologically at the point—and you young people know what I'm talking about—where they consider the cell phone and iPhone and others an essential part of their lives, which is why the majority of young people own such gadgets (funded by their parents). Forty-five percent of teens say that "having a cell phone is the key to my social life." They know that if they don't own a cell phone or can text, they're out of the loop, at the front of the geek line. They must keep in touch—constantly—to test the social waters.

Parents are naïve if they think their kids are sleeping at 1 or 2 AM. The studies show they're not. For one thing, 7 out of 10 have a television in their bedrooms (considering what's on TV, that's scary enough.) But, more than that: they're texting. Amid the pillows with laptop or BlackBerry, they chat with buddies in the 11th grade—or the next state. Photos fly back and forth, and their Facebook pages keep updating.

Gone are the days when being sent to one's bedroom was dire punishment. Most kids' bedrooms today are virtual control centers that would make Captain Kirk envious, with TVs, computers, and cell phones that constantly send messages and photos, download movies and music and rock concerts—and sometimes texting moves into sexting. Twenty-two percent of teen girls—and it's largely girls who do this—admit to sexting, that is, sending sexually explicit pictures of themselves via cell phone or via Facebook. (What is the need behind that?)

Teens, by nature, have always felt the need, the impulse, to keep in contact, to hang out with their peers, the need to know who's going with whom, who broke up, who's dating whom, who's the latest boyfriend or girlfriend, who's in and who's out, and so on—where they stand in the pecking order. Today's hyper-status Internet measuring carries its risks, what researchers call "Facebook Depression," a term describing teens with low self-esteem who can't measure up to the popularity of happy-looking kids having great times. Plus there are, as we know, the vile putdowns and cyberbullying of these hapless kids that have led to suicide. Do you recall the story of 17-year-old Jessica K. Logan from Cincinnati, who hanged herself after a nude picture of herself that she texted to her boyfriend was sent to the phones of hundreds of her classmates?

I remember reading the *Rolling Stone* article about a 13-year-old lonely girl who created an online persona of Kiki Kannibal—the name she chose should tell you something—posting photos of herself, sometimes in her underwear, sometimes with lurid makeup; in short, copying the media's concept of a desirable woman. She became a MySpace sensation with two million people logging on to her live, steamy video. Then came copycats claiming to be her. She became the object of celebration, and then ultimately ridicule, viciousness, and hatred. She received mob-like threats of sexual reprisals and vile threats like "I'm gonna kill you." The word "slut" was painted on her garage. An 18-year-old-kid named Danny, with a history of seducing young girls, forced himself on her. Her family pressed charges. As he was being arrested, he jumped off a garage roof, went into a coma, and died two months later. Addicted to the attention, Kiki couldn't get off-line. Finally, bankrupt, the family had to move away. Thus the dark side teens have to be aware of.

Well, in past times the kids had a counterweight to all this electronic absorption. Yes, they hung out after school or weekends, but that was pretty much it. In the pre-gadget tech age, however, they couldn't hang out or call all the time. All they had was the land phone at home. And they had chores. They had to be home for dinner. They had to sit at the dinner table and listen to their parents talk about shopping, vacation plans, the president, gas prices, and the news. Limited in peer contact, they were forced to notice, be aware of, and even participate to a certain extent in a world beyond themselves.

Today, with the availability of 24/7 networking and texting, kids can live almost entirely in a private, self-contained, peer-connected, and self-absorbed world. The clear social and moral danger, the social scientists point out, is that everything gets measured by the details of their lives, and that can lead to a self-centered, narrow, desensitized, narcissistic existence. In short, digital technology can and does deliver good content to teens. The problem is that's not what the majority of teens are using these tools for. They're using them for what 15-year-olds care about: other 15-year-olds.

After all, if you're talking to or texting with only your peers all of your waking hours, day after day, week after week, month after month, your frame of reference shrinks, your world grows small and constricted. The point: the texting teenagers who corral their peers almost 24 hours a day into a very closed, almost exclusive, circle, are unwittingly constructing a world that leaves little room for outsiders, for anyone else.

Teens have as much intelligence, ambition, nobility, and talent as any previous generation—and you are here today and I salute and admire your presence—but they exercise these qualities too disproportionately, too narrowly. There is too much interfacing with one another, undermining, I repeat, a sense of others, of larger issues, of empathy, of Lazarus at the door. And that's not good for democracy, or, as we shall explore in a later homily, for spiritual growth. Not to mention, as Pope Benedict points out, the danger that "the supremacy of technology tends to prevent people from recognizing anything that cannot be explained in terms of matter alone." Nor is life really that simple or neat. Mike Hayes writes in his book *Googling God* that young adults "live in a world of immediate gratification, the world of Google. Answers can be arrived at by the touch of a button or the click of a mouse. The result is a world that young adults live in where they expect answers that are simple, clear-cut, and require little thought."

There's a wonderful bounty to living in the digital world, and txtese or text talk is here to stay—"CUl8r"—but like all things, it is two edged. Parents must see that their children live in a balanced world where beauty, friendships, and truth are to be celebrated face to face, where awareness of God, nature, and others in need have their place.

59. *Trivial Pursuits*

If we're going to talk about trivial pursuits today—the title of the fourth homily in our Lenten series—we could take no better example than to cite America's obsession with celebrities. We could point to the over 5 million who subscribe to *People* and *US* magazines, the millions who track the ups and downs of their favorite celebrities on *Entertainment Tonight, Access Hollywood* and the E! network, or those who, 24 hours a day, hang breathlessly on every tweet from their idols. Our appetite for celebrities is apparently insatiable, as is our desire to be celebrities.

Yes, today's social media constantly forces us to collect friends ("join me on Facebook"), elevate our status, and market ourselves. We are out to get attention. "Look at me! Aren't I wonderful?" This comes as no surprise. After decades of self-esteem programs and everyone getting a trophy, it is not surprising that, when in 1950 a personality test asked teenagers if they considered themselves an important person, 12% said yes, but by the later 1980s, 80% said yes. By the 2000s everyone was a celebrity or wanted to be.

People have always had, of course, a place in their hearts for heroes, whether in the movies or sports. I can remember avidly collecting and trading the baseball cards of favorite ballplayers. What is different today, however, is the total saturation of the celebrity market due to the technology of the mass media, the lack of counterbalancing real heroes from ordinary life, and, as some social scientists observe, the inner loneliness many people, especially kids, feel as their families scatter or fall apart and so have less family and community affirmation, support, and presence.

Whatever the case, these experts point out that our obsession with celebrities is not a good thing for our human and spiritual growth, because it

259

distorts our perspective about what is important; because there is only so much time and space in a person's life, and celebrity obsession pushes aside too much of what we should be paying attention to.

And celebrity obsession tends to make us insensitive to gospel values. Take reality shows. They thrive on other people's humiliation, pain, weakness, and betrayal. Values like education, building community, honesty, transparency, and sharing are qualities that will often get one ridiculed and voted off any reality show. Fellow competitors for prize money and a chance for fleeting fame elect to "disappear" the unwanted. Those cast aside become, at least to the television audience, non-persons. Those who win are the best. Those who lose deserved to be erased. Those who fail, those who are ugly or poor, are belittled and mocked. That's not what Jesus is all about.

Yes, celebrity worship distorts. Jake Halpern is the author of the interesting book *Fame Junkies*. He tells about the time he was to appear on CNN precisely to talk about fame junkies but his appearance was canceled because of "breaking news." The breaking news? Britney Spears lost custody of her children. He later learned that the Spears story got three times as much coverage on that network as did the war in Iran and 37 times more coverage than the heart-rending conflict in Darfur. Something's wrong.

Another survey revealed that more than one third of young girls want to be famous and intend to be so, and famous not for discovering a cure for cancer or anything like that, but famous in the sense of being famous for being famous, or, in other words, famous for being a celebrity who can tweet their every thought to a waiting and adoring world.

Psychologists try to fathom the reason for celebrity worship. One popular theory is that it reflects our own yearning to be well known. They say that as communities and neighborhoods decline and families fall apart and affirmation fades and there's no one home to talk to and the act of socializing becomes more isolated by being done through gadgets, we become, as we have noted before, less present to one another and so have no way of being recognized. That's why Twitter is so popular. We are so anxious to be recognized that we feel we need to tell our every move to anyone willing to read about it.

When I hear things like that I think of the old story of the exceedingly unattractive orphan whom no one in the orphanage liked or paid attention to, especially the staff. One day the staff spied her scratching out a note and going and hiding it in a tree on the edge of the property. The staff was overjoyed. Perhaps she was communicating with a distant relative who might come and take her away. So when the child wasn't around they crept towards the tree, seized the note, opened it, and eagerly read it. It said in a child's scrawl, "Whoever finds this, I love you." It was, as the psychologists would say, her "tweet."

Celebrity worship and emulation also leave us open to the suffocation of the trivial. First, recall that we live in a world that subjects us to some 7,000 to 10,000 overt and subliminal commercials every single day—we have long since become unaware of this constant indoctrination to consume, but it works. And to support our insatiable consumption, we have advertising that by nature trivializes everything. For example, we honor our Presidents' Day how?—by holding sales and having actors dress up as Washington and Lincoln hawking automobiles, wine, insurance, or sleeping pills.

Advertising levels everything, even the sacred, to a marketplace value, and accordingly has a vested interest in keeping us in perpetual adolescence. You know: we know the names of the Brady Bunch but can't name more than three apostles. We hang on every word of Lady Gaga but can't recall any words of Nelson Mandela. We dumb down all distinctions between noble and frivolous, profound and stupid, worthy and unworthy, impulse and reflection. It is distressing to hear how many kids, inured by countless, incredibly graphic scenes of violence, think that torture is "cool."

The trivialization of society, as we said, keeps us in perpetual adolescence. The social scientists note that more and more young people desire never to grow up. They point to today's backward-baseball-cap-wearing, video-game-playing, cartoon-network-watching thirtysomethings. They hit us with their surveys that show that more adults, ages 18 to 49, watch the Cartoon Network than watch CNN; the average age of people buying and playing video games in 2006 was 30, as opposed to 18 in 1990; and one-third of the audience of Nickelodeon's Sponge Bob Square Pants is between the ages of 18 and 30. It's a Peter Pan world. Women write articles in national magazines with titles like, "Where have the good men gone?"

The thing is, we are by nature spiritual people, pilgrim people, noble people, decent people, good people with good instincts and yearnings, but we are trivialized to death by a celebrity culture, round-the-clock advertising, selfish competition, and some rather frightful anti-gospel messages. This steady diet dulls our spiritual, moral, and aesthetic sense.

Listen to this parable. Once upon a time, a young Chinese lad went to the Master's house because he wanted to learn how to make jade into beautiful objects. So he knocked on the door and told the Master that he came to sit humbly at his feet and learn. So the Master took a piece of jade, put it into the boy's hands, and then just sat there. He went on to chatter about his wife, his children, his job, and things like that. All the while the boy is sitting there, minute after minute, hour after hour, holding the jade. The next day the lad came back and the same thing happened. The Master put a piece of jade into the boy's hand, and then once again began to chatter about all sorts of things. The boy was starting to get agitated but he was too embarrassed, too hesitant, to say anything. And so this routine happened day after day, week after week until one day when the boy came as usual, the Master put a stone into his hand. "Hey!" the boy cried out, "This is a stone!"

He had learned the feel of jade.

Get it? All right, if you're not sure, let's turn the story on its head. Once upon a time, a young Chinese lad went to the Master's house because he wanted to learn how to make jade into beautiful objects. So he knocked on the door and told the Master that he came to sit humbly at his feet and learn. So the Master took a stone and put it in the boy's hand and then just sat there. He went on to chatter about his wife, his children, his job, and things like that. All the while the boy is sitting there, minute after minute, hour after hour, holding the stone. The next day the lad came back and the same thing happened. The boy was starting to get agitated, but he was too embarrassed, too hesitant, to say anything. And so this routine happened day after day, week after week, until one day, when the boy came as usual, the Master put a piece of jade into his hand.

"Hey!" the boy cried out, "What this?" And he quickly dropped it and the jade broke all over the floor.

The meaning of the story is clear: If we keep holding and cherishing something valuable and beautiful, we'll eventually get a feel for it, and therefore we will recognize the banal and the counterfeit when we see it. By the same token, if we keep on holding something shallow in our hands and hearts—the trivialities of our culture—when something genuine and beautiful comes along, we won't recognize it, and we will destroy it.

If, in other words, we keep on filling our minds and hearts with *Nip/Tuck* and *Jersey Shore* and Howard Stern and celebrities and bad art and slasher movies and soft- and hard-core porn, books and magazines that don't have a calorie of wisdom in them, we won't recognize virtue, truth, and real beauty when we see them, and we will become humanly and spiritually diminished, the mindless crowd, the consumer.

This, friends, is why we have Lent. We need time apart to take stock, to learn the feel of jade once more.

60. iPod and I, God

As we end our series, let us say an overdue word about the wonderful benefits of our electronic gadgets. One special one that quickly comes to mind is how grandparents and grandkids connect these days. Once when kids went off to college they saw seldom saw their grandparents, or when families moved, as so often they did, young grandchildren and grandparents lost connections. Now with technology they're reconnecting as never before. One website, readeo.com, lets Grandma in Maine read a bedtime story to her grandkids in California. As one grandparent said, "Nothing will replace a hug, but this is as close as it gets." Families can even celebrate virtual Christmases or birthdays. And there's scientific research, the ability to respond to emergencies, politics, such things as the Arab revolutions, all fueled by cell phones. Even parishes in which they tell you to "Please silence your cell phone and other electronic devices" before Mass can use it to advantage. One parish, for example, told their parishioners to turn on their cell phones and to text-message basic information, and within minutes hundreds of people had electronically registered with their parish. The Church has been very positive about the new technologies, pointing to the many blessings from the new electronic age, and we're grateful for them.

At the same time, the virtues of our electronic world also create a new set of serious social vices, such as targeted ads, the loss of privacy, tracking, hacking, stalking, bullying, and the Internet's first and most enduring success, the phenomenal $13.2 billion pornography industry. Anyway, that brings us to the summary point of this series: our over-busy, overstuffed lives preclude the growth and development of faith, hope, and love. The sheer saturation of our devices, commercials, entertainment, and general noise presses us into 16- and 17-hour workdays, locks us into our gadgets, and hectors us to shop till we drop. All those odd "spaces" in between focused activities that we used to call idle time, relaxation, daydreaming, or just "goofing off" are now invaded by faxes, cell phones, and emails. The phone, the Blackberry, and the iPad come with us to the garden, onto the porch, into the bathroom, in our cars.

Some cars have become mobile offices. We have arrived at the point where we can stay plugged in 24 hours a day. And many do. We're addicted to busyness; and busyness, by definition, is the enemy of the interior life. Neuroscientists also note a distinct loss of focus. They say our ability to focus is being undermined by bursts of information. Heavy multitaskers, especially, have trouble focusing and shutting out irrelevant information, and they experience more stress. They say technology is rewiring our brains as impatience, forgetfulness, and distraction take their toll on spouses and children.

I think of the article in *The New York Times* citing studies of children's frustration because their parents are on the cell phone and they can't get their attention. The subheadline was "Mommy, put down the cell phone and talk to me!" Studies also show that children of heavy cell phone users have a far smaller vocabulary and weaker verbal skills than those whose parents don't use them excessively.

In the March/April 2010 issue of *AARP* magazine—for you young ones, it's a magazine for senior citizens—among the ads for hearing aids and vitamins, there was an article by a man named David Dudley, who writes:

On a sparkling Sunday afternoon recently, I found myself in our local Baltimore park, sitting on a blanket with my 5-year-old daughter, consumed by an e-mail that appeared on my brand-new iPhone—a legitimately important communication from my employer that demanded a timely response. She chattered on (my daughter, that is, not my boss) about peanut butter and birds and how to sing 'This Land is Your Land' while I tapped out my reply. Hitting "send" I felt a flash of satisfaction—that's one less e-mail to deal with tomorrow morning—and plowed back into my box looking for more chores to dispatch. Then I blinked up to see all the other silently staring parents, slumped on benches or standing around, buried in the screens of their own smart phones. The kids ignored them; they ignored the kids; the birds sang, and the sun shone, and that flush faded into something closer to a chill.

Thus it is across America; he described it well: clever devices have replaced or diminished people, fractured community, and constricted our moral and aesthetic world. Another author describes the situation this way: "We have all these invisible walls built by iPods and cell phones." That is to say, we live less and less face-to-face. As one psychiatrist puts it, we have, simultaneously, connection and isolation.

What's the attraction of such busyness? For one thing it gives us a certain "kick," a rush of adrenaline, when we swing into action or race the clock even if what we're chasing doesn't matter much. It's the challenge. Second, it makes us feel important. "I'm so busy," we complain tiredly, all the while knowing that's the way we want it, all the while looking for the affirmation "but what would we do without you?" We're productive, a quality much prized in America regardless of what we're producing. We are efficient. In fact, we're so good at being busy that we can't say no to more busy things.

Third, all this activity is reinforced by the culture that prizes busyness and rewards quantity not quality. We can't afford to stop. Besides, some people actually get antsy and restless if they try to slow down. Unfilled time fills them with anxiety, not to mention guilt. After all, the ever-replenishing to-do list needs attention. Fourth, and perhaps more spiritually sinister, something we mentioned before: busyness doesn't allow us to be affected by the pain and suffering of our world. We're too distracted.

There we are. What I propose to counteract all this over-activity is simple. It's the ancient wisdom. It is that silence, a little reflective time, would help us get our priorities right. Silence is a time-honored practice of all the great religious movements, including Jesus—who often withdrew from the crowds and spent the whole night in prayer—and the first Christians who followed suit.

Remember Jesus cautioning Martha, who complained about her sister's silent attentiveness to Jesus: "Martha, Martha, you are anxious and troubled about many things: one thing is needful. Mary has chosen the good portion and it shall not be taken away from her" (Luke 10:38). Think of St. Anthony and St. Benedict, who took themselves to the desert where they lived simply and made time for God, and who gave us monasticism, a place and a condition where one could find the time for prayer and where times of silence could be honored and encouraged.

Think of the prophet Elijah at a cave on Mt. Horeb and the Lord passing by: "The Lord said, Go out and stand on the mountain before the Lord, for the Lord is about to pass by. Now there was a great wind, so strong that it was splitting mountains and breaking rocks in pieces before the Lord, but the Lord was not in the wind; and after the wind an earthquake, but the Lord was not in the earthquake; and after the earthquake, fire, but the Lord was not in the fire; and after the fire, a sound of sheer silence. When Elijah heard that, he wrapped his face in his mantle and stood at the entrance of the cave" (1 Kings, 19:1–12). That's where God was.

Think of Henry Thoreau in the famous passage from Walden: "I went to the woods because I wished to live deliberately, to [con]front only the essential facts of life, and to see if I could not learn what it had to teach, and not, when I came to die, discover that I had not lived." Think of his other famous saying, "Most men live lives of quiet desperation." Only today he might revise it by saying that most people live lives of hectic desperation.

Yes, without silence we cannot live, much less grow. Plants, animals, and children need fallow time to put down roots. That so many people are shallow and rootless today testifies that we have neglected this simple truth. Without silence we are at the mercy of the hawker, the demagogue, the peddlers of empty promises, and the widely seductive and dangerous power of group-think.

Reaction is setting in. More and more people are seeking "black-hole" resorts that do not have television or wi-fi. More people are trying to flee the electronic world and get some down time. They buy what is called Freedom software that enables them to disable, for up to eight hours, connections that seemed so emancipating not long ago. There are Internet rescue camps in South Korea and China that try to save kids addicted to the screen. With the average American spending at least eight-and-a-half hours a day in front of a screen and the average American teenager sending or receiving 75 text messages a day, there is an urgent need to slow down. Marshall McLuhan had it right half a century ago when he warned, "When things come at you very fast, naturally you lose touch with yourself." And we have lost touch.

And our creativity. Jonah Lehrer, a neuroscientist, says that our brains often need to become inattentive to figure out complex issues, and we need to daydream and let the mind wander. He says, "There is an importance to being able to put it [the computer] aside and let those daydreams naturally perform the cognitive functions your brain needs." A professor of psychology adds, "daydreaming and boredom seem to be a source for incubation and creative discovery in the brain and are a part of the creative incubation process."

The need for silence is deep, even though the culture discourages it. The fact is, we can't find silence in our gadget-filled, commercial-loaded world. We need to find it in a separate space if we have a mind to. Such as: we can pray daily and even create or join prayer groups. We can meet once a month for quiet prayer and reflection. We can learn how to pray the Divine Office—it's the time-honored prayer of the whole Church—and there are simple editions that one can use to pray twice a day for a short time.

We can schedule in days of recollection and a retreat with the same fierce determination and foresight with which we plan our vacations. We can if we have a mind to. Some of you, even now, are making summer and fall plans. Why not plans that include a retreat? There's even retreats for entire families. Your pastor can provide some suggestions in the bulletin. We can use car tapes or CDs—this is not the distraction of the cell phone or monitor screen. This is more like background music. There are many splendid tapes and CDs that nurture the spiritual life.

Finally, one effective traditional Lenten antidote for all this over-busyness and clutter, one way to turn down the noise and shut off the commercials for a while, is spiritual reading. Reading the gospels meditatively or some good spiritual book for ten or fifteen minutes or a half-hour a day, will go a long way to giving you a renewed sense of self.

Ask your pastor to recommend some good spiritual books or, even better, ask him if he could put a short list of suggestions in the bulletin. These books lift us above what's being said and introduce us to things that aren't often said. They take us gently down the road less traveled. They re-introduce us to Jesus Christ and the saint-in-the-making we are called to be, and, after all, isn't that what Lent is all about?

In short, we need a deliberate alternate world to take the edge off the unreflective life that has become habit, and which, as Socrates said long ago, is not worth living. We have to pull back from the ubiquitous and spiritually deadening consumption and mass homogenization of advertising that makes us all dress, think, and live alike. We need to reclaim our humanity, our relationships, our spiritual life.

Remember David Dudley at the beginning of this homily, how his busyness in the park made him blind to his daughter, the birds, the sky, others? He's lucky. He had an "aha!" moment of insight into what he was missing. Taking time apart can bring us that "aha!" moment too. We also might rediscover beautiful people, beautiful things, and—not the least of which—who we are and who God is.

61. Fatal Attraction

MARK 1:1–21

The Internet has brought many blessings, but pornography is decidedly not among them. Already widespread in print, movies, and videos, the Internet is a natural venue for pornography. Three factors make it so. First, there is the belief that the user remains anonymous. No one will know you're accessing it. Which, of course, is absolutely untrue. Every time you turn on the computer you are tracked electronically. Second, pornography is available 24 hours a day, 7 days a week—anywhere where there is an Internet connection. Third, there is its affordability. Many Internet pornography sites are free. So, with the coming of the Internet, pornography has enormously expanded its presence to all countries and all ages at all times. Internet pornography is, depending on how you look at it, the world's most profitable business or the world's biggest epidemic.

Thus, in 2006 the pornography industry was estimated to earn annually 97 billion dollars worldwide. To put that in perspective, these revenues are larger than those of Microsoft, Google, Amazon, eBay, Apple, Netflix, and Earthlink combined. Here in the United States the pornography business earns annually from 11 to 15 billion dollars. That's billions. There are 430 million pornographic web pages, of which 89% are based in the U.S. Forty million adults visit pornographic websites regularly. A 2008 study of undergraduate and graduate students found that more than two thirds of the men and one out of every ten women viewed pornography more than once a month. Studies show that 90% of 8- to 16-year-olds have viewed porn online and that children ages 12-17 are the largest consumers of online pornography.

Gail Dines, in her book *Pornland,* cites market research suggesting that

270

the average age a boy first sees porn is 11; one-third of 13-year-old boys admitted to viewing porn; a third of 14-16-year-olds have first seen sexual images when they were 10 or younger. Often, because it's so pervasive, kids stumble on it by accident. They may not even be looking for it. It can pop up on an ad. Some researchers say two to three children out of five are approached on the Internet with some kind of sexual proposition. Child porn thrives, and the FBI made more than 10,000 arrests between 1996 and 2010 of those who make and distribute it; the numbers are growing.

Porn spills over to the workplace. In July of 2010, the U.S. House of Representatives voted to block pornography from government computers after a series of embarrassing incidents in which Securities and Exchange Commission workers were caught spending hours at work looking at pornography. (No wonder they have no time to check on Wall Street.) On July 23 of that year *The Boston Globe* revealed that a child pornography investigation has exposed offenders in the Pentagon, including the National Security Agency.

So porn is a big elephant, and, statistically, it means that the problem is deeply among us, part of our lives. But people say, so what? It's a private thing. Big deal. No harm is done. What's the problem? Let's answer those questions

The problem is that pornography is not a private matter. It has serious social and spiritual fallouts. Let's look at the data. Studies and surveys show that, due to pornography, many marriages are lost or in tatters; sexual addictions multiply; there is the constant slide, on account of higher tolerance, into ever edgier kinds of porn; and children and teenagers are lured into participating in it in various ways. Three separate studies, for example, have found that among teenagers a strong correlation exists between pornography consumption and engaging in various sexual activities. They are far more likely to test positive for sexual diseases.

As for marriage, let's note that 62% of the lawyers who are members of The American Academy of Matrimonial Lawyers say that the Internet plays a distinct role in divorce. Other social scientists cite the negative impact on other aspects of marriage; for example, among individuals who have been married, those who say they've seen X-rated movies in the past year are 25 percent more likely to be divorced and 13 percent less likely to identify themselves as "very happy" with life in general. Porn, as someone said, is the quiet family killer. Trust is porn's biggest casualty.

A popular online blog called "Getting Serious About Pornography" has a woman deploring porn for the role it played in the destruction of her marriage. Her blog elicited this response from a military man:

> I absolutely agree it's damaging. It damages my respect for my wife, and she has done nothing to deserve that damage. It damages my self-esteem and respect for myself because I know it's not helpful to our life, to our marriage, to our love. It reduces my satisfaction in a wonderful woman. It makes me yearn for things I should not want. It is disruptive of my inner peace. I don't like myself when I'm looking at porn. I don't like the way I feel about myself when I am looking at porn...But I can only do without it for about six months...It's been an endless cycle.

Yes, that's the other thing about porn: it is highly addictive, and neuroscientists are beginning to map the biological basis for it. Doctors treating men for porn addictions find it a common refrain that men are no longer able to relate to their wives. One doctor writes: "Pornographers promise healthy pleasure and relief from sexual tension, but what they often deliver is an addiction...and an eventual decrease in pleasure. Paradoxically, the male patients I worked with often craved pornography but didn't like it." Peter Kleponis, a psychologist, says, "Every day I talk to people who are struggling with this addiction."

Porn users require more and more hardcore stuff to get the same kick. Sooner or later they begin to look at things they once considered appalling, like child pornography and torture, but even though they know it's wrong, they can't help themselves. That's addiction.

In addition to degrading women, porn harms guys. Pamela Paul, a reporter for *Time* magazine and the author of *Pornified: How Pornography is Transforming our Lives, Our Relationships and our Families,* writes: "Countless men have described to me how, while using pornography, they have lost the ability to relate to or be close to women. They have trouble being turned on by 'real' women, and their sex lives with their girlfriends or wives collapse." They also have a tendency to see women as commodities or sex objects. When your teenage daughter walks down the beach and, of the guys looking at her, half have been watching sex on the Internet in the past few days and half have not, which ones do you want watching her?

Finally, people say, it's only pictures of consenting adults. But, of course, porn is never just about pictures. Every single person is someone's daughter, sister, cousin, son, or mother. They are diminished by what they do. They are not persons. They are paid mannequins divorced from real relationships. Nor should we forget the connection between pornography and prostitution, and pornography and the sordid sex trafficking that plagues the world. And then we must ask, why are so many daughters "sexting," or putting themselves exposed on Facebook? Where does that come from but from a culture saturated with pornography?

So pornography is not a victimless crime, as people like to say. Broken marriages, the inability to love, the commodification of women, and serious addiction are some of its fallouts. Did I mention that child sex offenders are more likely to view pornography regularly and be involved in its distribution? Yet, each year, with the help of the media, the culture lowers the moral bar or, as we say, pushes the envelope further and further, as we get headlines like "Super Bowl Ads Get Racier" and the Supreme Court wrestles with the "freedom of speech" issue of whether nudity and cursing are permitted on public television.

People caught up in pornography need help. The good news is that treatment of pornography addiction is effective and accessible. There are social support, 12-step groups like Sexaholics Anonymous or Sexual Compulsives Anonymous that offer peer group help. There is a website with links listed in our Sunday bulletin that will provide good resources for help [www.flrl.org/TrueFreedom.htm]. Check it out. Finally, as you would and should expect, a deeper spiritual life and a good spiritual director can help one move toward a more mature sense of who she or she is. As in today's gospel, some demons can only be expelled by Jesus.

Pornography flourishes in a world that has lost its center in God and so has lost the true notion of love, of the beauty and meaning of human relationships. We pray at this Mass for healing that mends hearts and minds and offers a better vision of life.

62. Confession and Community

The sacrament of confession has gone the way of Catholic weddings, ordinations, and church attendance. Statistically they have bottomed out. Those long confessional lines of my early priesthood have long since dwindled. In a culture where therapeutic categories have replaced the seven capital sins— "I steal because my mother smoked pot," or "the kids picked on me" sort of thing—a sense of sin and conscience has evaporated. There is no need to confess a faulty gene, and how can it be wrong if Snooki does it and gets paid a lot for doing it? Yes, John Newton lost his chance when he sang of "Amazing Grace," that gracious grace of Jesus that saved a wretch like him from his terrible sins. He could have had fame and a mini-series instead.

Yet sin in its original biblical meaning of "missing the mark" seems the only adequate word for what Sergeant Clyde Lobdill wrote at the liberation of the Nazi concentration camps: "We arrived at Dachau 29 April at about 1200. There were thirty-nine boxcars on the railroad siding next to the camp so we checked them out. They were loaded with the naked corpses of men. These men had all starved to death. The guards didn't have time to cremate them before we arrived. They were stacked, five and six deep, in the box cars. The bodies had gray-colored skin stretched over their bones. The faces of the top bodies on the piles were the shape of a skull. Their mouths were open as if they were gasping for air. Their eyes were open and had a look of despair. They appeared to be looking for someone to come to their help; but no one came...."

Somehow "naughty" or "bad karma" or "bad parenting" or "indigestion" or "poverty" alone don't seem to cover the evil of the Holocaust, the genocide of Rwanda, the routine bombings and beheadings we read about every day, human trafficking, the degradation of the planet, the torture of children, and daily betrayals that fracture families and foreclose households. Sin seems the only adequate word to suggest a deep and penetrating offense against God's creatures and against what God has in mind for the family he begot.

So much of the problem, of course, is precisely that: We have lost the sense of being a global family, a united people, a tribe deeply and intractably connected and whose actions, therefore, like an earthquake in Japan, can affect the entire globe. Our pathological individualism—the world revolves around me; profit at any cost; if I think it's right, it's all right—undermines any sense of solidarity and therefore of sin. We are no longer aware that sin, while at times it may be secret, is never private. Sin is always communal. I repeat: sin is always communal.

And that concept is as hard for us to grasp as it was normal for our ancestors to understand. Because it is, let me give you a homely example of communal sin thought to be private. I go to Walmart, and because I want something and don't have the money (or even if I do), I steal it. Why not? Everybody does it. I didn't harm anybody, and besides, Walmart is rich, and they'll never miss what I took. But think: Walmart, like Target and Sears and all the rest, are in business to make money. That's a no-brainer. Therefore, when customers and employees steal from them and eat into their profits, what do they do to compensate? They do what you would do. They raise prices. So every time you and I shop, each one of us is unknowingly paying higher prices to cover someone's so-called "private" thefts.

The fact is, if nobody stole, prices would be nearly half of what they are. We all pay for evil. The shameful, secret manipulations of the Wall Street meltdown have, I need not tell you, deeply wounded this entire country. What Bernie Madoff did in secret affected thousands of lives.

But what about what people do in their bedroom? That is personal and private. Personal, maybe, but what people do anywhere is never private. The public assistance to young unwed mothers, for example, costs every citizen in this county almost $500 annually. The massive aborting of female babies in China has produced an unbalanced and dysfunctional society. Massive contraceptive and abortion practices have left Europe way below replacement level—think Italy, Spain, France, Germany, and so on—leaving the way for Muslims and others to take up the labor slack. That has public ramifications.

Yes, sins, like the fluttering of a butterfly in Korea that is felt in California, are never private. They affect the public, the entire human race, the community. What wrong we do has public consequences, as does the right we do.

And that truth brings us to the biblically minded Catholic practice of confession, a practice based squarely on the belief that we are all united. You heard the gospel. Jesus cures the leper and then he gives, what seems to us, a strange directive. "Go and show yourself to the priest so that he may certify the cure." In our way of thinking, why should the leper go to the priest? He was cured, and so he should go home and tell his wife. Why waste the priest's time?

The answer is that, because leprosy was thought to be contagious, lepers were ostracized, excommunicated, severed from a frightened community. To be cut off from community was the worst penalty of all in a society deeply grounded in family and tribal ties. But now that the leper had been cured and was able to reenter community, he had to let everybody know. He wanted to be restored. But since he couldn't go to every citizen in the land to show himself—he'd die of old age before he finished the rounds—he went to the community's official representative: in this case, the priest. The priest didn't cure him, of course—he was already cured—but in his official capacity as the people's spokesman, on behalf of the people, the priest pronounced him officially clean and fit to be restored to the community, which rejoiced at his return. The community was made whole again.

The same thing happens civilly. To return to our example, the thief, to make amends, must apologize to all the Walmart or Sears customers, but since that is impossible, he meets with a representative of the people he has betrayed, the one we call the district attorney. Notice the official court announcement of the charge: "The People of New Jersey versus John Doe." Yes, the people, all the citizens, have been violated and penalized by this so-called private theft, and the district attorney is their representative, their priest if you will, the mediator of reconciliation.

So it is with confession. The process has nothing to do with the priest's worthiness or intelligence—for which you should be grateful. The priest doesn't forgive you your sins. Only God does that. But he, as the community representative, as representative of the whole Church, certifies your spiritual cure and, on behalf of the people, celebrates your return. You "went to confession," or, in today's politically correct phrase, you celebrated the sacrament of reconciliation, remembering now that that reconciliation was not only with God but, through its representative, the priest, with God's people, whom we have wounded with our sin.

Bottom line: confession is about sin and repentance and how they relate to God and the community. It's not about me. It's about us. It's not about my healing. It's about community healing. In any case, embracing the concept of the Mystical Body, the Communion of Saints, the solidarity of the human race is the first step to a mature spirituality.

This concept, I admit, is hard to realize because the system we have today is such a secretive affair: sneaking into a quiet church on a Saturday afternoon and anonymously whispering our sins in a dark box. That's relatively new. How confession moved from a very public community affair to this private encounter is the topic of next week's homily.

63. A Brief History of Confession

Some years ago I was helping out in a parish that recently had had a series of teachings on confession and I was pleasantly taken aback to hear some of the openings when people came to confession. Here are some I recall:

"Rejoice with me, Father, I wish to rejoin the People of God."

"Congratulate me, Father, for I want to be reconciled with the people I've hurt."

"Bless me, Father, for I want to be restored to God's family."

"Father, I am here to confess my sins to the entire Church."

"Celebrate with me, Father. I am here to acknowledge my sinfulness and my need for Christ my savior."

These words may sound stilted to us but these people were at least trying to bring the ancient sensitivity to the demands of community to the private confessional box.

That we saw last week. This week, we take a quick thumbnail sketch of the history of confession. As we go back over the record of confession in Church history, we find a very mixed bag. For example, we find that there is no explicit reference to any kind of confessional format as we know it before the third or fourth centuries. This is not entirely to be wondered at. These were the beginnings of Christianity and the era of persecutions, and people had other things to think and write about. It seems that sin and

278

repentance were simply accepted as a normal part of the average Christian life and needed no special reference. Yet, even if the details are lacking, the literature of the time shows that the Church was aware of its power to forgive sin, no matter how grave, as long as the person genuinely wanted to return to Christ and the Church community.

With the third and fourth centuries came certain heresies, and these provoked more precision on doctrine and practice, including that of sin and forgiveness. One development has perplexed historians, the issue of "unicity." It means "only once," which in turn meant that the Church at one time had the practice of forgiving certain sins—three of them to be precise—only once. Commit them again and you're through. No second chance.

Now, of course, you want to know what those three are. The first was not contributing to the support of your pastor. No, I'm kidding. Actually the three were centered, not surprisingly, on how badly they fractured community. Church leaders asked, "What did the most harm and gave the most scandal? The answer: apostasy—denying publicly the faith; adultery—it fractured the community by fracturing its basic unit; and murder. These three made people take notice and comment, "Well, if that's the way Christians live, forget it!"

So once a person committed any of these sins, confessed, and did penance for them, there was no second chance for reconciliation if they fell again. Now, this wasn't a doctrine—after all, Jesus said forgive 70 x 7—but a discipline. And a harsh one. Church leaders should have foreseen what actually happened: People cunningly postponed penance until near death.

Furthermore, in the fourth and fifth centuries—again with their stress on community—the Church leaders invented official, canonical, public confession. This meant that the process toward forgiveness was a public, community affair. The sin was publicly acknowledged. Penance, long and arduous, was public. People publicly prayed for these penitents and took part in the public reconciliation. Again, in actual practice, because it was so rigorous and so prolonged, only a small number of penitents took part in it. Most, again, waited till they were sure they were near death. Clearly the system needed improvement.

It came, surreptitiously, with the Irish monks in the seventh and eighth centuries. Christianity first came to Ireland in its monastic form. There were no large cities and so no bishops and no dioceses. But there were in due time hundreds of monasteries, with the abbot and his monks as the center and definers of religious life. It was a close, paternal, almost family relationship. Gradually the more pious Irish would seek out the monks for advice and guidance on daily matters—remember, monks, except for those ordained to celebrate Mass, are laymen living in community. Many times in these encounters, issues of the spiritual life would naturally arise and incited what we might call spiritual direction. In the course of such direction the issues of spiritual progress or regress, sin and virtue, came up, and the client and the monk would discuss them, with the monk ending up giving advice, and an assurance of God's mercy, forgiveness, and a blessing.

It wasn't long before this process between monk and client transmuted into an exclusive focus on virtue, sin, sorrow, and repentance. In a word, monk and client gradually evolved into that of confessor and penitent. At that moment, confession, private confession, as we know it, was born. Moreover—and this was a plus—unlike the old, canonical, public, one-time system, this private, one-on-one system could be repeated over and over again. Eventually the Irish monks, on their great missionary journeys, brought this new private form of confession to Europe, where Church leaders resisted and forbade it; but it became so popular they finally gave in.

Soon there developed the Penitentials, books containing the sin on one side and a fitting penance on the other. It wasn't three Our Fathers and three Hail Marys. The penance might be the donation of five sheep, a pilgrimage of some two or three years, clearing land, or a year's free labor, depending on the severity of the sin. The monks were tough, but the change had been made. Private confession was here to stay.

The post-Reformation sixteenth century added some much needed clarity and, also, unfortunately, a more restricted legalistic approach, as it bequeathed to us four precise steps to a good confession, steps that Catholics here from another age will remember—I should offer a prize for anyone who gets it right. Ready? Examine your conscience, be sorry for your sins, confess your sins (number and circumstance) to the priest, and be willing to do the penance the priest gives you.

This was helpful, but there were serious drawbacks. The extreme focus on sin, especially what was considered sexual sin—you know, "I had impure thoughts," when they were only normal sexual thoughts—the sharp legalistic approach that made the goal of confession not a personal encounter with the Jesus of the gospel but the verdict of the confessor or the textbook, which meant in turn getting absolution by hook or crook—one sought out the priest who was deaf, senile, or foreign, and if he was all three, you drew a winner—the promotion of a state of perpetual guilt (greatly enjoyed by the Irish), and, most serious of all, the loss of that communal sense that Jesus enjoined when he told us to go to the community's priestly representative.

These are the pluses and minuses of history.

Well, Vatican II came along in the 1960s and tried to recapture the best of the past and made more changes. Unfortunately it was not in time to counter the cultural upheavals of the '60s and '70s, the decline of a sense of sin, the rise of an almost pathological individualism, and the exodus of many of its members.

And today? Well, today, says the modern Vatican, when going to confession, have your iPhone ready. Really? More on that next week.

64. An Apt Confession App

Like most people, we prefer to forget our failures and sins. Who wants to be like Charlie Brown, who's always reminded of his shortcomings, especially by loudmouth Lucy? It doesn't make for a happy life. But what if, without wallowing in guilt, we did in fact keep a record of them, tracking the habitual ones and getting real about where we are most vulnerable, checking on the sins that keep us from being all we are meant to be? Well, today, as we say, there's an app or application, for that, and the Catholic Church has claimed it. It's called the confession application or confession app, for short.

Yes, as you may have read, someone, with Church approval, has come up with a confession app or an application for smart phones. You download the app, register and log in, click on your status—married, single, nun, priest—and your preferred act of contrition. Before you know it, the screen pops up with a customized examination of conscience. For example, if you sign up as a married person, your examination is divided into issues of responsibilities to your family, the workplace, society, and so on. Tap one of those areas, and you're given a list of possible sins that allows you to check off the ones you've committed.

You then take your iPhone or iPad into confession (the app gives you the prayers to say) and then you confess your sins. You can then tap on "prayers" and choose your act of contrition. The Church insists that this is a tool to help you and that you must confess to a real priest. There is no confession via iPhone. There must be a personal encounter between person and person or at least between a person with an iPhone and the priest. The confession app is simply an aid.

As in the old devotional books, so it is in the app: the general guide or standard for one's examination of conscience in preparing for confession is the Ten Commandments. The app needs to show them on the screen, because the reality is that most people today don't know them. They can't name them all. Surveys show that while 35 percent of Americans can recall all six Brady Bunch kids and 25 percent could name all seven ingredients of the Big Mac, only 14 percent could accurately name all 10 Commandments.

"Thou shall not kill" and "Thou shall not steal" are the two that are always remembered. The rest, not so much. That's where the digital app comes in. The 10 Commandments are right there before you to check out.

The first three Commandments are about our faithfulness to God. At the root of all our sins is that first commandment concerning idolatry: setting ourselves up as the center of the universe, worshiping our computers, our adored celebrities, our brand names and cars, our status. These are the gods we worship. They dictate and hold up a mirror to ourselves and our priorities. Recall the story of the stockbroker. As he got out of his BMW, a speeding car slams into the door shearing it off. When the police arrive, the stockbroker is apoplectic.

"See, what that idiot did to my beautiful car?" he shouts, "Do you know what this car costs?"

"Sir," says the officer, "you're so worried about your car that you haven't even noticed that your left arm was ripped off."

The stockbroker takes a look at where his arm once was and screams, "Where's my Rolex?"

That's idolatry.

Using God's name as a swear word, and making every day a consuming day with no day special to God and God's works show how far we have strayed.

The other seven commandments concern our relationships with one another and how to live honestly in community. Violating them by individualism, disrespect, stealing, betraying, jealousy, lying, committing adultery, bullying, or murdering fractures community and sows the seeds of distrust, anger, and revenge; and no community can long survive those. The

Commandments are a good checklist.

As are the seven capital sins. Anyone remember them? Pride, greed, lust, gluttony, anger, envy, and sloth. Pride and greed are all around us, so much so that they make movies about them. They are, of course, behind so much of our current grief caused by the Wall Street meltdown and outsized paychecks. Gluttony is another popular sin that we live with every day. Why else would some restaurants serve up enormous outsized portions and obesity be a major national problem?

One food chain defends its practice, "We find that when people dine out, they want every calorie they pay for." Why are we not surprised to find that there is a Kentucky Fried Chicken stand just a hop from the 4,500-year-old Sphinx in Egypt? Deep down, as one perceptive writer put it, "a glutton is one who raids the icebox for a cure for spiritual malnutrition."

Lust is everywhere, and pornography is its banner. According to statistics, every second—every second, mind you—over three million dollars is being spent on it. Every second some 29 thousand are viewing pornography, and every second 372 Internet users are searching for it. The pornography business has bigger revenues than Microsoft, Google, Amazon, eBay, Yahoo, Apple, and Netflix combined. That's lust, and it's hiding the profound spiritual emptiness of our times. Someone wisely said, "Lust is the craving for salt of a man who is dying of thirst." That is to say, a yearning for fulfillment that is misdirected.

So it goes with anger and the rest. They are sins to check, to bring to Jesus for healing.

So, to summarize, as someone has put it, the whole confessional process revolves around the "three Rs":

Regret—This includes empathy towards the other person, trying to understand the pain or hurt we caused them, how we have fractured community.

Responsibility—not blaming anyone else, making excuses or, like the politicians caught in evil, using, as one crooked governor did, the passive voice: "Mistakes were made." Not, "I made mistakes. I take the blame." No some mysterious force did this. Not me.

Remedy—what we would call a firm purpose of amendment, not repeating the sin, making restitution.

For some, this process of checking the app on your smart phone or other lists to test your moral progress smacks of an undue focus on guilt. For others, it's what our long Catholic tradition calls an "Examen of conscience," a process that people who want to grow in faith, hope, and love use, much the same way dieters keep a record of their weight loss progress—or regress, as the case may be—or people like me with high blood pressure check it frequently to keep tabs on our health.

In any case, the Examen of conscience is a time-honored program practiced by the saints, and that's enough of a recommendation to make us look at it next week.

65. The Examen

The feast of St. Joseph this past week reminds me of the story about the time Jesus was walking by the Pearly Gates when St. Peter asked him to watch the gates a few minutes. Jesus agreed and very shortly he saw an old man approach. He walked very slowly, and had a halting gait and long white hair and a beard.

"How did you spend your life on earth, my son?" asked Jesus.

"I was a simple carpenter for sixty years," replied the old man.

"And what do you hope to find here in heaven?" asked Jesus.

"I hope to find my son," said the man.

"Well, there are millions upon millions of people here, how will you find him?"

"I'll recognize him by the nail holes in his hands and feet," said the man.

Jesus did a double take, thoughts for a moment, and said, "Father?"

The old man looked at Jesus and said, "Pinocchio?"

Not quite what we expected, was it? But the story segues us into the notion that we all hope to find something, and, within the context of our series, that something is "how do we stand?" How do we stand at work, with our friends, in popularity, in the pecking order, in health, and so on. Only our question is, "How do we stand with God?"

One of the time-honored ways to answer this question is what is traditionally called the "Examen of Conscience." That phrase is a bit inaccurate, because what it really means is an "Examination of Consciousness," which is to say, a seeking of ways to discern or be conscious of God in our lives.

Anyway, this Examen, as we'll continue to call it, has developed a certain routine, certain steps. They have been around a long time but it's the Jesuits who perfected them. There are five of these steps, usually done in the evening. It's a discipline; and right away, I warn you, there's the problem of distraction. Social scientists have shown how addicted we are to our digital gadgets, and that one of the sorriest casualties of this addiction is lack of sustained attention to serious matters.

In our Pavlovian response to every beep and ring, we never explore anything in depth. Say something triggers a thought, an invitation to ruminate, a notion or experience to explore, to ponder, to think it through, to savor and enjoy. We're momentarily enticed. The allure is there. We pause, but then we decide that we don't have time for any of this to happen. Why? Because like the alcoholic or drug addict, we feel the compulsion to access our cell phones, check our email, and answer our messages, and so the noble urge to go deeper, the wonder moment, if you will, fades away, and we continue to skim the surface and live off sound bites and surface glitz. The result is that we have become a shallow and therefore an easily manipulated people. And it shows in our harried, shallow lives.

Processes like the Examen demand quiet time and are an antidote to shallowness; for it is, as I said, a discipline and does require us to disconnect from the consumerist world. It requires solitude, being digitally disconnected. Think of the Examen as a spiritual evaluation. Just as professionals and workers are periodically evaluated to determine competency, progress, or lack thereof, so the Christian pilgrim needs the same scrutiny, needs to look at his or her life on a larger canvas. Just as AA or support groups are encouraging personal inventories for noting success or failures, so the person serious about growing spiritually needs the mentoring of the Examen for the same reason.

So let us consider the first step of the Examen, one that may surprise you. It is gratitude. Here you recall the good things that happened to you during the day. Yes, the day may have been a mess but maybe during the day there has also been a tender moment—a bird flew by, sunlight poked through the window, the sandwich you had for lunch, work completed. Think of these. Turn them around. Such savoring slows us down as we pause to enjoy what has happened and take note of the hidden joys. Noticed gratitude is the first step to noticing God.

The second step is asking for the grace to know our sins, to see where we have turned away from God during the day, been less than we should have been. We ignored someone, shot off the sarcastic remark, cheated a bit. Sometimes our failure is as simple and hurtful as failing to bother. I could have held open the door, helped a friend, phoned a sick relative, but didn't. Why? This part of the Examen is not designed to make us feel guilty—we've had enough of that—but designed to make us become more sensitive, more loving. By asking such questions we are making ourselves see our need for God. This step's goal is not to condemn ourselves for our human weaknesses but to challenge us for the strengths we failed to use. And that's a different matter.

The third step is to review your day over all. It's rewind and playback time. You think you know what happened today, but go over it. You may have missed something: a passing joy, a sight, a pleasing sound, someone who crossed your path. Doing this regularly will in fact unearth new facets of your day. Like the detective looking at the video the hundredth time you might spot something you missed before.

The fourth step is asking for forgiveness, the idea being role-playing the Prodigal Son, knowing the Father's love, compassion, and mercy, emphasizing not how bad I am but how good God is.

The fifth and final step is asking for the grace of God's help for tomorrow. It's another day. Then you close with a prayer.

These five steps gradually make a difference in one's life. These five steps of gratitude, knowing one's sins, reviewing your day, asking for forgiveness, and petitioning for help for the next day don't have to take long—20 minutes, a half-hour—and you can vary the steps; but done routinely, this Examen of Conscience is an excellent tool for spiritual growth.

It is important, and you must be loyal to its practice, resisting the temptation to view it as simply a task to get done by remembering that it's time with God.

The Examen is also a good antidote for people who say, "Why go to confession? It doesn't do me any good. I confess the same old stuff over and over again. It doesn't work for me." The answer is that, first, the Examen helps refine one's conscience so that the scope of one's examination of conscience is broadened beyond the same old sins.

Second, the Examen reminds us that the purpose of confession is not to acquire moral perfection. No, it is, rather, a "prodigal son" moment. That is, it is primarily the occasion of meeting with the Father in which you learn how much he loves you, how strongly he seeks you out, how far he will run to embrace you. The very act of confession expresses your need for God, your astonishment at his mercy. With these attitudes, the time will come when you will lose those "same old sins."

So the five-step summary of the Examen might go like this:

1. Begin with gratitude by recalling anything you might be especially grateful for and give thanks.

2. Review any moral failures, times perhaps when you turned away from invitations to grow.

3. Sorrow. Recall any actions you regret.

4. Forgiveness. Ask God for forgiveness and decide if you can make amends to anyone you have hurt—and if not tomorrow, another day.

5. Grace. Ask God for the next day's opportunities.

Will you change? Yes. Will it be long? Yes. It takes time to notice patterns and for patterns to form. It takes time to become aware of God more and more in your day but the transformation is worth it.

66. Confessional Postscripts

In the short time we have had each weekend for our homilies on confession, we could not cover everything. We highlighted some points; namely, that sin and reconciliation are communal; that we are genetically, ecologically, and spiritually connected to one another in what we Catholics call the Mystical Body, the Communion of Saints; that we must be conscious that confession is about community healing and restoration. Here, today, we add some significant postscripts, three of them to be exact. The first is that we cannot neglect to add those old Catholic jokes about confession. The jokes, of course, disguise our nervousness and fears about going to confession even when we sought out the priest who was a visitor, foreign, or deaf. Here's an old one that has long made the rounds.

O'Malley goes to confession and confesses that he has had his way with a girl.

Fr. O'Shaughnessy says, "I know your voice, O'Malley. Tell me the girl's name."

O'Malley says, "I'll not be telling. It wouldn't be proper."

"You'd better or you're not getting absolution. Was it the Morrissey girl?"

"No."

"Then was it the Murphy girl?"

"No."

"The Kelly girl?"

"No, I said I'll not be telling you."

"Then you'll not be getting absolution. Out with you."

O'Malley goes outside looking dejected. His buddy Sean asks, "Did you get absolution?"

"No," mutters O'Malley sadly. But then he brightens up and says, "But I got three good leads!"

Enough of that. For our second postscript we move to the serious side: we need to focus, not on the mechanics of confession but on confession as an encounter between sin and mercy, between the prodigal son and daughter and a Father who runs to meet them. John Grisham, in his book, *The Testament*, captures the spiritual and emotional dynamics when he describes a scene in which Nate, the alcoholic attorney, is in church. Grisham writes:

> The young [minister] in the pulpit was praying, his eyes clenched tightly, his arms waving gently upward. Nate closed his eyes too, and called God's name.
>
> God was waiting.
>
> With both hands, he clenched the back of the pew in front of him. He repeated the list, mumbling softly every weakness and flaw and affliction and evil that plagued him. He confessed them all. In one glorious acknowledgment of failure, he laid himself bare before God. He held nothing back. He unloaded enough burdens to crush any three men and when he finally finished, Nate had tears in his eyes. "I'm sorry," he whispered to God, "Please help me." As quickly as the fever had left his body he felt the baggage leave his soul. With one gentle brush of the hand, his slate had been wiped clean. He breathed a massive sigh of relief, but his pulse was racing…He opened his eyes and wiped his cheeks. Instead of seeing the young man in the pulpit Nate saw the face of Christ in agony and pain dying on the cross. Dying for him.

No one will ever know the millions of people who, like Nate, have found peace and forgiveness in the experience of repentance and confession. We should not focus on the horror stories of the arrogant or harsh priest but on the many stories of spiritual refreshment and renewal, the continuing mercy of Jesus.

The third and last postscript is a much-needed review of a much-abused phrase, "Follow your conscience." True enough, except that conscience today has degenerated into, "If I feel it's all right, it's all right," a common attitude. In the summer of 2008, for example, Christian Smith and his research team from Notre Dame conducted interviews with young adults about their moral lives and how they figure out what's right and wrong. The vast majority's response came down to, "It's up to the individual. It's how you feel. Morality is personal. I would do what I thought would make me happy."

Limited and narrow answers, but these young people are not immoral. They are simply steeped in contemporary individualism and relativism. They have never been given the tools to make proper moral judgments, so conscience for them is solely what each person feels. There's no one right and wrong for everybody, an attitude that leaves university professors complaining that their students have a hard time saying Hitler was evil.

But, as we might now suspect, conscience is always more than what I think. Conscience is communal, and therefore the correct reading of the dictum, "follow your conscience" is "follow your informed conscience." You are not the sole arbiter of right and wrong, as if you were the only person on earth. That would be the ultimate pride: to make oneself God. An informed conscience is the key.

So, in practice, what does an informed conscience mean? It means that, even though we are born with an innate sense of fairness, we must consult four people to test ourselves, especially today when our consciences are molded by a mass media of the lowest common denominator.

First, in a serious matter, we must consult the Holy Spirit. That is, we must humbly pray for guidance, pray that we are doing the right thing. Second, we must consult the community, that is, other people's experience. Not that they are necessarily always right but they offer stories and other points of view that we can learn from. Third, within the community, we consult the wise. There are always certain people who have more wisdom and insight than others. We know instinctively who they are. We need to talk to the wise ones. Finally, we must consult the Church. Not that the Church is always right either, but it has two thousand years of teachings to draw on and the wisdom of its saints—sources not to be neglected.

So sincerely consulting God in prayer, the community, the wise, and the Church constitutes the workings of an informed conscience so that, when you do decide, it is an honest, moral decision even if it turns out to be wrong. But you did your best and you stand right before God. This is far, far better than the arrogant "I feel it's right."

One wise man sums it up this way:

> I know I'm doing right if I try to be pure in my intention in all I do—what Jesus called being "single-minded"....I know I'm doing right if I consult the teaching of Jesus...I know I'm doing right when I consciously make my love for God through my concern for others, for the common good—this man, this woman—the measuring stick for every choice I make. I know I'm doing right when I consult the whole Church...its religious thinkers and the holy and learned people of my own acquaintance. In all I do I mean to seek the counsel of the brotherhood of believers—and not theirs alone but that of any men and women of good will. I know I'm doing right when I remain faithful to my conscience, which I have done everything in my power to inform.

And there it is. All the words I have shared are the simple and profound reminders of the truth that we are not the center of the universe. We are part of a whole, not meant to go it alone. To be moral persons we must not just follow our conscience but an informed conscience, informed from sources beyond ourselves.

Conscience, like life itself, is a communal affair.

67. The Local Church

The children begged for a hamster, and—after the usual fervent vows that they alone would care for it—they got one. They named it Danny. Two months later, when Mom found herself responsible for cleaning and feeding the creature, she located a prospective new home for it.

The children took the news of Danny's imminent departure quite well, though one of them remarked, "He's been around here a long time. We'll miss him."

"Yes." Mom replied, "But he's too much work for one person, and since I'm that one person, I say he goes."

Another child offered, "Well, maybe if he wouldn't eat so much and wouldn't be so messy, we could keep him."

But Mom was firm. "It's time to take Danny to his new home now," she insisted. "Go and get his cage."

With one voice and in tearful outrage the children shouted, "His cage?!! Oh, no! Danny?!! We thought you said Daddy!"

Well that's my funny introduction to a far more serious misunderstanding we all harbor, and what I'm about to say is challenging and maybe perplexing to some of you. It will probably give you a headache, but it's all brought about by a phrase from today's epistle. It's the opening line, which you probably didn't notice. It goes, "Paul, Silvanus and Timothy to the church of the Thessalonians…" The church of the Thessalonians? Later, St. Paul would write "to the church of God which is in Corinth" (1 Cor. 1:2).

Notice Paul said the church, the full church of Jesus was in Thessalonica and Corinth. Understand what he is saying. These churches were in no way subdivisions of the church in Jerusalem. They were full, independent churches united with the others by a common faith, baptism, Eucharist, and apostolic preaching. They didn't take orders from Rome. There was no Rome, as we know it, then. They were not branches of the mother church in Jerusalem. They were fully church in themselves. And they were a diverse lot.

I point this out because our concept of the Church is miles away from that. It is, I suspect, that of an industrial complex model with its clones all over the world. That is to say, the average Catholic, both clerical and lay, thinks of his or her parish as a subsidiary of the Vatican. The local parish—say, this local parish of St. Catherine's—is looked upon in relationship to Rome as the local Chevrolet dealer is in relationship to General Motors at its corporate headquarters in Michigan.

In fact, the only reason we have parishes, we think, is that the pope, who is the pastor of the universal church, obviously can't handle the whole world, so he has CEOs called bishops who oversee the carved up smaller units called dioceses. But the bishop can't handle all his territory either, so he in turn subdivides it into parishes. The parish is the last subdivision, with the implication being that the parish exists only at the behest of the next higher level. It has no innate justification. It is but a branch office with all of its standard "products" bought from the parent company. Most people like yourselves, as I said, subconsciously understand the local parish this way. It's what we call a vertical ecclesiology or vertical church structure. We're a franchise under the brand name of Roman Catholic.

But this is clearly not so. You heard St. Paul. The local church exists in its own right, not just as an organizational, administrative subunit of the Church universal though connected to it. Vatican II's doctrine of collegiality was very clear about this. The bishops in their *Dogmatic Constitution on the Church* (26) say: "This church of Christ is truly present in all legitimate local congregations of the faithful which, united with their pastors, are themselves called churches in the New Testament."

Let me repeat this teaching: "This church of Christ is truly present in all legitimate local congregations of the faithful which, united with their pastors, are themselves called churches in the New Testament." Let's continue: "For in their own locality these are the new people called by God, in the

Holy Spirit and in much fullness. In them the faithful are gathered together by the preaching of the gospel of Christ, and the mystery of the Lord's Supper is celebrated....In these communities...Christ is present. By virtue of him, the one, holy, catholic and apostolic church gathers together, for the partaking of the Body and Blood of Christ...."

Think of that. The full church of Jesus is present here in Farmingdale. The parish of St. Catherine's, with its pastor, the bishop's representative, is not a mere subdivision of Rome or the diocese. It has its own integrity, shares a common mission, and is the full church of Jesus Christ. Moreover that church—this church—is the People of God, to use the phrase of Vatican II, who have been called and commissioned by their baptism to be full, adult members presided over by a pastor who has been given Holy Orders; that is, his task is to orchestrate or bring a holy order to the gifts of the people, which they possess, not by delegation, but by their own right as baptized members. Take note of that.

In other words, the pastor's task is not to share his or the bishop's power with the laity but rather to call forth and remind them of the power they already have in virtue of their baptism. The laity, in short, are collaborators—equal co-laborers—in the common task of the Church. Indeed, when you come right down to it, being 96% of the Church, the laity are its most public element.

Listen to the United States bishops: "One of the characteristics of lay men and women today is their growing sense of being adult members of the Church. Adulthood implies knowledge, experience and awareness, freedom and responsibility, and mutuality in relationships... thanks to the impetus of the Second Vatican Council, lay women and men feel themselves called to exercise the same mature interdependences and practical self-direction which characterizes them in other areas of life."

Well, I hope I'm making my point, perhaps novel to some of you. And it is this: were St. Paul writing to us today, along with box number and zip code, he would address us as "the church of God which is in Farmingdale." Yes, we don't go to church. We are the Church, today, as it happens, the Church gathered.

In the "so what?" department, all this means that the nineteenth-century cleric who said that the extent of the laity's contribution to the Church was "to pray, pay, and obey" was wildly wrong. On the contrary, the laity has rights and responsibilities: the right to a good pastor, good preachers, ministerial and fiscal accountability, the right to speak up, to be consulted and heard. They have the responsibility to be church by their witness and participation in spreading the gospel where they are. Again, the Church is the people, all the people, not just the hierarchy. Together we are the Church.

I have a dream—to use a familiar phrase—and it is this: I dream that someday this conversation will take place at St. Catherine's. You and a few other parishioners happen to be in the vestibule when a group of visitors stop by to look around at the lovely buildings and grounds. After coming from the place where we worship, as they step into the vestibule where you are, you overhear them exclaim to one another, "What a beautiful church!" And then you have your shinning moment when you interrupt and add in all sweet sincerity, "Yes, and the buildings are nice too!"

68. The Foursquare Church

I don't know why my friend sent me this email. It states that starting in January the federal government will start deporting old people instead of illegals in order to lower social security and Medicare costs. The reason is that old people are easier to catch and will not remember how to get back home. He says, "A tear came into my eye when I thought of you…see you on the bus."

Well, so much for friends. Let's get to the homily that builds on last week's when we discussed a deeper understanding of ourselves as Church. Today we want to view why we're here and the four pillars that undergird our presence.

Many years ago a sharp man named Jack Shea said that Sunday is about three things, to which I have added a fourth. Sunday is all about: gather the folks; tell the story; break the Bread; and share the experience. Gather the folks; tell the story; break the Bread; share the experience.

Gather the folks. All week long we have been individual Christian disciples in our homes, neighborhoods, workplaces, and schools. We felt the human need to build larger buildings so that on Sunday we can gather in them to praise God corporately and publicly—something forbidden to us by a secular society—and revisit those weekday experiences, both noble and ignoble, and to find safety in numbers, mutual encouragement in worship, and the strength of the Eucharist in living a holy life. Furthermore, in our assembly, we are most conscious that we are more than the sum total of our individual selves. We are Church. Yes, on Sundays we, some three hundred lay folk and one priest, are the public face of the Church.

And there's more. Unlike the "I am spiritual but not religious" crowd, we take the Church as it comes. We don't get to pick whom we sit next to or like-minded partisans. We don't get to hear the sweet things we prefer, do our own spiritual thing, or solely make up our own consciences in ways that happen to agree with what we like to do. The self-centered, self-justifying "If it feels good, do it" is the opposite of the wisdom and challenge of the communal Church. T.S. Eliot caught the truth of the Church when he wrote:

Why should men love the church?
Why should they love her laws?
She tells them of life and death
And all they would forget.
She is tender where they would be hard
And hard where they would like to be soft.
She tells them of evil and sin
And other unpleasant facts.

Then, too, there's that precious fact that we are a Catholic—universal—family where the CEO sits next to the plumber, the Democrat next to the Republican, the Englishman next to the Irishman, and the celebrity next to the nobody. Here we are all equal before God. No pretense, no frills. We all equally proclaim Jesus Christ is Lord and, we all cry out equally, "O God, be merciful to me, a sinner."

Here also in this family, the joyous among us pray for the depressed among us, the saints for sinners, the faith-filled for the doubtful, the hopeful for the depressed, the loving for those who can't love, the healthy for the sick, the employed for the unemployed, the happily married for the unhappily married. This motley mix of sinner and saint is Church. When we say we come to "Gather the Folk," that's who we are—an imperfect pilgrim people of all stripes. And in our midst stands Christ, who takes us as we are.

So, if you are tweeting right now, for example, you are pulling back into a private space and undermining the communal worship. It's like hiding in a closet while all the others outside are singing "Happy Birthday." Your deliberate emotional and moral absence ill prepares you for the long, fallow stretches of life—workplaces, friendships, marriages—where ennui and dry periods are truly necessary to prepare us for the next oasis, for newer and unexpected renewals and depths. Life is not about you. It is about us even when you're bored.

Tell the story. We're here to hear the God story, the Jesus story. Sometimes it's told well. Other times badly; and, as I said last week, you have to demand that it be told better. But nevertheless it's a story we seldom hear elsewhere: what will it profit you to gain the whole world and lose your soul? Turn the other cheek. Pray for your enemies. Do not return evil for evil. Love your neighbor as yourself. Do not commit adultery or lie. Beware of the greed that blinds your soul and hardens your heart. Rejoice in being God's child. Know that every hair of your head is numbered. You are worth more than many sparrows. I no longer call you slaves but friends. I will not leave you orphaned. I have loved you with an everlasting love.

The story includes the story of the saints, the endless centuries-old chapters of care, charity, and compassion and those of sin, scandal, and shame. Through the stories we are reminded of what we have been, and that God cares, not for what we have done, but for our striving for what we can do. It's a story to live by.

Break the Bread. Ah, yes, sharing a meal is traditionally one of the highest forms of companionship and bonding. But we have forgotten a significant fact of the Eucharist. "Take and eat" is the command. But what are we taking and eating? The answer is Christ. Yes, but remember, it is the whole Christ. When we receive Jesus we receive his mystical Body as well. That is, all who are united to him. In Communion, to put it badly, we swallow not only Jesus but our neighbor, and that prompts thoughts of charity and reconciliation.

Share the experience. Go forth, the Mass is ended. Go in peace. "Mass" is the Latin word for "sent," for mission. When we are finished here, we will be sent forth to be Christ's disciples the rest of the week, as we go out to seed the world with the good news.

So, there we are, and here we are: the Church celebrating the Sunday experience which, once again is: gather the folk; tell the story; break the bread; and share the experience. So far, we've done two of them, and are about to begin the third. The fourth remains to be completed after you leave here. Hold these four elements in your hearts and "going to Mass," as we say, won't seem so bland. In fact, it's downright exciting.

69. The Full Circle Church

In Advent of 2011 the official Church leaders decided to give us a new English translation of the Mass so that both priest and people had to go through a new learning process with hand-held cue cards for a while. Some people loved the new changes; others loathed them; but one thing we know is constant: the liturgy of the Mass has never been constant. It has always been changing. There are still some here, for example, who can remember when the Mass was in Latin, the priest's back was facing the people, guitars were unheard of, and there was a palpable sense of mystery.

But even that, at one time, was novel. In fact, generally speaking, there are four broad changes in the history of the Mass, and, to put things in perspective, very briefly it might be helpful to examine them.

The first phase was, at the beginning, the Simple and Flexible Mass. Remember, this literally was the beginning: a fledgling minority group, sometimes persecuted, with no firm structure meeting quietly in homes. The one who presided—usually the home's host—faced the people and talked to them in their everyday language, which usually happened to be Greek. Modeled after Jewish tradition, he said a simple prayer of thanksgiving and all partook of the bread. Soon the reading of the Scripture was joined to this meal. It was, as I said, a simple affair of thanksgiving, consecration, and communion. Not unlike the Last Supper. It was flexible, and the presider (whoever he was) would make up the prayers as he went along.

Now fast forward to the second phase, which brought us the Long and Complicated Mass, say, around the fifth and sixth centuries. A lot has happened. Christians are now liberated and legal and largely Gentiles. Mass is now held in a large building or cathedral. The altar is still a simple free-standing table, and the priest—the old presider had morphed into a priest when the old defunct Jewish Temple concept of sacrifice and priesthood was applied to the Mass—is still facing the people, but everything is larger, grander, and more solemn. The spontaneous prayers have been standardized into canons. Prayers for the living and the dead have been added, plus ceremonies borrowed from the Byzantine court ceremonial, including what Christianity had formerly rejected; genuflections, bowing, kissing, incense, and candles. The cult of the saints and martyrs also became prominent in this era. The Christians freely borrowed from the culture, using new interpretations of things like anointing, foot washing, baptism by immersion, sacred images, and processions, They even borrowed the clothing of Roman state officials and reinterpreted them as clerical clothing and vestments. It was all quite elaborate. Something was gained but something was lost too.

The third phase of the Mass came to be called the Far Away and Silent era. This is around the 9th and 10th centuries and for the first time in a thousand years there is silence. No one is talking or singing in church anymore because no one but the clerics knows Latin. So the choir, now segregated from the sanctuary and pushed to the back of the church, took over the singing parts, and altar boys took over the people's speaking parts. Furthermore, with the sanctuary being highly decorated, the back wall became a backdrop for the altar that was shoved against it, forcing the priest to come to the other side and have his back to the people. He whispered the Mass.

No one but the clerics went to Communion. The laity were too unworthy. Eventually a Church council had to force the people to go once a year. Standing way back in the cathedral the people could not see what was going on, so they clamored to have a look at the host and chalice, and eventually forced the introduction of the elevation of the sacred species after the consecration. That's where we get it. When you consider there was no sound system and how large the cathedrals were, you get a sense of the physical and emotional distance between the people and their Mass. The laity were passive. The clergy took over. It was now a long way from the Last Supper.

The fourth phase until the 1960s was the Mass of the Rubrics—the word "rubric" in Latin means red, which stands for the rules and directions printed in red among the black text. Minute rules were put in effect after the sixteenth-century Council of Trent, which was attempting to correct abuses. Everything but everything was governed by strict rules, from the way the priest held his arms and wore the maniple—remember the decorated cloth he wore on his arm? It started out as his handkerchief pinned to his sleeve and morphed into a vestment part—to what to do if the priest dropped the host. Trent froze the Mass into a precise ritual passively watched by the people who, to while away the time, said their rosaries or private devotions.

Some brought their missals to church so they could follow in an English translation. Some missals even had little pictures so you could know what part of the Mass the priest was at. Like abstaining from meat on Fridays, the beloved missal—and it was that—became the dividing line between Protestants and Catholics. The Protestants brought their Bibles to church and the Catholics their missals.

The phase we're in now, promoted by Vatican II in the '60s, is the result at looking back into history. Vatican II wanted to recover the shared worship of the Mass, so the rail separating the sanctuary from the people was removed. And it wanted to restore participation, so the Mass was returned to the language of the people, and emphasis was put on singing, harking back to the Last Supper where it is recorded, "And after reciting a hymn, they went out to Mount Olivet." Recovered were the proclamation of the readings and the distribution of the Eucharist by the laity, the prayers of the faithful.... In short, the Mass had come full circle and was restored as a public celebration of all the people—the word in Greek for "public celebration" being liturgy.

It is into this context that you must place the recent corrections of language. Whether you approve or disapprove, they are meant to further unity and participation, to enhance the liturgy of the Church, meaning both priest and people. So, to return to a now familiar mantra: gather the folk; tell the story; break the Bread; and share the experience—a formula that goes back to Jesus and has fluctuated throughout the ages for better or worse, and still challenges us in new ways to be the People of God.

70. The Right Place

I want to tell you about Lana Peters, who died in 2011 at age 85 in Wisconsin.

Why should we be interested in her, a woman we never heard of? Because in fact we have heard of her or at least her father.

She used various names throughout her life but she was born Svetlana Stalin, the only daughter of one of the most murderous dictators in all of history—something she never forgot nor would people let her. Joseph Stalin's real name was a long, unpronounceable one. In his 20s he adopted "Stalin," which means "prince of steel," and it turned out to be an apt title.

Svetlana was born in 1926 when her father was already general secretary of the Soviet Communist Party. Her mother was Stalin's second wife. Her mother died six years after Lana was born. She committed suicide after being brutalized by her husband. Talk about traumatic beginnings! Imagine being born of a militant atheistic, murdering father and an abused mother who committed suicide.

But there was a grace hidden in the background. Her father's mother was a devout Orthodox Christian who had sent her son Joseph to an Orthodox school and then an Orthodox seminary. In one of history's depressing moments he dropped out and went on to abolish religion. Later, at his mother's deathbed in 1939, the old woman lamented, "What a pity you have not become a priest." It was this grandmother who secretly baptized Lana.

Lana's obituary says that she, Lana Peters—the name of her fourth husband—spent most of her early life under intense scrutiny as "Stalin's princess." She was in the public eye and was often photographed with her father and held up as a role model for other children.

At 16, this wounded girl fell in love with a Soviet filmmaker, but her father disapproved and had him exiled to Siberia. She then married a fellow student whom her father also disapproved of, and the marriage collapsed under his pressure. In 1949 she was married a second time to one of Stalin's henchman, had a daughter, but quickly divorced. Then her father died. Nine years after her father' death Lana was baptized into the Orthodox Church because, as she said, she "did not want to live without God."

As a young woman, she worked as a translator while bringing up her two children. She was a well-known and connected figure in the USSR. Her third marriage to an Indian Communist, who interested her in Hinduism, ended when he died in 1966. Finally, anxious to put her past behind her, in 1967 she caused a sensation by defecting to the United States. She first sought asylum in the U.S. embassy in India, but the American authorities, fearing she might be a Soviet spy, were reluctant to allow her to fly to the U.S., so she spent a month in a Swiss monastery. After her pious grandmother, this was the second touch of grace in her troubled life. She would always remember the warm hospitality and piety of these Catholic monks.

Finally she was admitted to the U.S., wrote two well-received but ghost written autobiographies, and married William Peters, who lived in a commune. She left him and his strange commune and moved to Princeton, where she enrolled her daughter in a Catholic school. Still, she always remained under suspicion as "Stalin's daughter," not-to-be trusted, a defector, a curiosity. That intolerable pressure finally drove her to move to Britain.

But even there she could not live down her name, her history, the fact that she was a Russian, the daughter of a wicked dictator. The old prejudices and suspicions dogged her, so she returned briefly to the Soviet Union in 1984, but it did not work out. And so, by this time alienated from her children, she went back to America in 1986 to Wisconsin. It proved hard for her there and so, four years later, in March of 1990, penniless and reviled, she was back in London, moving from convent to convent and finally to a day care home. She had enough of that, and in 2007 she returned to Wisconsin where, in touch with her daughter Olga, who lived in Portland, she died of colon cancer four years later.

What sustained her? It was the third grace after her grandmother and the Swiss monks. When, in 1982, she relocated to Cambridge, England, she met a Catholic priest in West London through a mutual acquaintance.

Through him she became more and more interested in the Church, and in her autobiography she describes "my constant desire and persistent admiration towards the Church of Rome and a desire 'to be there.' Like a compass that always turns towards the North Pole, I keep turning all the time towards the same direction: Rome."

She began attending Mass at a local Catholic Church in Cambridge and was impressed by the simple piety of the people. She wrote of observing how they returned to their seats after Communion with transformed faces and hearts. It was something she wanted for herself. She got her wish and was received into the Catholic Church on December 13, 1982.

Ten days after her reception, she wrote to the priest, saying, "Thank you again and again for having opened this door for me. I cannot describe to you in what darkness I have been the last years, and what a great joy and inner peace I possess now." Ten years later her commitment remained firm: "I feel stronger and stronger after these ten years, that I am in the right place," she wrote.

Thus the story of a woman with a horrendous start: a maniacal father, a mother driven to suicide, a godless Communism, four marriages, alienated children, lionized or reviled wherever she went—all making her a restless pilgrim. But hidden grace was working: a faithful grandmother, a devout monastery, simple people at a parish church. They all led her to find "the right place" in the Catholic Church.

For us her story is a reminder that, no matter how fractured our lives, healing grace is calling us. Her story is also a reminder of our calling to be a grace for those people who, out of the corner of their eyes, are secretly looking for the right place and hope that, by our witness, we can give them a clue where it is. So we pray for Stalin, since we are commanded by Jesus to do so, and we pray for Svetlana, who embraced what her father cruelly rejected.

71. Olga and Darran

Let me introduce you to two people I saw in two articles, one in *Commonweal* magazine, the other in *USA Today*.

First, Olga. Like most farm workers in the United States, Olga is from Mexico, where she worked in a stationery store to raise her three kids, but the grinding, unrelenting poverty of Mexico led her to the United States, where all day she plants onions in holes made by a tractor on a farm in western New York, about an hour's ride from Rochester. Olga is one of the 60,000 to 80,000 farmworkers in western New York alone.

It takes her about three hours to fill a row, and for this she earns $32. She wears a red bandanna to protect herself from the dust and the pesticides. She works 8 to 10 hours a day, 6 or 7 days a week. She never planted onions before coming to the United States and endures the heat, the sun, and the dirt. She says that the work was so hard and long that she cried for months when she first came here. But her labor in the fields is just one part of it. Even with that back-breaking work she is also expected to take care of the children, cook, and clean.

Farm work is among the most dangerous in the country. I don't know if you know this, but farm work consistently ranks as one of the three industries with the most accidents and injuries. It is also one of the lowest paying jobs. Farm work is hard for anyone, but especially for illegals. For them, life becomes almost a case of house arrest where they hide in fear of deportation. Yet year after year they daily endure incredible hardship.

So why do they stay? Every parent here knows the answer to that question. It's always the same. They want to give their children the chance of a better life. So they go on working hard under terrible conditions, saving

308

and hiding from the authorities, whatever it takes, to give their children something they themselves will never fully possess.

That's Olga's world. Now we move to the world of Darran Dubose, age 21. He's a student who lives in Detroit's west side. It's a Saturday, and he's standing outside of a hip store called Burn Rubber. It's not just a sneaker store. It's a sneaker boutique. Darran has been in his spot in line since Tuesday along with dozens of others, mostly young men. Why are they standing there for days and nights? What are they there for? They are all waiting —are you ready for this?—all waiting to buy Kanye West's Nike Air Yeezy (yes, that's the marketing name of the latest must-have sneaker) at a 400% markup. That comes to exactly $1,000 for an already inflated $245 pair of sneakers.

Darren, by the way, also pays someone $400 an hour to keep his place in line while he goes home to shower. He returns with his computer, iPhone, and headphones, along with a zebra-print Snugglee, gummy bears, and a book. I'm not sure who pays his school tuition. The article didn't mention.

So, there we are: the stories of Olga and Darran—one laboring for 32 dollars, the other forking over a 1,000 bucks for a pair of designer sneakers, which probably cost $50 to make. These stories aren't about the immigration debates or politics. They are simply two stories there side by side, to make us think; and if we can't think about them here, where else can we?

So, let's begin by assuming that Darran isn't bad. He's just a typical American. Which means that his world and his worldview and his value system are profoundly shaped by a society that is thoroughly consumerist. In a sense, he has little chance of resistance to the 50-60,000 subliminal and overt commercials he sees and hears every single day—just as we do. The trend setters, the celebrities, Jersey Shore, the Kardashians, sitcoms, mainstream pornography, music, and entertainment are permanently plugged into his brain via his ever-present iPhone, iPad, Facebook, and Twitter and make him the perfectly conditioned consumer living in a self-enclosed world.

Darran is Darran, and Darran is us. Pause and think of what and how much TV (with its endless commercials) we watch, how much time we spend on the cell phone or computer, what magazines we read, what our shopping habits are, how many sweaters or shoes we have, how many gadgets and toys we have—what is our everyday input? What fills our time—and shapes and conditions our minds—without our realizing it?

We will find that, with every minute filled with clever and seductive distraction, we have no knowledge of Olga, no clue as to how the majority of the world lives. It's not that we're bad or insensitive; it's just that we are conditioned consumers. Behind our physical and moral gated communities we're tunnel-visioned into what is called the American Dream of endless consumption. With those spiritual blinders on, the Olgas of this world are out of our line of vision. We just don't see them. Or if we do, they are an unsightly and disturbing distraction from the beautiful bodies with perfect abs and perfect measurements and perfect teeth and perfect hair and perfect health and perfect clothes and the perfect income we are told to aspire to if we want to be "successful."

Again, our conditioning began from the day our parents set us in front of commercial TV, and just like trying to get free of a cult, now it's hard to overcome. We don't even see the problem. It's what the gospel calls spiritual blindness. Why else we would we pay $1,000 for a pair of designer sneakers or $800 for a pair of designer jeans or several thousands of dollars for a designer watch unless we wanted to be a part of an exclusive brand name club to show how rich and cool we are? A $50 pair of sneakers, a $40 pair of jeans and a $20 Timex would serve just as well and maybe free us up to see Olga. But we worry: without our brand names, how would others know who we are? How would we know who we are?

Socrates had it right: the unexamined life is not worth living. Everything in a consumerist society is designed to make us not examine life. Rather, we are to respond to impulse and stimulation. But that wide contrast between Olga and Darran tells us that we really do need to step aside often and examine our lives, our Christian lives to be precise; and that's why we're here and why I related the two contrasting stories.

Take inventory. What do we read, what do we watch, what do we listen to? How much time do we give to these things? What is our spiritual diet or lack of it? Do we ever do some spiritual reading, or read the New Testament or a thoughtful book or read one of our fine Catholic magazines that, like Dickens' ghosts, show us another side of life?

If we are Christian, how do we habitually stand on Jesus' criteria for salvation? That's a good test: feeding the hungry, giving drink to the thirsty, clothing the ill-clothed, visiting those imprisoned within walls, addictions, depression, poverty, injustice. What part do these things play in our lives? What percentage of our lives is dedicated to being a Christian, to looking past the commercials and celebrities and profit at any cost and, as we might put it, noticing Olga? Or, to put it another way, in our lives, do Olga and Darran ever meet?

If not, the unexamined Christian life must be examined.

72. The Fourteen Generations

In today's epistle, as you heard, St, Paul wrote, "Brethren, I urge you to live in a manner worthy of the call you have received…"

"A call you have received." Let's circle in on that by mentioning something that has affected us all. It is this: the recession and the ones who caused it. Like you, I read in the press of scandals—bankers manipulating the interest rates, packaging billions of dubious mortgages into a bond and having it stamped Triple A rating to sell to some unsuspecting buyer, or forging documents to foreclose fraudulently on countless homeowners. Not only do I read that—and I don't understand it all—I learn that the surprising thing about all this stuff is that no one is surprised, that we have come to take such hurtful wickedness for granted, as the routine way of doing business. The polls tell the story: Americans distrust not only banks but big business itself, which they believe is corrupt. And nearly three in four Americans believe that such corruption has increased over the years.

One analyst I read says bluntly, "Company executives are paid to maximize profits, not to behave ethically. Evidence suggests that they behave as corruptly as they can." This kind of talk takes me aback. He goes on to cite a 20-year study that points out that the most lucrative strategy for executives at too-big-to-fail banks would be to loot them to pay themselves vast rewards, knowing full well that the government would save them from bankruptcy. We all see that some banks are too big to fail and some bankers are too big to jail, and we live with that and pay for it. Then there is the other depressing statistic that shows that in 1980 the CEOs of large U.S. companies made 42 times the average wages of workers. Thirty years later, in 2011, that average has ballooned to 380 times more! That's astounding! No wonder society is so split between the haves and have-nots.

This is not good. Then there's institutions like the Catholic Church and Penn State University that grossly betrayed trust. Drug companies inflate prices and inflate claims. The British giant GlaxoSmithKline just paid $3 billion in fines for doing so. Some large corporations plunder the earth and pollute the air. Politicians are routinely found to illegally profit from their positions. Some go to jail. Students and teachers together are caught up in cheating scandals. Then there's the average American who delights in beating the system: healthy people get sham prescriptions from their doctors so they can get free rehab. People brag how they bilk the government or cheat on their taxes, not realizing that their conduct raises costs for all of us. The goal seems to be looking out for No. 1, finding loopholes, bending the rules, cutting corners, and it all adds up to a huge drain on society. The all too familiar litany goes on.

What's happening? We can't go on like this. We ask: what has been lost here besides trust, without which no society can survive? The answer, in a word, I suggest, is a sense of stewardship.

So many of today's CEOs are a talented, privileged group but they are captains of industry without a moral rudder. As one columnist put it, they know how to succeed but not how to be virtuous. They have totally lost any sense that they are guardians, not owners, of our institutions. They have no consciousness of their larger social or moral role, that they are but stewards.

I suppose we should not be surprised at all this. It's the way they're brought up, the way we're brought up. Over the past half century, religion has slowly been removed from the public square. Schools cannot mention God. Moral values have been reduced to anyone's opinion. Virtues are ridiculed. Any remnant of solidarity has been buried under a media avalanche of self-esteem and "I'm Number 1," "It's All About Me," and "Whatever Works for Me." Any sense of the Common Good has evaporated as we celebrate greed and greedy people.

The thing is that, as a result, we have lost any sense of God, of a sense of calling, of vocation, of mission, of stewardship, a sense that we have been given custody of the earth and others for a time only in order to enhance them and pass them on to the next generation, that we owe the past and we owe the future, that we are connected.

This kind of talk shouldn't be news for Catholics because we have all these concepts buried in our ancient metaphors like the Body of Christ, the Vine and Branches, the Mystical Body. We speak of the Church Triumphant, the Church Militant, the Church Suffering, the Communion of Saints. All these venerable phrases have but one moral, spiritual point: we are all connected. We are all co-responsible for one another. We have a vocation, given to us at baptism, to be brother and sister to one another and to the planet on which we live, and the mandate to leave both better off for the next generation. We are stewards of God.

All this calls to mind something said by the late Sister Jose Hobday, a Franciscan nun whose mother was a Seneca Indian. She said that her mother taught her many Native American traditions, and one of them was the concept of the Fourteen Generations. The idea, she writes, seems simple—deceptively so:

> you pay reverence and respect to the seven generations that have gone before you and the seven generations that will come after you. According to this tradition, you keep seven generations, forward and back, in your mind and heart in everything you do, and live accordingly. When my mother first told me about this, I responded primarily to the part concerning the seven generations who had gone before me. I liked the idea that for seven generations my ancestors had lived with me in mind. Knowing that, I felt I had been loved and cared for even before I arrived. My mother explained that if I lived with my ancestors in my memory, it would give me power I would not otherwise have. This proved correct. Being aware that these ancestors went ahead of me, and knowing they wanted to pass on to me what they had, has been a real gift. It gives me strength.

> As I grew, so did my understanding of the Fourteen Generation tradition. As a child I had been enamored with the part of the tradition concerning those who had gone before me. But as an adult, I became more aware of keeping in

mind and heart the seven generations who will come after me. Now, instead of being on the receiving end, I moved to the giving side. Instead of being empowered, I saw myself as trying to empower. Instead of being imagined (as the seven generations before me had done) I tried to imagine those who would come for seven generations after me. I now wanted to pass on what I had to those who would follow me…I feel connected not only with those who went before me, but with those around me, as well as with those who will come after me…Sadly, many people cannot say that today…but this idea of the Fourteen Generations helps me to see that I am not alone and challenges me not to live only for myself….

This notion of the Fourteen Generations should be recited in every boardroom, every bank, every school, every home. We Catholics especially should embrace it—we, the Communion of Saints, the Body of Christ. We must tell and retell the story of the Fourteen Generations to our children and grandchildren so that when they grow up they may be ready to honor their calling and be faithful stewards of what God, for a brief time, has entrusted to them.

So, let's end our message with a prayer from Cardinal Newman:

God has created me to do him some definite service.
He has committed some work to me that he has not committed to another.
I have a mission.
I may never know it in this life
But I shall be told it in the next.
I am a link in a chain,
a bond of connection between persons.
He has not created me for naught;
I shall do good—I shall do his work;
I shall be an angel of peace,
A preacher of truth in my own place.

Amen.

73. Dorothy Stang

We're familiar with enough gangster movies to know that the underworld and sometimes even the government put out contracts on someone's life. Still, 74-year-old Dorothy Stang didn't seem like the kind of person to have a contract put out on her. Short, gray-haired, glasses that slipped down her nose, a daily Bible reader—and a nun. Who would want a contract put out on her? Let's go back a bit.

Dorothy Stang, a Catholic girl from Dayton, Ohio, eventually joined the Sisters of Notre Dame de Namur in Cincinnati. It was a religious order whose mission was—and I quote—"to take our stand with poor people, especially woman and children in the most abandoned places." Think of that: that's a challenging and courageous mission to take on. Anyway, that's how she found herself in one of the most remote places in the world, 30 miles from the nearest village in the jungle in northern Brazil. She would spend more than 30 years there with the landless peasants who eked out a living by subsistence farming in the rainforest.

The landless peasants, like others in so many parts of the world, including our own, seldom have a voice to speak for them. They are vulnerable to exploitation from the government and the industrial barons. Illegal loggers and ranchers, with greed and profit as their only goals, were cutting huge swaths out of the rainforest—some 20% of the region's 1.6 million acres. It was not only a long-term harm to the ecology of the entire planet but the destruction of a way of life for these rainforest people, the poorest of the poor, who were being driven off their land by threats, intimidation, and violence.

Sister Dorothy refused to be silent at such injustice. She continued to teach the local peasants how to farm the land without deforestation while at the same time mounting a campaign against illegal land grabbing. She lobbied the Brazilian government and named those who were exploiting the people and the land. In no time she became a threat to the loggers and was marked for death.

Even though she knew this she refused to flee. "I don't want to flee," she said, "nor do I want to abandon the battle of these farmers who live without any protection in the forest. They have the sacrosanct right to aspire to a better life on land where they can live and work with dignity while respecting the environment."

She was often seen wearing a T-shirt that said in Portuguese, "The death of the forest is the end of our life." She hoped her nun status would protect her.

On February 12, 2005, Dorothy was walking to a meeting in the Boa Esperanca settlement, where she was to discuss a new settlement for the area that had been granted to the peasants by the Brazilian government, but which was in a proposed tract of land valued by illegal loggers. As she walked to the meeting along with two peasants from a nearby village, two gunmen emerged from the bushes. They asked her if she had any weapons.

She said that her only weapon was her Bible, which she opened and began to read. "Blessed are the poor in spirit, blessed are the peacemakers." A second later, one of the men opened fire shooting her once in the abdomen. As Dorothy fell to the forest floor, the gunman fired another round into her back and four more into her head.

We are shocked and grieved at the brutality—but sadly it's become so commonplace: the hundreds of murdered Mexicans routinely found in open graves, for example, the drug-related killings, the almost daily car bombings, and the murder of women and children that go on in Iraq and Afghanistan and Pakistan and in Syria—and in Chicago. Will it ever end?

Will the greed and profit-only creed that spawned our own United States recession and pain ever end? Will the death list of Dorothy Stangs ever cease? More to the point, will we raise up the Dorothy Stangs, committed to the gospel to bear witness to truth, who speak for God even though they know the old saying that "Those who speak for God must get used to the sight of their own blood."

I must add that, in the wake of Dorothy's brutal death, the Brazilian government increased its presence in the forest region to shut down illegal logging and protect the peasants. It's still a hard place to be but some changes have been made.

You should know the story of Sister Dorothy Stang and the many like her who, often at the peril of their lives, bear witness to the gospel. We are challenged to put our own lives alongside of hers to see how we witness at work and school and home, whether we're part of the problem or part of the solution, what kind of Christians we are. While we're pondering the question, we might add a name to the litany of the saints: "St. Dorothy Stang, pray for us."

Notes & Credits

The Preface

Regarding the Bible as an inventive story form I recommend the following books:

Sidney Lumet, *Making Movies* (Vintage Books, 1995).

William J. Bausch, *In the Beginning There Were Stories* (Twenty-Third Publications, 2004), and William J. Bausch, *Touching the Heart* (Twenty-Third Publications, 2007).

Chapter 1, The Sunday After Thanksgiving: Five Kernels

This is good for the Sunday following Thanksgiving. In 2011 that Sunday happened to be the first Sunday of Advent, so I tied in an Advent reference. And even though it was Advent, as the preface I chose to use the First Sunday, Ordinary Time I, with its reinforcing motif of "a chosen race, etc."

Chapter 2, The Legacy

The quote about Mme Ramotswe is taken from the *Reader's Digest Select Editions*, 2005, page 438.

The New York Times front-page story on coach Urban Meyer is dated November 29, 2011. *The Wall Street Journal* story is dated November 21, 2011.

Chapter 3, Three Cups of (Weak) Tea

This is so entitled because there has been controversy over Mortenson's book, some claiming that his account is fabricated and that he defrauded donors. I wrote this homily before this exposure and have included it in case he is vindicated and, even if not, because the homiletic dynamics would still be valid. It should be noted that, in April 2012, Mortenson was acquitted of fraud.

Chapter 4, Testimony of Two Women

The Sito story comes from *The Four Gospel Journey as a Guide for the Spiritual Life* by Alexander J. Shaia, published by Now You Know Media (Copyright © 2010 by Now You Know Media. Used herewith by permission of Now You Know Media, Inc.).

Chapter 5, Mary Moments

The man who tells the story about his son is Christopher deVinck in his book, *The Power of the Powerless* (Crossroad, 2002).

The one reference to the Rutgers fresco comes from Barbara E. Reid in her book, *Abiding Word* (The Liturgical Press, 2011), p. 10.

Chapter 6, Christmas or Xmas?

This chapter I owe to Fr. Mike Sullivan, pastor of St. Martha's church in Point Pleasant, N.J., who runs this wise piece in his parish bulletin each Christmas season. I have reworked his article somewhat. If you can find it, it might be helpful to show a visual, say, of an old vestment or missal with the Chi-rho symbol on them.

Chapter 7, Two Images For Christmas

What you have here in this homily is an adaptation of other homilies for the special Christmas mix of the faithful, the strangers, the visitors, the once-a year Catholics, very few of whom have heard the material here in other Sunday homilies. So I have no hesitation is using here the story that will appear in chapter 12, "Encounters." You will notice that I will do the same at Easter time: repeating a routine Sunday story and pressing it into the service of the special occasion.

Chapter 8, Lent is Calling

Timothy Radcliffe, *The Tablet*, August 7, 2010, p.17. The "one writer" is Matthew Kelly. The reference is from his book *Rediscover Catholicism; A Spiritual Guide to Living with Passion and Purpose* (Beacon Publications, 2010), p. 32

Chapter 9, Tale of Two Cities

I suggest that the celebrant use Reconciliation Canon number 2 in connection with this homily. This homily, given to the regular weekend crowd, will be expanded and recycled for the Easter crowd on Easter Sunday. It was too good not to share with the visitors who may not be regular churchgoers.

Chapter 12, Give Them What They Want

The story is from Andy Andrews, *Mastering the Seven Decisions That Determine Personal Success*. As 15-minute fame goes, the name Charlie Sheen might be obsolete at this reading, but he was a star of a TV sitcom and an off-screen, out-of-control, motor-mouth druggie.

The "Tommy'" story, which I have used on other occasions, is a condensed version of an old one from John Powell, S.J.

Chapter 14, Encounters

As I mentioned in the text, this version of the Samaritan Woman at the well preaches better. The story, an old gem, is from Arthur Gordon's marvelous *A Touch of Wonder* (Fleming H. Revell, 1996), pp. 122ff. I have used it before and it fits in well here. The people were deeply moved by it and its gospel parallel.

Chapter 15, The Untying

Because the gospel is long, this homily is somewhat shorter. For greater impact, leave off the last line of the gospel ("This caused many of the Jews who had come to visit Mary, and had seen what Jesus did, to put their faith in him"). I further suggest that, in connection with this homily the celebrant use the preface from the funeral Mass.

Chapter 16, The Easter Church

The *Times* Op-Ed article is by Nicholas Kristof, April 18, 2010. Although the material was used previously in another homily (chapter 9, "A Tale of Two Cities"), at that time it was given for the regular Sunday crowd. This enhanced repetition was for an entirely different congregation, the Easter Sunday crowd; and it was very well received.

Chapter 17, Why Is This Meal Different?

My icon references are, of course, peculiar to the parish church I serve. The reader will have to make adjustments to his or her own church.

Chapter 19, As I have Loved You

The fishing story is from James P. Lenfesty, "The Catch of a Lifetime."

Chapter 21, Gospel Mirrors

I suspect this controversy of exhibiting the 9/11 cross will be settled by this reading. For the American Atheists' arguments see *The New York Times*, July 29, 2011.

Chapter 24, Five a Day

It would be most helpful if the Sunday bulletin contained a listing of some suggested spiritual reading and retreat houses to take advantage of. It is frustrating for the people to be admonished to do both but with no resources to tap. This homily is based on an article, "Five a Day for a Healthy Soul" by Sheila Hollins, *The Tablet*, April 20, 2010, p. 11.

Chapter 25, Enough

Alan During's book is published by W.W. Norton & Co, 1992. "One writer" is Matthew Kelly. See the reference to his book above.

Chapter 26, The Cost of Discipleship

This sandwiching of the gospel between the homily commentaries is innovative but it proved to be quite effective.

Chapter 29, Spiritually Teasing Stories

The dialogue with the man is a "made for Catholics" version of a story that Methodist Bishop William Willimon told.

This retelling of the bagel story is called "Fresh Bagels" by Zane Chait from *Storytelling Magazine*, November/December, 2009, p. 6.

Chapter 30, Becoming Rachel

The Sandy Vietze and Doughterty stories were headlined in the media in August of 2011. Kristof's article was in *The New York Times*, "Rachel's Last Fund-Raiser," August 11, 2011. I have no doubt that the homilist can find contemporary bad examples to contrast with the Rachel story.

The Scripture reading is not to be found on a Sunday. I took it from the Tuesday of the 19th Sunday of the Year, 1 & 2. Leave off the last paragraph about the 100 sheep, since it's another, distracting thought. I substituted this gospel for the Sunday one because of its topical relevancy at the time.

Chapter 31, The Woman who Taught Jesus

This homily insight I owe to John Shea. I have taken his reflections and woven them into this homily. John Shea, *The Spiritual Wisdom of the Gospels for Christian Preachers and Teachers* (Liturgical Press, 2004), pp 252ff.

Chapter 32, Hospitality

The Tom Long story was recorded by William Willimon, August 29. 2010.

Chapter 33, Ruth's Legacy

I took my material about the Japanese internment from *The Wall Street Journal*, August 20-21, 2011, p. A4). I suggest that the celebrant use the second canon of reconciliation with its apt phrases, "take away everything that divides us" and "Gather people of every race, language and way of life to share the one eternal banquet..."

Chapter 35, Wellsprings

The background of this homily is the attempted assassination of the Congresswoman Gabby Giffords of Arizona and the killing of six others at a political rally in January, 2011.

The local paper referred to is the *Asbury Park Press* (N.J.), December 28, 2010. The story comes from B.G. Kelly, "Christmas in Paradise," *America* magazine, December 20-27, 2010, p. 88). I suggest that the celebrant use the second reconciliation canon in connection with this homily.

Chapter 36, Hereafter

The material is taken from an article by Paul Meyers in *Portland Magazine*, Fall, 2010.

Chapter 37, Doubt

The woman is found in *The Tablet*, April 14, 2012.

The first atheist is Alian de Bottom and his words are taken from his book, *Religion for Atheists* (Pantheon, 2012).

The wistful atheist is physician and author Richard Seltzer.

Nicholas Kristof's column was in *The New York Times* Op-Ed section, April 12, 2012.

Chapter 38, New Year (Solemnity of Mary)

The no. 1 bestseller is *Go The F--K to Sleep* by Adam Mansbach (Akashic Books, 2011). Cee Lo Green won a Grammy for Best Urban/Alternative Performance for his song, "----You."

Chapter 40, The Guns of August

Two books on Jägerstätter are *In Solitary Witness: The Life and Death of Franz Jägerstätter*, 1964 and reprinted by the Templegate Press, Illinois in 1986, and *Franz Jägerstätter: Letters and Writings from Prison*, Robert Anthony Krieg (Orbis 2009).

Chapter 42, A Reflection on Mary

This can be used on any Marian occasion. I just used the catch-all phrase "On this patronal feast..."

Chapter 43, Trust Dies in Brooklyn

On July 11, 2011, the country was horrified when a little 8-year-old Hasidic boy from Brooklyn, Leiby Kletzky, lost and seeking help, was abducted, drugged, smothered to death and dismembered by another Jew of the community, 35-year-old Levi Aron. This homily was exceptionally well received. The phenomenon of betrayal "by one's own kind" was horrifically replayed when Anders Behring Breivik killed some 90 people on July 24, 2011 in Norway. It called to mind our own domestic betrayals: 14 killed at the University of Texas in 1966, 13 at Columbine High School in 1999, 32 at Virginia Tech in 2007. We have met the enemy and he is us.

Chapter 44, Trust Revisited

I did not want to overload the chapter with too much distracting detail but here I note Joe Nocera's Op-Ed column in *The New York Times* (July 26, 2011). He writes about how Wells Fargo was deep into the subprime illegal abuses that had a direct connection to the financial meltdown that affected the lives of millions of people. Yet for all of the clear evidence of criminal malfeasance, there has been no criminal investigation by the Justice Department. The Federal Reserve made Wells Fargo pay a fine of $85 million—pocket change: they made 20 billion in one quarter. That was it. It seems that not only are banks too big to fail, bankers are too big to jail. No wonder people have lost faith in our institutions.

In 1802 Thomas Jefferson was prescient when he wrote, "I believe that banking institutions are more dangerous to our liberties than standing armies. If the American people ever allow private banks to control the issue of their currency, first by inflation, then by deflation, the banks and corporations that will grow up around the banks will deprive the people of all property—until their children wake up homeless on the continent their fathers conquered." One thinks of the massive home foreclosures.

As for money corrupting the news, "checkbook journalism" has always been with us. See the news article, "Paying for News? It's Nothing New" by Jeremy W. Peters in *The New York Times*, August 6, 2011.

For a recent view of education see Naomi Schaefer Riley's book *The Faculty Lounges and Other Reasons Why You Won't Get the College Education You Paid For* (Ivan R. Dee, 2011). Note headline in *The New York Times* for August 23, 2011: "Under Bloomberg [mayor, New York City], a Sharp Rise in Accusations of Cheating by Educators," p. A17.

Chapter 47, St. Dad: Father's Day

From *Wisdom of our Fathers* by Tim Russert, copyright © 2006 by Tim Russert. Used by permission of Random House, Inc.

Chapter 50, Zaire D'Avella

This homily is perhaps too personal to be of use but I include it for its opening story and (although a bit worn now) its closing story.

Chapter 53, Michael Savoia: Fingerprints and Heartprints

The reader will notice that the gospel is an amalgam of different sources brought together to make a homiletic point.

Full disclosure: the Italian folktale is actually an Irish folktale that I've heard in several versions and have adapted for the occasion. That's ok because, like all tales, the Irish version is likely a retelling of the general common lore.

Chapter 54, Bill Barth and the Little Tin Box

Bill died on 9/10/11, the day before the tenth anniversary of 9/11. Hence the opening reference. The homily is personal but I have included it only because of the use of the Ed Hayes's story, "The Little Tin Box" (from his book, *Twelve and One-Half Keys* [Forest of Peace, 1981]), which may supply the homilist with a lead to develop his or her own personal thoughts.

Chapter 56, Cell phones and Cars

It's good to announce the series beforehand and by all means, before that first homily, be sure to ask the people to turn off their cell phones so that no one gets embarrassed. Material comes from *The New York Times*, December 7, 2009 and January 17, 2010, and the information on "doctor distraction" from the December 14 and 15, 2011 issues.

Chapter 57, The Dives Syndrome

Material comes from *The New York Times*, January 26, 2010, August 10, 2009, and from *America* magazine, October, 2009.

The Huffpost reference and Readeo.com references are cited in the July, 2011 issue of *Reader's Digest*, p. 28.

Chapter 58, Alien Voices

The data comes from *America*, October, 2009. An excellent article on the dark side of iPhones is "Selling Our Souls: Of Idolatry & iPhones" by Andrew J. Bacevich in the August 12, 2011 issue of *Commonweal*.

The *Rolling Stone* article is by Sabrina Rubin Erdely, April, 2010 issue.

Chapter 59, Trivial Pursuits

The *Our Sunday Visitor* source is May 25, 2008, p. 106.

Chapter 60, iPod and iGod
References to "black hole" resorts" can be found in the article "The Joy of Quiet" by Pico Iyer, *The New York Times Sunday Review*, December 29, 2011 and the quote from Jonah Leher from an article by Nick Bilton, *The New York Times*, January 2, 2012, page B3.

Chapter 61, Fatal Attraction
The web site is www.flrl.org/TrueFreedom.htm
   Check the books mentioned in the homily. A really good social background book is *Manning Up: How the Rise of Women has Turned Men into Boys*, by Kay S. Hymowitz (Basic Books. 2011). I took the three factors that makes pornography popular from *Lukenotes*, October-December, 2011, "Understanding Cybersex Compulsion" by Bryan Silva, OMI, Psy.D, and Nancy Kluge,PhD., LCPC.

Chapter 62, Confession and Community
The "Snooki" referred to in the opening paragraphs is a character from the wildly popular TV show *Jersey Shore*, which features the amoral, terminally self-absorbed antics of a half-dozen twentysomethings. To check the global impact of fertility see David Brooks' article, "The Fertility Implosion," *The New York Times*, Op-Ed page, March 13, 2011.
   The concentration camp quotation is featured in *Portland Magazine*, Autumn, 2011, page 10.

Chapter 64, An Apt App Confession
The two quotations on gluttony and lust are from Frederick Buechner.

Chapter 65, The Examen
The sources are varied, with a special nod to James Martin, S.J., in his book, *The Jesuit Guide to (almost) Everything* (HarperOne, 2010).

Chapter 66, Confessional Postscripts
The John Grisham quotation is from his book *The Testament* (Doubleday, 1999, p. 306).
   Christian Smith and his colleagues' book is *Lost in Transition: the Dark Side of Emerging Adulthood* (Oxford University Press, 2011).

The quotation is from Gerard Sloyan, *How Do I Know I'm Doing Right?* (Pflaum, 1966).

Chapter 67, The Local Church

The quote from the *Dogmatic Constitution of the Church* comes from section 26.

The source of the United States Bishops' document is *Called and Gifted: The American Catholic Laity*, November 13, 1980.

Chapter 68, The Foursquare Church

The T.S. Eliot citation is from his work, *The Rock*.

Chapter 69, The Full Circle Church

This all-too-brief summary of the history of the Mass I have resurrected from an old book of mine, *Renewal and the Middle Catholic* (Fides Publishers, inc, Notre Dame, 1971), which in turn I had gleaned from Gerard Sloyan's book, *Worship in a New Key* (Herder and Herder, 1969).

I am aware that, although most people won't catch it, some few alert ones might be scandalized at the words saying that in the primitive church the household leader probably presided at the Eucharistic gathering, implying that he—or she—could be a layman. It won't help when they hear those later words saying that this presider morphed into a priest as we know him today when Christians began to interpret the Mass in terms of the now defunct Jewish Temple sacrifice (which seems to be the case).

The official statement of the Catholic Church affirming the traditional stance is found in the Catechism (#1337), which states that Jesus "instituted the Eucharist as the memorial of his Death and Resurrection and commanded his apostles to celebrate it until his return; thereby he constituted them priests of the New Testament."

But historically this is not true. As Francis J. Mahoney, S.J., speaking for other mainline scholars, writes, "There is no literary or historical evidence for this tradition…a historical link between the Last Supper and priestly ordination is unlikely… the earliest literature we have from the emerging Church provides no evidence of any individual who functioned as a 'priest,' a person set apart to preside over the cult of the Christian community…While there may have been some sense of hierarchy there does not appear to be any hiereus (priest) in the early Church ("The Catholic Priesthood: A New Testament Reflection," *New Theology Review*, August, 2004, pp. 6ff).

I'm always hesitant to upset people but sooner or later they will learn of this history, and sooner or later, in discussing the hot button issue of women's ordination, someone is going to say that the issue is moot anyway. "Jesus did not ordain women. [Cheers from the con side.] Then again, he didn't ordain men either." [Cheers from the pro side.]

Duck.

Chapter 70, The Right Place
Source: "From Communist Princess to Catholic Penitent," by Peter Stanford, *The Tablet*, January 7, 2012, pp. 11ff.

Chapter 71, Olga and Darran
Source: The Olga story is from the article "¿Vale la pena?," by Joseph Sorrentino in *Commonweal*, April 20, 2012, pp.14ff. The Darran (Dairante) story is from *USA-Today*, June 8, 2012, "Fans willing to pay 400% markup for Kayne West sneakers."

Chapter 72, The Fourteen Generations
Source: "The Spreading Scourge of Corporate Corruption" by Eduardo Porter, *The New York Times*, July 12, 2012; "Why Our Elites Stink" by David Brooks, *The New York Times*, Op-Ed page, July 13, 2012; the much condensed version of the Fourteen Generations is from Sister Jose Hobday, *Stories of Awe and Abundance* (Sheed & Ward).

Chapter 73, Dorothy Stang
Source: *Homiletics* magazine, July, 2012, p. 15.

MORE BOOKS BY
WILLIAM J. BAUSCH

Once Upon a Gospel
Inspiring Homilies and Insightful Reflections

This book contains over 100 homilies reflecting the liturgical year, special occasion homilies for holy days, holidays, and other celebrations. A great resource for homilists, but also a source of spiritual reading for all on your parish leadership team.

624 PP | $34.95 | 978-1-58595-683-8

Funeral Homilies

Father Bausch brings a deep pastoral presence and much thought and preparation to each of his homilies. Each homily is crafted to reflect the person remembered as well as the message of Scripture and reflects the communal nature of a Catholic funeral and is sensitive to the status of the mourners. Father Bausch's words are faith-filled and compassionate, comforting and challenging, communal and personal.

208 PP | $19.95 | 978-1-58595-727-9

Touching the Heart
Tales for the Human Journey

Here in this landmark work, Bausch's goal is to help readers see the centrality of stories, to read and hear Scripture as story and not as history, and to learn to enrich and expand their lives by looking at the "story behind the story." As always, Father Bill weaves social commentary and engaging stories to demonstrate the challenging truths that shed light on the human journey.

272 PP | $24.95 | 978-1-58595-617-3

A World of Stories for Preachers and Teachers
And All Who Love Stories that Move and Challenge

These 350 stories aim to stimulate the reader and listener, to resonate with the human condition, as did the stories of Jesus. They originate from different cultural settings literary genre including Scripture, lives of the saints, and family stories.

534 PP | $29.95 | 978-0-89622-919-8

1-800-321-0411
www.23rdpublications.com